# Hillbillyland

J. W. Williamson

What the

Movies

Did to the

Mountains

and

What the

Mountains

Did to the

Movies

# Hillbillyland

The

University

of North

Carolina

Press

Chapel Hill

& London

© 1995 The University

of North Carolina Press

All rights reserved

Manufactured in the

United States of America

The paper in this book

meets the guidelines for

permanence and durability

of the Committee on

Production Guidelines

for Book Longevity of

the Council on Library

Resources.

99   98   97   96   95

5   4   3   2   1

Library of Congress Cataloging-in-Publication Data

Williamson, J. W. (Jerry Wayne), 1944–

   Hillbillyland: what the movies did to the mountains

and what the mountains did to the movies /

J. W. Williamson.

      p.   cm.

   Includes bibliographical references (pp.   –   )

and index.

   ISBN 0-8078-2195-0 (cloth : alk. paper).

—ISBN 0-8078-4503-5 (pbk. : alk. paper)

   1. Mountain whites (Southern States) in motion

pictures.   2. Mountain whites (Southern States)—

Social life and customs.   I. Title.

PN1995.9.M67W54   1995

791.43'6520624—dc20                    94-33817

                                 CIP

for Pammy Lou

and for The Ski King

and for all the gang

at the Troublesome Creek

Olympics and Chair Toss

but especially

Hague and Quinlivan and Collins

and Anne and Swarpetta and Pat

and Jim Wayne and Gurney

and yes Mike too

# Contents

# Preface. The Argument

This book defines and analyzes our ambiguous need for hillbillies. It begins with laughter and ends in pain.

The hillbilly lives not only in hills but on the rough edge of the economy, wherever that happens to land him. Meanwhile, in the normative heart of the economy, where the middle class strives and where cartoon hillbillies and other comic rural characters have entertained us on a regular basis since at least the mid-1800s, we take secret pleasure in the trashing of hallowed beliefs and sacred virtues—not to mention hygiene. Secret pleasure is guilty pleasure, and guilt begs containment. So we have made the hillbilly safely dismissible, a left-behind remnant, a symbolic nonadult and willful renegade from capitalism.

As rural memory, the hillbilly is not so easily dismissed. Hillbillyland is coated in barnyard, and the residue sticks like mud. Its denizens perversely refuse to modernize, obliviously miss the need to be embarrassed. Free of our squeamishness, the hillbilly thrives in squalor. He's the shadow of our doubt.

And he is, most frequently, male. Even as a she, the hillbilly is often a mock male. As a man or a woman, he/she stirs ambiguity about what is "natural," whipsaws us between our patriotic belief that sheer gonads built the Republic and our terror that sheer gonads might also rape the last living organism on the planet.

# Acknowledgments

In 1984, on the way to the beach, I popped the question to Pam. "Why don't we collaborate on a book about the hillbilly in the movies?" And she was willing and sat through umpteen really awful but archived movies at the Library of Congress and lost her temper only once and took good notes and has helped in innumerable ways, but I ended up writing this thing by myself. Without Pam, though, I wouldn't have started on this decade-long effort. And without her, I certainly wouldn't have finished.

Laura Schuster and Sharyn McCrumb laid the foundation for this study in 1984 with their Appalachian film list, which I was fortunate to publish in the *Appalachian Journal* (vol. 11, no. 4 [Summer 1984]: 329–83), and which got me focused.

The *Appalachian Journal* itself had already been helping to focus me for about a decade, since the first issue in 1972. Virtually everyone I have had the privilege of knowing and publishing during that time has taught me something. But in the preparation of the final typescript, I was especially guided by lengthy comments from Henry Shapiro and Archie Green. I also salute the work and influence of many others: Bob Henry Baber, Pat Beaver, Jim Branscome, Ron Eller, Steve Fisher, John Gaventa, Jack Higgs, Helen Lewis, Gordon McKinney, Bill McNeil, Borden Mace, Jim Wayne Miller, Burt Purrington, Bob Snyder, Jean Speer, David Walls, Jim Webb, David Whisnant, Cratis D. Williams, and a host of others whose work is cited more specifically in the sources. They shouldn't be blamed for my tangents.

I am much in debt to Judy Ball, Eric Olson, Dean Williams, and the staff of the William Leonard Eury Appalachian Collection at Appalachian State University. Eric Olson and Dean Williams, especially, have funneled to me valuable clippings and other hot tips over the years.

I am grateful to Loyd Hilton, retired chair of the Department of English at Appalachian State University, and to the College of Arts and Sciences and the Cratis D. Williams Graduate School for supporting this research with released time, research assistance, and travel grants. My colleagues Edwin T. Arnold (past associate editor of the *Appalachian Journal*) and Dan Hurley have read much of this book in early drafts and have made many suggestions for improvement. John Higby was instrumental in obtaining books for my benefit, as well as the complete run of *Moving Picture World* (1907–29).

I am especially indebted to many students who have taken my "Hollywood Appalachia" class over the years, most notably the Spring 1993 class, who happened along at a crucial moment before the final drafting of this book: undergraduates Jay Casey, Dierdre Cecil, Angie Lewis, Pat Moss, Meredith Oehler, Betsy Sanders, Wes Saylors, and Shawn Wilkerson, and graduate students Debbie Bell, Nancy Collins, Randy Crutchfield, Andrea Frye, Suzanne Moffitt, Julie Mullis, David Reynolds, Deanna Shelor, Steve Smith, and Josh Wood. They taught me.

Eileen Burt Carbia proofed the manuscript and found several errors and made good editorial suggestions and helped locate illustrations. Jennifer Levine helped in the preparation of the final typescript, and Thomas Wayne Eidson helped with illustrations and made valuable editorial suggestions.

Finally, I am much indebted to Anna Creadick, whose suggestion produced the final arrangement of these materials in the chapters that follow. Anna pointed out some sentences that wrapped their tails twice around their heads. She also launched the search for illustrations, and she convinced me of the inevitability of writing Chapter 8. I have taken several of her marginal comments and incorporated them into the text.

# Hillbillyland

Figure 1.1.
(Courtesy of Jim Harris)

I'm a lazy

drunken

hillbilly with

a heart full

of hate.

—Hunter S.

Thompson

# What "Mountain" Means, What "Hillbilly" Implies

That's the fellow, the classic American hillbilly, the dark one with the black pelt and dangerous ways. He is found on ashtrays, plates, trivets, placemats, plaques, figurines, cigarette lighters, cups—in plastic, tin, ceramic, copper, plaster-of-Paris, wood, and coconut shell—in a thousand knick-knacky venues all across this hugely rural continent. The hillbilly provokes a range of responses, from an odd kind of comfort to a real kind of terror. When he looks like Figure 1.1, like an ultimately harmless cartoon, we indulge him, even take on his identity in public and become boundary-crossing fools-for-freedom ourselves. But put the hillbilly in *Deliverance*, and he can fill us with hor-

1

Figure 1.2. "Hey, Paw—s'posin' I *do* git married—would there be room for me here?" (Cartoon by Paul Webb; reproduced courtesy of *Esquire* magazine)

ror. In both roles—in safe cartoons and in believable depictions of reality meant to scare us—he's the same hillbilly serving different purposes, our richly symbolic American country cousin.

My assumption is that the hillbilly mirrors us, and like most mirrors he can flatter, frighten, and humiliate. As a rough-and-ready frontiersman, he can be made to compliment American men. He can also terrify. Put him in the same woods, but make him repulsively savage, a monster of nature, and he now mirrors an undeniable possibility in American manhood. In other words, we want to be him and we want to flee him.

Think of what the hillbilly does, his rank country disregard for all propriety. He drinks hard liquor—and not at cocktail parties (Fig. 1.1). He's theatrically lazy but remains virile (Figs. 1.2, 1.3, and 1.4). He near-

Figure 1.3. Ceramic decanter with four plastic cups, topped by a ceramic hill-billy-head stopper. Two resting hill-billies frame the words "WILD CAT JUICE."
(Private collection)

ly always possesses the wherewithal for physical violence—especially involving dogs and guns (Fig. 1.5). He's gullible when skepticism would be wiser (Fig. 1.6), and he's stupid when smart would be safer (Fig. 1.7). He reminds us symbolically of filth, of disgusting bodily functions. Why else is he so frequently pictured with outhouses (Fig. 1.8)? That particular prop links the hillbilly to what William Willeford calls our "developmental past," an uncomfortable and unwelcome opening into a history we have tried to forget, our conflicted memory of the pain and heartache of living in the dirt on the frontier. So the hillbilly's outhouse is a pig's bladder at the American garden party, an abstracted and ironically glorified memorial in plain sight of the utter democracy of human hygiene (Fig. 1.9), a symbol of the plain fleshly equality of all people. And when the hillbilly is depicted as sexually loose—another

Figure 1.4.
Metal trivet.
(Private collection)

category of symbolic filth (Figs. 1.10 and 1.11)—isn't his easily available Moonbeam McSwine a fantasy of that same democracy?

Clearly, some groups in American society take to the hillbilly more readily than others. After all, who buys the tourist items, the wall hangings, and the yard art? That is, who besides me? (My hillbilly bona fides are detailed later in this chapter.) I find my hillbilly mirror in every flea market and at every tourist stand in this broad country, from barbecue joints to national park gift shops. Who buys these icons of negative identity, these decorative snapshots of the subconscious? Not the upwardly sashaying urban class, the managers, the professionals, the office warriors. Hillbilly souvenirs do not find a home in condos but in countryside abodes where ground sense is acknowledged and accommodated. Stuck-working people buy them, the purely salaried buy them, and *they* get the joke. The hillbilly takes his durn ease right in the middle of all these working people. He gives the horse-laugh to middle-class respectability. He's absurdly and delightfully free.

Which accounts for the potential flattery in him, the things that draw his constituency. His dangerous freedom can seem at times a hopeful

Figure 1.5. Postcard, lithograph on wood. Reverse side contains a penciled message sent from Hendersonville to Asheboro, North Carolina, in 1943. (Private collection)

human possibility, because he seems never to suffer. He thrives in filth, is impervious to weather and to dominant economics. Yet that same free hillbilly can quickly turn dangerous, become the Whang Doodle of dread who lives "in the darkest corners of our consciousness alongside cancer and cannibalism," as Josh Wood put it.

The hillbilly is often a useful negative object lesson, a keep-away sign on the far edge of our own deniable possibilities. Here is an example of the common context for the word *hillbilly* in the mainstream culture:

A dimwitted hillbilly inadvertently gets _____ed.
— *TV Guide*

Fill in that blank from one of many sitcom plots on American television, from *I Love Lucy* to *Father Knows Best* to *The Andy Griffith Show* to *The*

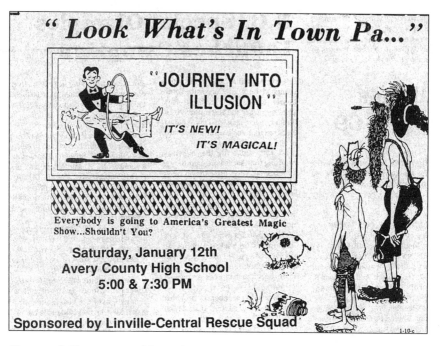

Figure 1.6. Newspaper ad from the *Avery Journal* (North Carolina),
10 January 1991.

*Doris Day Show* to *Lobo* (whose "dimwitted hillbilly" got involved in an
armored-car robbery). The assumption in these contexts is that the word
*hillbilly* names something different from us. Consider this congregation:

> . . . monsters, hillbillies, psychotics, and drunken brutes.
> —Dr. Lee Salt in *TV Guide*

Salt, a psychiatric caseworker, was describing, rather clinically, the
make-believe men who—most other men want to assume—commit the
crime of incest. Salt's point: we in our suburbs are not so safely immune
from our natures, which may not be what we think. Our secret dread is
that the dark, drunken hillbilly is no Other, but us.

The truth is that most popular-culture hillbillies probably induce no
such teetering ambiguity. In 1977 historian John Higham said that
hateful American nationalism, xenophobia, thrived longest "among the
hicks and hillbillies"; in 1984 novelist Elmore Leonard joked that Alba-
nians were the hillbillies of Europe; in 1985 the political cartoonist
Herblock skewered the anti–family planning triumvirate of Jesse

Figure 1.7. "Pa musta got the damn gears in backwards—she goes mighty good though, don't she?" (Cartoon by Paul Webb; reproduced courtesy of *Esquire* magazine)

Helms, Orrin Hatch, and Jack Kemp as hillbillies (Fig. 1.12); in 1989 the *Texas Monthly* explained away a neo-Nazi, KKK-allied skinhead in Dallas as "one tough hillbilly" with roots in *Tennessee*, not in Texas. In other words, human beings with something to lose—which means most of us—usually move in the direction of personal comfort, which makes us keep our psychic distance from hillbillyland.

In the countryside, denials of the hillbilly identity can get even more heated, probably because so many people understand the power of the image as a class marker, hence a fighting word:

> We are afraid that, once again, we will be portrayed as a bunch of hill-billies.—Johnny Fullen, mayor of Matewan, W.Va., worrying about John Sayles's movie *Matewan* (1987)

Figure 1.8. Particle-board plaque. The center button originally held a movable arrow, now missing. (Private collection)

Meanwhile, others from the country and even from the city inhabit parts of the identity and find it, well, profitable—especially in, say, Nashville. According to Minnie Pearl, Nashville's business community dismissed the Grand Ole Opry as just "a bunch of hillbillies," until they realized in the 1950s that country music could make big bucks for them, too. Steve Earle, Buck Owens, Ronnie Milsap, Dwight Yoakam, and most recently Marty Brown have all embraced the word and found real-seeming freedom plus a surge in their personal fortunes as a result.

Dwight Yoakam was born in the coalfields of eastern Kentucky, and he plays the smart-alecky country hellraiser, prancing in "strategically ripped jeans and dirty-dancing his guitar." He titled his 1987 break-through album *Hillbilly Deluxe*. "That's one smart hillbilly," said Ken Tucker in the *Philadelphia Inquirer*. The Judds were fetchingly humble in accepting Nashville's Horizon Award in 1984, calling themselves just "two red-headed hillbillies" as they strolled off with the industry's heart. Recently Marty Stuart grabbed the word, despite his Tina Turner hair-style. Stuart was born in Mississippi, cut his musical teeth in fundamen-talist tent revivals, learned his licks from country legend Lester Flatt, was married for a time to the daughter of Johnny Cash, and self-con-sciously talks about "the importance of passing wisdom to each new generation of juvenile hillbillies" like a country-culture Moses.

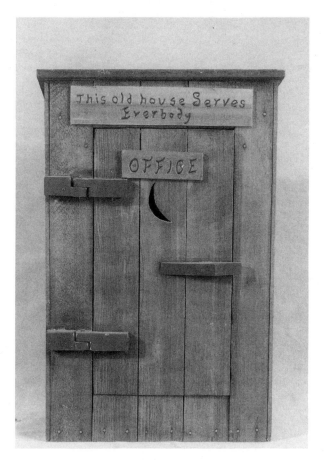

Figure 1.9. Handmade wooden outhouse, 12" tall. Sign over the door reads, "This old house Serves Everbody." (Private collection)

But *hillbilly* as positive identity hasn't been totally ghettoized in Nashville, nor is it based purely on geographic location. Nonsouthern rocker John Mellencamp, born and raised in the Midwest, explained to an interviewer: "I hated Seymour [Indiana]. The first time I came to New York I was embarrassed that I was from that town because the first thing everybody said to me is, 'What kind of accent is that?' . . . Let's face it, I'm a hillbilly and there's nothing I can do about it." Nothing to be done but let it fill the wellspring.

Not surprisingly, politicians in Kentucky and Tennessee and other states far removed have also embraced some part of the identity for generations—usually the dirt sense without the danger—since at least Andrew Jackson and David Crockett on up through Estes Kefauver, Albert Gore Sr., and Ned Ray McWherter. Playing dumb but showing

smart was just good sense in a politician, a purely symbolic but useful leveling of power in the eyes of voters so that power could continue to be unlevel. The political expediency of playing the hillbilly is common, too, in places not even remotely associated with Appalachia or the Ozarks. In Montana in 1989, freshman Republican senator Conrad Burns was said to be turning the Big Sky Country red with embarrassment for the way he was playing the egregious rube in Washington.

An extravagant and institutionalized example of hillbilly role playing can be found among the Shriners. The Grand and Glorious Order of the Hillbilly Degree was launched in 1969 as a "side-line degree" by Shriner Jim Harris of the El Hasa Shrine Temple in Ashland, Kentucky. He wrote out the requirements and the ritual based on hillbilly jokes remembered from his boyhood in West Virginia and from living in the

Figure 1.11.
Newspaper ad from
the *Wisconsin State
Journal,* July 1980.

Kentucky hills. By 1970 the Grand and Glorious Hillbillies from Ashland were parading in their officially sanctioned hillbilly garb and driving their moonshine still–equipped jalopies at the Imperial Shrine
Convention in Miami, Florida. Immediately, Shriners at the Hejaz Temple in South Carolina saw the fun of it all and installed the Hillbilly Degree in their own local temple. Clans quickly followed in several West
Virginia towns and in Cincinnati, Cleveland, and Roanoke as well as

towns in many other states far outside the South.. By 1981, 60 hillbilly clans rollicked in Shriner parades—two clans were in Canada—and by 1992 the number had grown to 137 separate units.

In no time, the Grand and Glorious Order had a newsletter, the *Hillbilly News*, and a copyrighted mascot (Fig. 1.1, as a matter of fact). It then launched the first annual Hillbilly Days festival and street parade in Pikeville, Kentucky, in 1977 (Fig. 1.13). Here were middle-class men, upstanding citizens, professionals of one sort or another, dressed as hillbillies and driving their comically disreputable jalopies down the main drag, occasionally being as vulgar as imagination allowed. Such goings-on horrified some. But the hillbilly display celebrated self-affirmation and regional pride. Here is how the Pikeville Shriners invited people to their sixth annual Hillbilly Days in 1982: "Come all of you including Jack Grace from California and Paul McCutcheon from New Mexico.

Figure 1.13. Hillbilly Days, Pikeville, Kentucky. (Photograph by John C. Lowe)

Meet some genuine mountain people here deep in the Appalachian mountains. We were born and bred hillbillies before we ever heard of a Shriner or Mason. We are civilized, good common help your neighbor kind of people."

All true. But in that very year of 1982, the Grand and Glorious Order nevertheless caused a ruckus in Cincinnati. The Ohio Shriners planned a big convention and street parade and invited all the guys who had arrived for nearby Pikeville's celebration. But Cincinnati-based Appalachian activists made a point of objecting: Hillbilly Days, they said, implicitly and explicitly ridiculed and humiliated new arrivals to the big city from the mountains of Kentucky. The behavior of the Shriners would be considered "insulting and distasteful" to as many as 250,000 residents of Greater Cincinnati, Mayor David Mann was told. Mann had already agreed to stand on Fountain Square and officially welcome the Shriner hillbillies to the city and then review their parade, but under pressure he withdrew. The irony is clear: members of the offending group, thoroughly middle class and influential in their own hometown settings, adopt the hillbilly as a cheeky affirmation of regional identity in the *larger* American context, their own assertion of equality. Yet they end up endangering the self-esteem of their coregionists who *are* relatively powerless in the city setting and thus vulnerable to policymakers who act on stereotype. For the first group, the mirror flatters and energizes; for the second, the mirror mocks and diminishes.

The special thrill the Shriners get from playing the country fool in public comes not just from the big money they raise in the process for their crippled and burned children philanthropies. Their behavior is a rebellion, too. They are giving vent to a common human urge to kick over authority—what Willeford calls the urge to eat sausages in the cathedral. If you're a member of the church, after all, you can afford to pretend to be symbolically what demonstrably you are saved from being.

Consider also the non-Shriner, small-town hillbilly foolshows of octogenarian Estill Drew, who lives in wooded Hamilton County in southern Illinois. Estill, along with his septuagenarian brother Dale, has made a series of Super-8 mm home movies featuring hillbillies and their standard breakdowns of propriety—moonshining, drunkenness, failure to support the family, outhouse high jinks, and even murder. Estill's *We Live by the Code of the Hills*, the movie that got him on *Donahue* and on the *CBS Evening News* back in 1984, is partly a plotted story-film: a revenue agent stalks a moonshiner, is killed, and goes to heaven, where he is entertained by a circle of winged angels (one of whom looks pregnant). But the film is also an anthology of humorous turns, a filmed variety show including vaudeville bits by Estill himself with a ventriloquist's dummy, scenes of pie auctions, barn dances, hay rides, and church services—all portrayed by Hamilton County people playing themselves, sometimes intentionally trying to act funny but being funny in the best human sense.

Brother Dale always gets the dangerous hillbilly role. In *We Live by the Code of the Hills* and *Our Country Cousin*, Dale hams it up as a drunken, no-account moonshiner. In actuality Dale Drew, like some Shriners, is a shy, self-effacing, religious, Pat-Robertson-for-president teetotaler. He enacts a hillbilly character as an example of the worst he might fall to if he were to lose what he has. His hillbilly is a mirror image warped into caricature like the reflection in a funhouse mirror, outlandish but nevertheless recognizable.

I myself grew up in the Texas Panhandle. Everybody there scraped the soil to survive or depended on people who scraped the soil. Visible class divisions were rare. Some farmers made a lot of money when irrigation came in. Some didn't make much money at all. The point is, you could hardly tell one from the other. We were all pretty much in the same boat. Everyone worked hard. My father farmed and managed another man's three thousand acres of dry-land wheat. We lived in his houses on his land, grew gardens, raised chickens, milked cows. My mother's family, greats and grands, were around us everywhere. They'd gather, seventy-five strong, for a major dustup at Thanksgiving, Christmas, and Easter, and there'd be fiddles and guitars and, in a spot where the women and children couldn't see it, some drinking. We depended utterly on a network of goods and services, bartered and borrowed, and we had a good life.

I witnessed my first hillbilly foolshow in a west Texas "Womanless Wedding." I sat with my mother and my grandmother and several of my "aunts" (including two of my grandmother's sisters) in the auditorium of the local high school and watched while my uncles and cousins and cousins' in-laws conducted a raucous burlesque wedding, some of them taking the men's parts—the groom, the two fathers, the parson, numerous idiot kinfolk—but many of them starring as the women—the bride, the two mothers, the tarted-up sisters and aunts. One man came as a giant girl baby in a wheelbarrow.

Even a ten-year-old could get the plot. It dealt with a shotgun wedding between two clans, hillbillies of the classic cartoon guise. The bride, played by the biggest, most macho tub-belly in Silverton, was visibly, extravagantly pregnant. The groom, one of the smallest men in town, was forced to the altar by the bride's pappy, who was toting a rifle and swigging from a moonshine jug. The parson was a mis-namer and a mis-stater, a monumentally dumb hick, so the ceremony itself was full of interruptions accompanied by general vulgar high jinks—simulated drunkenness, belching, hiking of dresses and showing of underwear, poking of long rifles up other people's butts. The main course and centerpiece of the evening was unembarrassed pregnancy out of wedlock. It was the sort of village hoohaw that Huck Finn might have stumbled onto (Fig. 1.14).

These antics put us on the floor. We were country people who saw ourselves as ordinary, mainstream, middle-class, 1950s Americans who never would have laughed at such things in our real, day-to-day lives.

Figure 1.14. A Womanless Wedding underway in western North Carolina, 1993. (Photograph by Nancy Collins)

But these clowns helped us to release our dread, and these clowns were hillbillies.

So, as used in this book, *hillbilly* means rough, rural, poor but fruitful, blatantly antiurban, and often dangerous, but not necessarily hailing from the Southern Appalachians or even from any mountains. The hardscrabble of rural Arkansas or of rural Arizona, for that matter, can breed hillbillies just as well, and has (*Thelma and Louise* and *Raising Arizona* are both discussed later at length). It's the hilly sides of the American economy, the parts out of the mainstream, that I'm interested in, and the conflicted urban memory of necessary frontier rudeness that produces the rural fool who up-ends our complacent assumptions about ourselves.

In west Texas, the foolshow allowed us to make sport of what actually and truthfully frightened us, and our uncles and cousins performed the magic of our lives by acting out for our enjoyment the very antithesis of what we believed ourselves to be. In our world, when a pregnancy occurred outside of marriage, it was too shameful to speak of in the open. Drunks were werewolves who tore their own families apart. Country tatters were real; severe poverty was a part of recent memory for too many people, and it was no laughing matter, either. Sons got bailed out of jail. Families sometimes had to take extra people into an already crowded house but would fight for you if it came to that. Fathers yelled at their daughters and saw them married anyway to ducktails with loud pipes. Nobody made fun of such things because we were all too vulnerable—except in the foolshow of the Womanless Wedding. It was our safe mirror for seeing what we could not look at otherwise.

Were we allowed this vent so that the hillbilly in us wouldn't break out for real? Was the hillbilly fool part of our cosmos to keep us in line? Or was our public pageant a more innocent display to help us maintain our balance in a plainly unpredictable world? Some questions I cannot answer, but I think I can chart the emotions that hillbillies have stirred by way of the movies. And the beginning of that map is an examination of the physical environs of hillbillies, their special place in our mythology: anywhere the ground is uneven.

## Ambiguity and the Meanings of Mountains

Something in us is drawn toward what we are
ashamed of being drawn toward.
—George F. Will

*Ambiguity* comes from the Latin *ambiguus,* an adjective derived from the verb *ambigere,* meaning to wander about, to waver, to dispute. That word was a combination of an older verb, *agere,* meaning to drive, to lead, to act, to do, and the prepositional *ambi,* which added a severalness to the driving direction. When the word got Englished, that confusion of direction became the essence of doubt, the flip-flopping of cosmic possibility. Ambiguity is about running, but which way? The doubt clings not only to the thinker but also to the object thought about. Is it clown or is it painted monster? Such doubt threatens to tear us apart. Certainty is what we like. Guarantees are what we need. Give us lead-pipe cinches and clear maps drawn in the light of heaven.

The problem is that living in the world is highly productive of ambiguity, so we run into danger as much as we run out of it. And what we dread also fills us with exhilaration, and vice versa. But even with our great need for a comforting stability, the entertainments we devise have constantly shaken us with unthinkable possibilities. We often deliberately induce ambiguity on TV, in the movies, in the press, in stories and in pictures. We unbalance ourselves with horror. But because the object of our fears is on stage and in public, we can distance ourselves as a safe audience. We can dismiss our collective and private doubts even while experiencing them, feel a revolution of perception without running the risk of change.

The ancient Greeks (by which we commonly mean the men who wrote the codicils and regulated the religion for which the temples were built) agreed that the true nature of the world was order, harmony, and logic. Antiorder was unthinkable. Unfortunately, there were several inexhaustible sources of it. The Persians, for one. Women, for another. Mountains, for a third. All three seemed beyond mere logic and offered challenges to control. Mountains, especially, were the opposites of temples. No "reasonable"—that is, right-thinking—man went there, unless he was making a sacrifice of himself or of someone else.

According to Marjorie Hope Nicolson, the names of Greek mountains had root meanings like "tempestuous," "wild," "terrifying," "the hunger range." These names reveal a complicated (that is, ambiguous) feeling of simultaneous "awe and aversion." Nicolson says that the combination of conflicting emotions must have been common for many early peoples grappling with a real nature they didn't understand and the ideal one they composed their mythology about and worshiped.

The ancient enmity of Greek philosophy toward mountain chaos bonded with later European doctrines based on Christianity. "In the beginning was the *logos*," said St. John, "and the *logos* was with God and the *logos* was God." The Greek *logos* was translated in the King James Bible as "Word," but its real meaning was something closer to "the Informing Spirit of Divine *Order*." There was a certain ancient Hebrew belief that mountains were proof positive that the state of nature had been going progressively downhill since the Flood. Sinful Hebrews always ran willfully uphill, away from the *logos*. Pagan groves in the Old Testament were always in high places. Mountains suggested other people's sins of disobedience against Jehovah. The Christian Dante also felt that repugnance and often expressed it in *The Divine Comedy*.

To hate sin was to hate mountains, but an attraction to mountains was nevertheless inevitable. And when actual people went into actual mountains—where anything could happen at any moment, where literal survival was an active question and might be a matter of physical competence—the possibilities of mountains simultaneously thrilled and terrified. Does nature make us feel fully alive only when we are about to be eaten?

By the seventeenth century in England, mountains, for their inherent disorder, were regularly referred to as warts, wens, blisters, impostumes, Nature's shames and ills, deformities, excrescences, protuberances, and swellings (in the medical sense of *swollen* with infection). They were described as dark, gloomy, still, awful, unfathomable, ghastly, rude, unjust, hook-shouldered, insolent, uncouth, inhospitable, freezing, unfruitful, unfrequented, forsaken, melancholy, pathless, desolate, hostile, cruel, and later as abnormal, degenerate, and pathological.

An interesting case study of the outbreak of mountain-induced ambiguity in the white-men's club was the case of Thomas Burnet, the seventeenth-century English theologian who sat with monarchs and who wrote extensively on the meaning of mountains in his book *The Sacred Theory of the Earth* (1684). He preached against mountains because they were his weakness. According to Nicolson, Burnet knew, theologically and intellectually, that mountains represented evil, but he felt "rapt" and "ravished" when he ventured into the Alps. And like a sorely tempted saint, "he persistently fought the attraction" because "he felt before the monstrosities of Nature emotions he had believed legitimate only in the contemplation of God." Secretly, he longed for and was susceptible to the ravishment of monsters, not unlike the narrator in James Dickey's novel *Deliverance.*

I am aware that an early *aversion* to mountains came to be opposed by a fully romanticized *awe* for their beauty, etc., in the eighteenth and (especially) nineteenth centuries. But deeply ingrained aversion never disappeared and is the key to our modern ambiguity.

If we have no appreciation for the subversion of ambiguity and for the extremely useful release of it in public, we will not get beyond our imperceptive shudder at the approach of the hillbilly, failing to recognize ourselves in his mirror. But if we feel the pull, too, then the mountains and their hillbillies represent much more to us than Dogpatch.

## Everybody's Got One

Even as merely Dogpatch, however, the mountains will do very nicely.

Many hillbillies in the mass media are there to make the normative middle-class urban spectator feel better about the system of money and power that has him or her in its grasp. Someone is always beneath us, lending proof that the twig on which we stand is really the rung of a ladder leading upward to something we must defend with our lives.

For the English, the class on the lower rung was the Irish; for the Irish, it was the lowland Scots. For the lowland Scots, once they got to America, it was the Indians. Indians have been seen as hillbillies by many people. In Betty MacDonald's *The Egg and I*, the book that introduced Ma and Pa Kettle to the world, the Kettles are MacDonald's hillbillies, but the Indians are hillbillies to the Kettles. Everyone can feel reassured about his or her own standing and about the rightness of lining up on such a scale as long as someone else is standing underneath.

To someone in Connecticut, it's someone else in Maine. To someone in Austin, it's someone else in the Panhandle. To someone in Salt Lake City, it's someone else in southern Utah. To someone in Gainesville, it's someone else in the Everglades. In Carolyn Chute's *The Beans of Egypt, Maine*, it's someone across the street. There's always someone else. The "woodchuck" inhabitants of the Ramapo Mountains in New Jersey are "penurious and inbred." The shack-poor of Vermont are "slack-jawed hillbilly feebs." The "swamp Yankees" of New Hampshire participate in "sylvan depravity." The poor rural whites of Maine are "obnoxious, know-nothing, nativist nihilists."

Hillbillies live even in China. In November 1984, the official Chinese news agency denounced the peasants of Guizhou Province for their "shocking backwardness," caused by "narrow-mindedness." The Japanese have the "hairy Ainus," middle Europe has the mountain-dwelling Slovaks, the Iranians and the Iraqis have the mountain Kurds. And so on.

What all such characterizations share, whether applied by urban outsiders or worn as self-defining and defiant badges by the rural folks themselves, is a common need for economic reassurance through the spectacle of want. But buried within that reassurance for an urban audience is an appalling ambiguity: the sense that these people survive and even thrive despite our low opinion of their worth.

Folly is one of the

supreme facts about

human nature. . . .

Folly is an abiding

possibility.

—William Willeford,

*The Fool and His Scepter*

 ## Comedies
## The Hillbilly as Fool

        In English, *clown* originally meant a peasant, a rustic, a farm worker. According to the *Oxford English Dictionary*, cognate words in related languages (Dutch, Danish, Frisian) convey such ideas as clod, log, block, stump, or lump—as though farm workers were only marginally human, chaotic coagulations of undifferentiated manure and phlegm and sometimes amino acids—town dwellers' terms for another someone who lives outside the city walls, the idiot of urbanism.

        The word *idiot* derives from Greek *idiotes*, meaning "a private person," one who dwells alone outside the pale, presumably because of foolish or unnerving behavior. In the long recorded history of European fools and idiots, documented by Enid Welsford and others, some people called by these names may have been schizophrenics. Many were deformed from birth. Many were judged dangerous and locked up. But they were a presence in villages and towns all over western Europe and had been accepted by European society probably since neolithic times.

The word *fool* itself comes from the Old French *fou*, the corruption of Latin *follis*, meaning bellows, windbags. Fools were known as blowhards, mocking everything holy. The *stupidus* of the Roman Empire repeated the words of passersby incorrectly, tried unsuccessfully to imitate their actions, was deceived by everybody, and wore a long, pointed hat and a multicolored patchwork dress. It was this fool's duty to be "slapped at the public expense." In other cultures, the physical abuse of fools went far beyond mere slapping; they were whipped or stoned or deported or even killed. Fools were scapegoats, visually stigmatized by either outright deformity or outlandish dress—visual chaos as a fitting accompaniment to mental chaos (see Fig. 2.1). They wore "foxtails, cockscombs, calf-skins, long petticoats and feathers." Later, professional fools developed a guildlike jester's costume complete with ass's ears, bells, and a mocking scepter.

Fools often provoked ambiguity, the sometimes very unpleasant sensation of teetering suddenly between two truths rather than sitting comfortably atop one. The fool either dared to be or inadvertently was a boundary crosser, a cross-bearer, or even a cross-dresser in cultures frequently strangled by rules of class and church and state. A monolithic and tightly controlled culture could look upon the fool's antics—"the fool show," Willeford called it—and feel, not embarrassment or reproach, but something like relief.

The most stable of citizens might play the fool on occasion, solo or mixed chorus, enacting a ritual of chaos—a revolution, in fact—that might break out in one person or group but spread like an epidemic to others, fueled by whatever intoxicants were handy; revelers displayed an impulse to violate every law, to burlesque every hierarchy, to flout every decorum. The medieval state quickly caught on that to control the blooming-fool impulse, which seemed by definition uncontrollable, they need only *sanction* it, license it, and thereby effectively limit it. Hence the institution of All Fools Day, allowed on one day a year and no

Figure 2.1. Quentin Massys, *An Allegory of Folly*, oil on panel (ca. 1510). The classic European fool character with cockscomb, ass's ears, and scepter. (Courtesy of the Worcester Art Museum, Worcester, Massachusetts)

more. In some parts of France at Easter, the general run of society could put on temporary fools' garb and adopt fools' behavior and crowd the cathedral altars for free sausages while making humorous, rude, or vile comments about the powers that be (remember the Shriners). This did not mean that the people were free. Rather, it meant they were truly *not* free. Their one-day license proved it.

Some of Willeford's examples suggest that the more structured, hierarchical, or rigid the society, the more violent or obscene the fool's sanctioned behavior. Among Pueblo Indians of the Southwest, "'contrary behavior' was an important element of ceremonial clowning and was often sexual and scatological in character, as in sexual jokes, exhibitionism, transvestism, and mock sexual intercourse and in eating and drinking excrement and urine." Though the display challenged the otherwise unopposable, it did not weaken the dominant control one iota. By asserting the negative of what was standard and holy, the contrary fool performed an act of magic reversal—warded off the evil that

Figure 2.2. Tarot card, Austrian, ca. 1453–57. Inscribed, "Female joker, looking at her grinning idiot's face in the mirror." (Courtesy of the Kunsthistorisches Museum, Vienna)

would come from any sudden overturning of structure—for the benefit of his or her social betters.

European culture neatly rationalized the fool's presence as bitter but necessary medicine, a means for absolute power to practice humility. In sixteenth-century Belgium, the intellectual Erasmus issued this prescription: If I *recognize* someone else as a fool, I am in the act of assuming that I am a nonfool; and in thinking *that*, I become a fool in fact. In other words, the fool could act as a mirror image of power's absurd possibilities, a funhouse mirror image set up for medicinal purposes.

This concept of the fool-as-mirror emerges in European art. A fifteenth-century Austrian tarot card (Fig. 2.2) shows a grinning fool carrying a mirror in her hand, but the mirror is turned toward us, and hence the image it reflects is ambiguous; it does not belong to the fool alone but also probably to the spectator. The legendary German fool

Figures 2.3, 2.4. Title pages from two editions of the history of Till
Eulenspiegel: (left) Parisian, ca. 1580; (right) French, printed in Amsterdam,
1703. (Reproduced by permission of Carl Ed. Schünemann Verlag)

and trickster Till Eulenspiegel was always pictured with a mirror and an
owl (*Eulenspiegel* means literally owl-glass or owl-mirror). Both owl and
mirror were symbols of self-knowledge and wisdom, but Till's wisdom
was his recognition of folly. In Figure 2.3, Till rides blithely along, gazing at himself in the mirror, oblivious of the scrapes that lie ahead, the
owl of wisdom as his ironic banner. In Figure 2.4, Till is dressed as a conventional professional fool, a court jester. He stands to the side while his
owl gazes into the mirror, which is once again aimed at the reader: "To
get wisdom, look into this folly and see yourselves."

The fool's sanctioned role as a mirror is evident in Figure 2.5, in
which a fool hands a mirror to a prince. The ruler with his symbolic
power (the sword) must accept the fool's mirror, for the fool's power is
the right to represent chaos to the king's own face, the right to disclose

chaos *in* the king's own face. In his illustrations for Erasmus's *Praise of Folly*, Hans Holbein toyed with the mirror notion, showing a fool who wishes not to be a fool (he has pulled the traditional fool's cowl with asses ears off his head) regarding his image in a mirror; the image impudently sticks its tongue out (Fig. 2.6). Like the fool or the village idiot, the American hillbilly clown is an impudent mirror held up in front of us—both a reflection of and a window into something rarely glimpsed, the native deep and sable face of this creature we still are.

The European fool stood in opposition to intermeshing hierarchies based on inherited privileges, with king and pope at the top allowing the fool's privilege ironically to protect and even strengthen their own power. What the American hillbilly fool most often stands in opposition

Figure 2.6. "A Fool Looking at Himself in the Mirror," illustration by Hans Holbein the Younger for Erasmus's *Praise of Folly.* (Courtesy of Öffentliche Kunstsammlung Basel Kupferstich-kabinett)

to is capitalism. He is usually lazy, or inept, or an outlaw on the fringes of the economy, the idiot of capitalism. (An exception is Al Capp's Li'l Abner, who is the idiot of sex, though his Yokum kinfolks generally are thorns in the side of rich relatives like Mammy's sister and an irritation to captains of industry like General Bullmoose.) If capitalism operates by inducing its workers to believe in the virtues of work and by condemning the evils that interfere with work, such as strong drink, roaming the woods and hunting, and various social indiscretions including murder, mayhem, and bastardy—if, in other words, capitalism has indeed learned to control our collective imagery for our own good—then clearly the hillbilly fool is a warning, a keep-away sign enjoining us to avoid the rocky rural edges outside the grasp of urban economy.

# Hillbilly Clowning

Somebody's gonna push a button some day
  And it'll all go kerbang
No more women, no more wine
  Won't be a dadburn thing
But leaders and peters and dictator eaters
  With heads stuck up their rears
Still dumb
Still dumb
Still dumb
Still dumb
Still dumb after all these years
—Charlie Gearheart, "Still Dumb"

Charlie Gearheart's song, as performed by the Goose Creek Symphony, is a humorous hillbilly wail, a clowning stomp in which dumbness is universal, an attribute of "our leaders and peters and dictator eaters" and not just a consequence of living in the "never-never land of small town and countryside."

But *hillbilly*, as an opening to comedy, is a slippery slope. Just the word, let alone the gap-toothed grin, offends many people. So why would Appalachian State University in Boone, North Carolina, in the blooming Blue Ridge, have a cartoon hillbilly as its mascot?

Yosef is his name, though he originally spelled it with two *f*s. He's one of the few official hillbilly school mascots I know of (distinct from "mountaineers" represented as coonskin-capped frontiersmen) in what generally passes for the real American hillbillyland, which includes both the Ozarks and the Southern Appalachians (and, in my estimation, many other places on the American landscape).

Appalachian State University opened around the turn of this century as a "training institute" for mountain kids, offering a kind of workfare education with tough rules. The school grew and prospered and evolved, first into a teachers college in the twenties and finally into a full-fledged regional university in 1967. Today it has some 12,000 students, the majority of whom did not grow up in the mountains. But in 1942, from whence cometh the comic hillbilly Yosef, the majority of the university's 874 students did grow up in the mountains and foothills of

North Carolina, on farms and in small towns. The students who made *The Rhododendron* annual that year introduced Yosef, "a drawing of a mountaineer found at the bookstore" (Fig. 2.7), as a joke in the last slot for the last mug shot on the last page of the freshman class. They gave the portrait the name "Dan'l Boone Yoseff," all in all a stunningly paradoxical piece of undergraduate japery. The Dan'l Boone part joshed with public schooling's pieties about coonskin-capped frontiersmen and brave American empire builders. This Dan'l Boone suggested a wholly other pioneer of the mind. (Coonskin-cappers are the subject of the next chapter.) His last name was a sly piece of mirroring: Yoseff/ yourself. The editors liked the joke so well they also put him on the cover of that year's *Rhododendron.*

Yosef's appearance in the freshman class of 1942 might have been no more than a satiric jab at freshmen, literally a species of class judgment contained in a cartoon code, but his appearance on the cover of the annual is more intriguing. The editors were clearly doing more than poking fun at those lowly freshmen who since time immemorial have needed an annual ritualistic reminder of their worthlessness in the scheme of things. No, the upperclassmen were poking fun at themselves, too, as part of that "seff" and were incidentally throwing back at any potential pharisaical viewer out there an image that both satisfied stereotypical expectations and rebelled against taste. People who lived downstate not only set the budgets for mountain education but also the social standards. By comparison with those standards, Appalachian State Teachers College could be considered a podunk school in a podunk town that trained negligible middle managers—that is, *teachers* bred for other podunks. But students at ASTC were from the mountain middle class and had never run a ridge, most of them. But they knew they were the hillbillies in the structure of a larger power. Their own college president, rigid disciplinarian B. B. Dougherty, gave speeches in which he advised them to lose their rural accents before venturing into the world. In the face of that stigma, they chose to play the fool with Yosef anyway, to embrace the cartoon identity for the very cover art of their striving.

And Yosef caught on. Four years later, in 1946, *The Appalachian*, a weekly student newspaper, launched a regular editorial feature, a guest column mainly about athletics, written in an excruciating dialect and signed by "Yosef." After two or three installments, the editors paired

Figure 2.7. Yosef
first appeared on
the campus of
Appalachian State
Teachers College
in 1942, in the last
slot on the last page
of the freshman
class section of the
school's annual,
*The Rhododendron.*
(Courtesy of *The
Rhododendron*)

BOYCE RUCKER WHITE .... Rutherfordton, N. C.
ROGERS VANCE WHITENER ...... Spindale. N. C.
CARRIE LOUISE WHITESIDES ........ Shelby. N. C.
PAULINE JUNIE WHITLEY ...... Oakboro. N. C.
CHARLES WEAVER WILLIAMS .... Cleveland. N. C.
VERNA GLADYS WILLIAMS ... Granite Falls. N. C.
CLARA ELOISE WINKLER .... Yadkin Valley, N. C.
RALPH RICHARD WOOD ..... West Jefferson. N. C.
RUTH NELSON WOOD .......... Dobson, N. C.
FLORENCE ELIZABETH WOOSLEY . Clemmons, N. C.
IRIS DEANE YOUNG ............ Lansing. N. C.
THARON ELIZABETH YOUNG ...... Boone, N. C.
ROBERT RUSSELL YOUNT, JR. ...... Staunton. Va.
ALMAROSE YOUNTS .......... Lexington, N. C.
DAN'L BOONE YOSEFF ........... Appalachian

Yosef's thoughts with a new rendering of the 1942 *Rhododendron* debut picture of the character, wearing an identical hat and a similar thoughtful expression. This was followed by Yosef's second appearance in the annual in 1947, presiding over a photo layout of ASTC's most popular students. He was also briefly given a consort, "Mammy," who looked remarkably like the mother Yokum in the funny papers, and the following fall the students threw a Ma and Pa Yosef ball, requesting the company of "the most typically countrified and mountaineerishly dressed" couples, the most popular of whom were crowned "Mr. and Mrs. Yosef." But the female character did not last, especially after Yosef became more aggressively identified with athletic prowess.

By 1948 a male student playing the character was expected to put in an appearance at athletic events and pep rallies, and within a few years the students began electing their Yosefs by popular vote; these Yosefs in turn sometimes developed great followings. And why not? Yosef was performing the magic reversal for the tribe, and his power became such that his absence from a sporting event became an evil omen. Sometimes he withheld his presence, like a *deus absconditus* (a runaway god). A letter to *The Appalachian*'s editor, published in 1966, asked plaintively, "Why must Yosef be absent and silent game after game?" In 1968 an *Appalachian* staffer composed a letter in hillbilly dialect, supposedly written by the mama of that year's Yosef, saying that news of her son's laziness (in not attending basketball games) had reached Hollerin Holler, and the whole family was taking it hard: "Uncle Rasmus has even gone so fer as to *disinherit* Cousin Yosef."

In 1957 the men's "A" Club contracted with Roxboro sculptor Tony Duncan to create a monumental statue, and the following May the larger-than-life-sized Yosef was installed in the lobby of the Health and Physical Education Building (Fig. 2.8). In January 1966 the statue was destroyed in a fit of iconoclastic pique by a group of Western Carolina University students who had been shut out of a basketball game between Western and Appalachian. *The Appalachian* subsequently pictured three Western Catamounts (the rival mascot) going after the stoic Yosef with axes.

Standing for athletic team solidarity, Yosef was quick to take symbolic offense, always barefoot and evidently impervious to pain, deadly accurate with his gun, and reckless with his white lightning. Yosef embodied the very qualities, in other words, that any good school mascot is supposed to embody, a don't-tread-on-me potential for mayhem. And to boot, he was outlandish and not one bit ashamed of his outlandishness in the face of prevailing downstate urban style.

Bill Blanton, a popular Yosef for two terms in 1961–62, remembered the role as "a license to practice. . . . If you were dressed like Yosef, you could do anything you wanted to. . . . One time I got a firetruck, and we drove it around the stadium during a game with all these drunks falling

Figure 2.8. Yosef statue created by Tony Duncan, with student mascot of 1958. (Courtesy Appalachian State University)

off of it. . . . There was an *expectation* that Yosef would push the limits. And it was kind of like being a mountain shaman." Yosef was a symbol of talking back to the gods, including open satire of the faculty and administration, magically allowed but ultimately controlled because it was sanctioned by adults. How else can we understand the open imitation of drunkenness at a teetotaler's school?

The Western Carolina Catamounts who dismembered Yosef in 1966 were laughing, too, but as outsiders and as rivals to the identity. Essentially, there's laughter safe and dismissive, and then there's *laughter*—liberating in its implications, if not always in its effects.

# Hillbilly Archaeology

There was a time in the 1850s and 1860s when even urbanites seemed to see themselves in the mirror of rural fools—in fact, in the specific rural hillbillyland of east Tennessee. Gadabout writer and "extreme Southern conservative" George Washington Harris created the purely fictional mountain fool Sut Lovingood, a tall and lanky east Tennessee ridgerunner, to lambaste northerners and stir up southern solidarity. Sut was long on vulgarity and short on manners, intimate with dirt and ignorant of "progress." His clan included his father, Hoss Lovingood, the slovenly but fertile Mam, at least eighteen siblings, and assorted dogs and pigs and cows and chickens, found in tales featuring "fighting, laughing, hollering, screaming, caterwauling, and wild flight." Sut had a talent for sowing chaos, especially among the pretentious, the smug, and the sanctimonious—symbolic northerners. Sut acknowledged no shackles on his behavior, not money or class or town-dwelling or personal hygiene. His refusal to be embarrassed about base humanity shocked nineteenth-century northern urban propriety, and it sold like real estate.

Sut embodied the very idea of the recalcitrantly rural, of backwardness as a political act, of the rebel South seen through the North's eyes. He turned the tables brilliantly by surviving so exceptionally well, thriving in fact, in his willful chaos. At the time Sut became popular, only 15.3 percent of the population was "urban," according to the U.S. census for 1850, but it was from that 15 percent, mostly living in the North, that the appetite and the money to partake of the Lovingood phenomenon came. Many of the northern urbanites who bought the magazines that carried Sut's tales were still, in other words, within stout arm's reach of a good, long, intimate drubbing by stubborn country.

An illustration by Justin H. Howard from the 1867 edition of *Sut Lovingood: Yarns Spun by a "Nat'ral Born Durn'd Fool"* shows us a visual progenitor of Dan'l Boone Yoseff (Fig. 2.9). Yosef's hat has begun to take shape, and the ectomorphic body type is right, but see how happily this early rural clown witnessed the stinging chaos that surrounded him, whereas the original Yosef in *The Rhododendron* was almost an El Greco of suffering by comparison. (Thomas Main wrote: "With a shave, a trim, and a nice suit, Yosef could be mistaken for Abraham Lincoln."

Indeed, and what a country ape *that* president appeared to his political
enemies. George Washington Harris himself wrote devastating descriptions of Lincoln.) Otherwise the only feature lacking to make Sut a twin
of Yosef is the prominent black facial hair.

Another backwoods fool figure, Captain Simon Suggs, was created by
J. J. Hooper in the 1840s, about a decade before Sut Lovingood appeared. The illustrator Darley drew Suggs in a broadbrim hat tending
also toward the hillbilly's (Fig. 2.10). In demeanor Simon Suggs, a dour
personality, was more an *ur*-Yosef than a Sut. Yet in the Suggs saga, his
sour face was an ambiguous companion to a comic riot.

For some urbanites, apparently, Sut and Simon inspired recognition:
a revolt of taste, the liberation of something oppressed or at least suppressed. William Faulkner, who created his own Suts and Suggses in the
Snopes, commented once that Sut had "no illusions about himself, did
the best he could; at certain times he was a coward and knew it and
wasn't ashamed."

Figure 2.10.
Illustration by
Darley, from *Some
Adventures of Simon
Suggs* (1848).

Others did not perceive the image that way, of course. To them Sut reflected nothing at all, perhaps because their self-righteousness had grown perfectly opaque. Critic Edmund Wilson found Sut nothing but "a peasant squatting in his own filth . . . a dreadful, half-bestial lout" (never mind what Wilson's first three wives said about him).

Clearly, the distance between the hillbilly as comedy and the hillbilly as threat is amazingly short, representing the full masculine maturation of primitive rural America in pop culture. For example, the frontispiece to *An American Vendetta: A Story of Barbarism in the United States*, journalist T. C. Crawford's 1889 account of the Hatfield-McCoy feud, offers a representation of Devil Anse Hatfield (Fig. 2.11). This hillbilly has grown his full black beard and incidentally achieved a more immovable stance. Obviously the comic context of the Sut Lovingood picture (see Fig. 2.9) is far removed from this specter of "barbarism" leaning on his long rifle. He is not cartoonish exactly, but he is the next best thing: a graphic representation without context, an abstraction of rurality

Figure 2.11.
Devil Anse Hatfield.
(From T. C. Craw-
ford, *An American
Vendetta*, 1889)

meant to be taken seriously as a threat to American progress (and ironically, in some threatening way, a living embodiment of who we always
*really* were).

The hillbilly's hat may be another link to his distant comic genes. In
the 1960s Hans Bungert pointed out a connection between Sut Lovingood's comedy and an earlier New England comedy featuring "the Puritan Yankee"—"the earliest American comic type," according to Bungert—perfectly embodied in Ichabod Crane, who was, interestingly,

another backwoods ectomorph whirled about by chaos. The Puritan's hat, black and broadbrimmed and tall, became Ichabod's broadbrimmed but flatter hat, more like a nineteenth-century parson's. Both hats may eventually land on the heads of hillbillies, which may mean that hillbillies are, among other things, crypto-Puritans twisted by political isolation into parody.

Although the word *hillbilly* was no doubt in common parlance throughout the latter half of the nineteenth century, it did not appear in print until 1900 in the *New York Journal*: "A Hill-Billie is a free and untrammelled white citizen of Alabama, who lives in the hills, has no means to speak of, dresses as he can, talks as he pleases, drinks whiskey when he gets it, and fires off his revolver as the fancy takes him." The emphasis on race is interesting, even a little unnerving—"a free and untrammelled *white* citizen" with "no means to speak of." Poor, lower class but uppity, well outfitted with a dangerous insouciance: he shoots off his mouth as readily as his gun. The *New York Journal* was pinching itself in a racist way: the hillbillies it describes are *white* people indulging in the twin threats of whiskey and revolvers, by then associated comically with Indians and freed blacks. But if anyone was laughing at the use of *hillbilly* in the *Journal* in 1900, it must have been remarkably nervous laughter.

The word was in print again in 1902, 1903, and 1907, in the local presses in Georgia, Arkansas, and Texas, always with reference to characters on the poor rural fringes of the economy who did not seem to be accompanying everyone else into the dawning of the thoroughly modern twentieth century.

In 1915 William Aspenwall Bradley published a travel piece in *Harper's Monthly Magazine* titled "Hobnobbing with Hillbillies." Whereas such a title in such a magazine in 1990 might promise a forthright burlesquing of country manners, in 1915 the word still applied without a flicker of a grin to nonhumorous, hardcore rural denizens who were evidently quite comfortable with personal violence and demonstrated a shocking lack of "progress."

In 1915 the word also made its first appearance in the movies in *Billie—the Hill Billy*. No copies of this two-reeler survive, but we know the plot synopsis. A city man goes into the Ozarks "on research, and comes to a mountaineer's cabin. The old man's son has run away from home after a beating years before, and grieving over the result of his harsh treatment, 'Pap' got the delusion that every man who came there was his returning son." The city man humors the delusion, falls in love with Pap's tyrannized daughter, and at the end of the story whisks her away to the blessed city, far from Pap's fire-and-brimstone squalor. (This fictional Pap reminded Randy Crutchfield of Mark Twain's Pap Finn, another and much earlier bad hillbilly father.) In *Billie—the Hill Billy*, the keyword signaled something noncomic, not funny, but arguably a parody nevertheless, for Pap is so inhuman, so unlike us civilized people, that the city man's appalling breach of the ancient laws of hospitality (in carrying off the daughter) could be actually *applauded* as some sort of chivalric deed (although carrying off a man's daughter once started a very long war).

By 1915 the movie market was, as a matter of fact, crawling with noncomic hillbillies, by the hundreds if not thousands, though the use of that word *hillbilly* was actually exceedingly rare. The weekly programs at America's burgeoning nickelodeon theaters from 1910 through 1916 included no fewer than three hundred movies about moonshining and feuding, one- and two-reelers mostly featuring assorted mountain desperadoes. But in all the plots of all those movies, as well as in the publicity for them, not once until *Billie—the Hill Billy* did the word *hillbilly* appear, nor was there yet in vogue any Yosef-like comic character who bore that label.

And there were plenty of comic opportunities for a Yosef to appear. Naturally, all those hundreds of deadly serious one- and two-reel movies about moonshining and feuding mountaineers quickly prompted comic parodies, beginning as early as 1911. But I've found no evidence that any of the parodies on the program before 1926 came close to the Yosef cartoonized fool character we all now recognize as the classic American hillbilly. (See the sources to this chapter for an extended discussion of the "look" of nickelodeon hillbillies.)

Exactly when the Yosef type first emerged, when the black-bearded ectomorph from the backwoods first appeared in the pop culture marketplace as a comic figure with the hillbilly label—that precise moment eludes me. (Here and throughout this chapter I am talking exclusively of male hillbillies, though there is evidence that the female hillbilly clown, discussed separately in Chapter 8, was on the American enter-

Figure 2.12. Frame enlargement from the surviving trailer for *Rainbow Riley* (1926). (Courtesy of the Library of Congress)

tainment scene *first.*) Although the Yosef type may have been present in commercialized culture by the early 1920s, I can confidently trace him back only to 1926 in the movies. In that year Johnny Hines starred in the comedy *Rainbow Riley* (Burr and Hines/First National), playing a callow cub reporter from Louisville who is sent to cover a feud in eastern Kentucky. Although *Rainbow Riley* does not survive intact, the Library of Congress has a trailer for it that features a scene in which star Hines, as the bounce-back cub, demonstrates a golf swing for a yardful of identical black-bearded hillbillies of the Yosef type (Fig. 2.12). *Rainbow Riley* was a remake of *The Cub* (Brady/World Film Corp., 1915), which had also starred Johnny Hines, and both were based on an earlier common source, Thomas Buchanan's 1910 play *The Cub*, which had starred the young Douglas Fairbanks on Broadway. The original play was said to have been "extravagant to the last," a satire of feuding mountaineers, but I've found no evidence that either the stage play or the first filmed version in 1915 visualized the eastern Kentucky hillbillies in the Yosef manner. But the 1926 movie version suddenly did.

Very similar types menaced the heroes of *The Big Killing* two years

Figure 2.13. "Wonder if Maw's had her baby yet—I'm gettin' mighty hongry." (Cartoon by Paul Webb; reproduced courtesy of *Esquire* magazine)

later in 1928. *The Big Killing* was a story about two bumbling urban con artists, played by Wallace Beery and Raymond Hatton, blundering after the lure of money into the middle of an Ozarks feud between the Beagles and the Hickses, among whom money is meaningless (along with most other urban niceties). Like the hillbillies in *Rainbow Riley*, the Beagles and the Hickses are mere foils for the real stars of the show, the urban fools, who always descend into rural chaos in order to redeem the idea of town.

Paul Webb drew the Yosef hillbilly type to perfection, but he did not, as some suppose, invent the type. Webb premiered his "Mountain Boys" in *Esquire* magazine in 1934, about eight years after *Rainbow Riley*, whose hillbillies were similar to Webb's. And almost simultaneously with

Figure 2.14. "That's yer Oncle Rafe— Gran'maw jest had 'im the other day." (Cartoon by Paul Webb; reproduced courtesy of *Esquire* magazine)

Webb's debut of the Mountain Boys came Al Capp's *Li'l Abner* and Billy De Beck's Snuffy Smith, both of whom also hatched in 1934.

What was happening to make comic hillbillies mushroom so numerously again among the ever-growing urban majority? Economic collapse, for one thing. The early 1930s forced middle-class urban Americans to consider seriously the unthinkable possibility that the whole damn shooting match of the American economic system itself was about to land them back in Rural Subsistence Hell. So Paul Webb's hillbillies were the shadow of our doubt, a nervous clowning talisman to wave off the evil of failure. William Willeford wrote: "We feel that [fools] do not belong to the human image, [but] we are left to make what we can of the fact that in one sense or another *they reflect us*. . . . [Their]

Figure 2.15. "What d'ya reckon it is, Maw—Shucks— it tastes turrible." (Cartoon by Paul Webb; reproduced courtesy of *Esquire* magazine)

traits seem an opening into a past to which we have closed ourselves"— our own deniable possibilities.

Paul Webb (perhaps especially) saw the crank in advanced capitalism in sweetly rueful terms: his hillbillies might be inept with machinery (see Fig. 1.7), utterly dependent on the labors of women (Fig. 2.13), disastrously given to lechery (Fig. 2.14), or outrageously out of step with modern life (Fig. 2.15), but they were somehow at rest in the universe, utterly at home, blessedly oblivious; they were fecund, accepting their fate with placid equanimity and resiliency (Fig. 2.16).

Meanwhile, on the movie screen in 1935, Walter Lantz released the first animated short featuring the hillbilly type, *Hill Billys,* which was followed by a brace of cartoon visitations including *When I Yoo Hoo* (War-

Figure 2.16. "Shucks—Ah fergit—Ah think the little one is mah old bullet wound." (Cartoon by Paul Webb; reproduced courtesy of *Esquire* magazine)

ner Brothers, 1936), *A Feud There Was* (Warner Brothers, 1938), *Naughty Neighbors* (Warner Brothers, 1939, starring Porky and Petunia Pig), and *Musical Mountaineers* (starring Betty Boop, Max Fleischer Cartoons, 1939). Live-action movies presented the same visually cartoonized, Yosef-like hillbillies: *Kentucky Kernels* (RKO Radio, 1934), *Kentucky Moonshine* (Twentieth Century–Fox, 1938), *Murder, He Says* (Paramount, 1945), *Comin' Round the Mountain* (Universal-International, 1951), and *Feuding Fools* (Monogram, 1952). These movies starred such comedy teams as Wheeler and Woolsey, the Ritz Brothers, Abbott and Costello, and the Bowery Boys, or sometimes lone urban prospectors— idiots in the earliest sense—striking off alone into the mountains, as Fred MacMurray did in *Murder, He Says*. These stories were partly urban myths of solidarity, in which the boundary-crossing city fools were sent out like emissaries (scapegoats, Willeford would say) to deal with and symbolically survive the idiocy of rural life.

In *Comin' Round the Mountain* (1951), which drew its title, its look, and many of its gags from a collection of Paul Webb's Mountain Boys cartoons published in 1938, Lou Costello is the classic *stupidus*, the one who gets slapped. Only a tremendous fool would venture into the land of the fools. Costello's character supposes that he has inherited a Kentucky legacy, so he jumps from his inept showbiz job in New York to the inepter Kentucky hills, where instead of coming into a fabulous fortune, he inherits a ready-made feud and gets threatened, hurt, and humiliated. But through the crazy (magical) luck of the classic fool, he bounces back from it, is resurrected symbolically from rural hell, and is brought back home to the city at the end so that the urban and the standard are revalidated. We can walk away from Costello's hillbilly menaces as easily as from Halloween crepe paper.

But when the hillbilly fool gets out of that obvious symbolic cartoon uniform, shaves off the beard, eats a little better, and moves among us, he becomes much more capable, as a mirroring fool, of showing us ourselves. Think of the requisite new-car/furniture/discount merchandise tycoons who are always on television in major markets, mirroring our cupidity. Such a character in *Raising Arizona* is Nathan Arizona, the unpainted furniture king who bellows "Come on down!" to push his goods. People do come down and buy, too, and they make those low pitchmen rich, not because the people with the money to spend are alienated from symbolic rubes but because symbolic rubes can create the illusion of solidarity and collective power.

## The Hillbilly Fool as Troubadour

I like music if it's carried on right. It's got to be carried on right
before I'll associate with it. No cutting up and acting a fool.
—Mrs. Andy Webb, Rabun County, Georgia, 1973

In 1900 this nation was still overwhelmingly rural. Only 39.9 percent of us lived in what were defined as urban areas. But by 1920 a significant tilt had begun, one that is still occurring and that more than subtly altered America's mass-culture relationship with the hillbilly image: in 1920 the U.S. census found that 51.2 percent of us now lived in cities; by 1980 we were 73.7 percent urban. That urbanizing force seems irresistible, and as a result the urban majority is growing further and further removed from real rural experience and hence is freer to dissociate the hillbilly as a purely comic cartoon, something to be safely and unambiguously dispensed with rather than something symbolic of the banished rural memory that will not stay banished.

Failure to see self in the hillbilly mirror is a failure of humility on the part of the urban observer, whereas on the rural side, recognition of self in the hillbilly may be a paradoxical opportunity for metamorphosis. To willingly play the hillbilly fool, plime-blank, like the Yosef mascots at Appalachian State University, is to invigorate one's potential. Comic license is effervescent, allowing earthborn personalities to become airborne. Hillbilly boldness is a knowing flirtation with danger, a deliberate identification with the fool of yore who might just upset our applecart.

In its several manifestations, the spirit and practice of hillbilly music has made hundreds of fortunes in American commercial culture—in vaudeville, in recorded music, on radio, on TV, at concerts, and at the movies—even while it has often prompted the dismissive sneers of urban sophisticates: "a national earache," "the epidemic of corn," "that dreadful nasal twang."

But the spirit and practice of hillbilly music is a paradoxical amalgam of sincerity and clowning. In the countryside, the sincerity of performing the art of the tribe is balanced by a funny self-consciousness. That is to say, when a "gen-you-wine" country person gets up in front of his or her peers and *performs*—wags the butt and yodels—the performance is admired for its sheer outrageousness first and for talent second. According to social critic David Reisman: "Things that strike the sophisticated person as trash may open up new vistas for the unsophisticated." If the country clod has but one chance to interject himself or herself into the urban consciousness, into the symbolic company of American adults, let it be by clamoring, by showing off, by "blurting," as Bob Snyder calls it.

As a kid I saw that urge to play the hillbilly fool manifested at family gatherings, and music always started it—my grandfather's brothers and various in-laws with fiddles and bull-fiddles and guitars (but no banjos that I ever remember) far down there in the pecan groves of south Texas on the Nueces River in August. Deep into the night, with the incentives of many strings tuned together, eventually someone of that large family, either under the influence of the music or under the influence, period, would play the flat-footing rural fool for everyone's benefit. Either man or woman might play the hillbilly, dancing and falling down, and the men need not be drunk either, though the women fools might mimic male drunkenness.

Steve Smith, an expert on hillbilly music and a frequenter of country gatherings where such music breaks out, explains that, since clowning around is expected, it is also "overly exaggerated, so as to state clearly that it is not actual rebellion against the status quo. The clowning is too ludicrous to be taken seriously." Sanction the boundary-crossing, and it becomes safe.

Hillbilly music broke into American mass culture in a big way after 1923. The ubiquitous phonograph was responsible, followed by the gee-whiz discovery that rural music, made by rural people, had a whopping economic potential. That initial discovery belonged to marketing executive Ralph S. Peer of OKeh Records in New York City. On a scouting trip to Atlanta in the early twenties, Peer recorded "Fiddlin' John" Carson (Fig. 2.17) at the suggestion of a local music dealer who thought the "woolhats" who had been moving into Atlanta from rural Georgia to work the new textile industry might buy as many as 1,000 records. Frankly, Peer thought Carson's vocals were "plu-perfect awful," and the resulting field recording "was so bad that we didn't even put a serial number on the records, thinking that when the local dealer got his supply, that would be the end of it." But the jubilant dealer sold his initial 1,000 the day he got them, then ordered another 5,000 by express and 10,000 by freight. When national sales reached 500,000, Peer felt so ashamed of the poor quality of the record that he had Fiddlin' John come up to New York to rerecord the numbers.

Archie Green tells the story that as recently as 1962 it was the policy of the U.S. State Department to discourage too much familiarity with hillbilly music on the part of their foreign service officers. (Incidentally, the State Department also discouraged too much overt knowledge of the poetry of Walt Whitman, to raise the specter of another of our recent domestic demons.) But the music, if not the poetry, raised the sap

Figure 2.17. "Fiddlin' John" Carson (second from left) and friends, Atlanta, Georgia, 1919. (Courtesy of Tony Russell, Old Time Music)

in country people. It was a raucous caw-cawing in the face of urban tastes, a liberation of the spirit, a play-the-fool public breach of the peace, and worth whatever it cost for however long it lasted, including a night in the nearest jail. The people who bought those records by the thousands found an unexpected public mirror that flattered them. Urbanites might laugh at the spectacle, but country people smiled a deep and inward smile.

The first band to call itself *hillbilly* pulled into New York City in 1923. This foursome from the New River Valley of North Carolina and Virginia recorded six numbers at the OKeh studios. Ralph Peer handled them as he had Fiddlin' John Carson, with great skepticism, but he immediately recognized that these new guys had a broader economic potential. Out of the blue, Peer asked them what they wanted to call their group. Their leader, Al Hopkins, was unprepared. He stammered, "We're nothing but a bunch of hillbillies. . . . Call us anything." It can be an insider's word—*hillbillies*, just folks, all equals—a banner for the sincerity of their humility, so to speak, but Mr. Peer's laughter shifted the balance of power.

Al Hopkins, his brother Joe, Tony Alderman, and John Rector were not comic hillbillies in their own eyes, or in the eyes of their friends back home. They were accomplished musicians and firmly middle class. Al Hopkins was a hospital office manager. Joe Hopkins worked as a Railway Express agent. Tony Alderman was a barber, and John Rector kept a general store. They weren't rural Sut Lovingoods, nor were they college students overturning good taste. On their drive back home from New York, after Peer had officially named them The Hill Billies, Tony Alderman in particular expressed his disgust with Al Hopkins's popping off. "Hillbilly was not only a funny word; it was a fighting word," he later told Archie Green. Alderman said he thought his father in particular, a self-educated surveyor and civil engineer, might get unusually tetchy when he heard that his son was performing with a group called The Hill Billies. How intimate and powerful the word! How it pricked the sensibilities of middle-class mountain neighbors who were now officially a part of the American demographic minority, whose very second-classness now became somehow funny and marketable to the urban majority. The word *hillbilly* might still be used as a democratic touchstone between equals native to a place. But in the mouths of powerful men at record companies in New York City, it seemed to demand subservience, which in turn provoked anger.

Hillbilly music did something else that the movies had not yet attempted in the early twenties. In country music, the hillbilly clown became the star of his own foolshow, no longer the mere foil or silly menace in someone else's show. With hillbilly music, rurality rules the stage, and what a powerful illusory stage was early radio. By 1922 more than five hundred radio stations had signed on the air, and at least ninety were broadcasting in the more rural areas of the South. After 1923 those stations played the hillbilly sounds coming out of OKeh, Victor, Vocalion, and Columbia, and by 1930 a whole host of country performers could be heard on more than twelve million radio sets. By the early thirties there were hillbillies everywhere, including California (in the guise there of a popular band named, incidentally, The Beverly Hillbillies). Meanwhile, Vernon Dalhart became the first really big solo "hillbilly" singer and did "Hill Billie Blues" and sold seven million copies of "The Wreck of the Old 97," too.

*Variety* music editor Abel Green swam very much against this rural current flowing into the entertainment mainstream. Green expressed his contempt for hillbilly music in late 1926 and remained publicly dedicated to that position on into the thirties. But hillbilly took the country by gale force anyway. The music first made it to the movie screen in 1929 in a short subject featuring Al Hopkins and The Hill Billies, released as a trailer to Al Jolson's *The Singing Fool*, which was a jazz picture—hillbilly music impressively opening for the more dominant and hypercurrent urban music. Montgomery Ward was offering "hillbilly records" in its catalogs by 1930; and by 1933, *Variety* often headlined the word and admitted the music's popularity, though always with a contemptuous showbiz sneer: "Hollywood Goes Hillbilly," "Curse of a Sour Hillbilly Note," and so on.

It is a curious but so far inconclusive coincidence that hillbilly music arrived on the commercial scene at about the same time as my earliest traces of the Paul Webb-Yosef-type comic hillbilly in movies (*Rainbow Riley*, 1926; see Fig. 2.12). The music may have inspired the cartoonizing, innocently or deliberately, or it may have had nothing to do with it. But comic assumptions were obviously important in commercialized hillbilly music from the beginning. In the early years of the recorded sound, many string bands had regular designated clowns, men like Walter "Kid" Smith, Froggy Cortez, Toby Stroud, Slim Miller, Charlie Bowman, Coon Langley, Frank Welling ("Uncle Si"), Sleepy Carson, Abner Wilder, Jack Baggett ("Oscar McGooney"), Bill Carlisle, Dink Embry, Lazy Jim Day, and Rod Brasfield. Many women played the hillbilly clown, too (and see Chapter 8). Minnie Pearl is perhaps the most famous, but before her there was Elviry of the early vaudeville team The Weaver Brothers and Elviry. According to Mary A. Bufwack and Robert K. Oermann, Elviry's "drawling, deadpan comedy style" was a principal audience draw. Wrote a critic for the *New York American*: "Sis Elviry is the best straight-faced comedienne in captivity." The Weaver Brothers and Elviry made several movies for Republic in the 1930s and 1940s (*Swing Your Lady, Down in Arkansaw, Jeepers Creepers, Grand Ole Opry*), as did Judy Canova, one of the original Georgia Crackers, in the forties (*Scatterbrain, Sis Hopkins, Pudden'head*). (During the thirties and forties, hillbillies were proliferating everywhere. Arkansas vaudevillian Bob Burns made *Mountain Music, The Arkansas Traveler, I'm From Missouri,* and *Comin' Round the Mountain,* among other movies; and let us not forget the Lum and Abner opera from the same era: *Dreaming Out Loud, Bashful Bachelor, So This Is Washington,* and *Goin' to Town.*)

Ferlin Husky followed this troupe of country howlers to the screen in 1958 in the surprise hit *Country Music Holiday* (Paramount), a decidedly low-budget feature showcasing country music and a good venue for the improbable hillbilly to star in his own foolshow. When I arrived in Boone, North Carolina, in 1970, a dozen years after its initial release, *Country Music Holiday* was still playing an annual weekly run at the local downtown theater. It had been aimed initially at the peripheral southern drive-in and small-town trade, where it certainly found its audience and its audience presumably found its mirror.

Husky had started in the music business as Simon Crum, a conventional hillbilly music-hall clown, and in his film career he never strayed very far away from the mouth-twisting, eye-popping, lurch-strutting potential inherent in the hillbilly string-band clowns, the country goofballs let loose by music. (See, for example, Husky's performance of "I Feel Better All over More Than Anywheres Else, Baby, When I'm Out with You" in *Las Vegas Hillbillys*).

In *Country Music Holiday,* Husky plays sincere country boy and honorably discharged soldier Verne Brand. Verne gets discovered by a couple of hustling urban talent scouts, and he takes off for the Big Apple to reconnoiter, while promising to remain true to the hometown folks in Puffin Bluff, Tennessee, and especially to his devoted country sweetheart, who is played by June Carter, herself a member of a legendary mountain singing family that commanded a vast audience. His first night in Manhattan, Verne walks into a cocktail nightclub in a loud plaid suit, a country clown's outfit. He's slow, almost somnolent — a little like Li'l Abner in his obliviousness, especially to his own sex appeal. But naturally he incongruously attracts the most "bee-YOO-tiful" blond bombshell, major socialite Zsa Zsa Gabor, who for her own reasons considers him a conquest and gets him into high society duds (Fig. 2.18). This comic reversal, the dumb hillbilly getting the improbable doll-baby, became a kind of Husky trademark. A long time after his surprise

Figure 2.18. Publicity shot for *Country Music Holiday*, showing socialite Zsa Zsa Gabor with her country boy conquest, Ferlin Husky (center), all duded up for a fox hunt. (Courtesy of Wisconsin Center for Film and Theater Research)

success in *Country Music Holiday*, Husky did two other movies in which he played Woody Woodrow, who was in most respects pretty much like Verne Brand, except that Woodrow had a more cartoonized collection of hillbilly relatives. In the seriously low-budget *Las Vegas Hillbillys* (Woolner Brothers, 1966), he reversed expectations and attracted both Mamie Van Doren and Jayne Mansfield, and in *Hillbillys in a Haunted House* (Woolner Brothers, 1970), he had newcomer Joi Lansing under his spell.

In the Husky movies, the country-clown troubadour ventures into the big wicked city much as the urban fool Lou Costello ventured into the dark dangerous hills in *Comin' Round the Mountain*—in order to experience a symbolic death, only to be resurrected and restored to the innocent and wholesome country. No wonder *Country Music Holiday* was popular in Boone and in many another rural marketplace.

To his notorious biographer Albert Goldman, the gullible Elvis Presley was a pure hillbilly troubadour, and maybe the true original nat'ral-born durn'd fool, too. According to Goldman, Elvis was inept in the classic hillbilly way: he was so sincere he made Goldman's teeth ache. Elvis the Unconscious tried in his twenty-nine cookie-cutter movies to do something he couldn't consciously do at all, that is, *act*. The Elvis movie "formula," according to Goldman, was this:

> [He] was always cast as a handsome young stranger of working-class status who has just blown into town and stumbled over the most incredible looking collection of girls. His identity as a racing driver, a sailing captain, a helicopter pilot, a deep-sea diver, a boxer, an acrobat, a photographer, a roustabout, a ranch hand, a gambler, [an Air Force sergeant in *Kissin' Cousins*], etc., was simply a matter of the costume he wore. His silicone-cheeked face, his tooth-capped smile, his helmet of shiny jet-black hair ("five inches of hot buttered yak wool": *Time*) varied no more than does the head of a display window dummy. Though Elvis spoke lines, threw punches, and did a lot of driving in these pictures, his basic identity was that of a dummy.

Dummy indeed—as if Goldman were not—and a dummy stuffed with money, lots of it, animated by the heady sanctioning of millions of fans who felt better about themselves because of his success. Of course, their liberation was also Elvis's trap.

David Reynolds has pointed out that Elvis, the ultimate media hillbilly, was also the ultimate mountain mama's boy (the "mama's-boy syndrome" is discussed below in Chapter 7). He elevated his mother, Gladys, to the status of saint and icon and was himself the studiously devoted son. Yet alongside that cuddly boyishness one sensed the tension of his flaming-teen dangerousness. As Reynolds says: "But the person in the greatest danger from Elvis was himself, and he did a pretty good job of slaying that bloated Goliath."

The soundtrack of Warren Beatty's *Bonnie and Clyde* (1967) offers the best and certainly the most influential linkage between hillbilly music and the spirit of the (threatening) foolshow. Flatt and Scruggs's 1949 classic, "Foggy Mountain Breakdown," is played wide open for the first car chase out of town after that cute devil Beatty (as Clyde Barrow) has pulled off his first robbery to impress that other cute devil Faye Dunaway (as Bonnie Parker), and in 1967 this music provoked anarchistic glee among college audiences. Suggesting careening fun, the music makes crime and life on the run into a Dionysian celebration, wild-ass economic rebellion, the pleasures of chaos and easy cash.

According to Neil Rosenberg, *Bonnie and Clyde* was not the first film to induce the Dionysian spirit with bluegrass, which is a late development in hillbilly music, but it was the first fiction film to use the bluegrass sound for what might appear to be political meaning. In fact, ever since *Bonnie and Clyde,* bluegrass—that "folk music with over-drive," as Alan Lomax called it—has been used in many otherwise serious, even ponderous films to subvert the status quo through sudden eruptions of rebellious and balancing humor. *Where the Lilies Bloom,* the 1974 Appalachian pastoral scripted by professional mountaineer Earl Hamner Jr., used bluegrass music for comic chases, light episodes embedded in an otherwise sentimental story. Compare this with the 1984 Kurt Russell/ Goldie Hawn vehicle *Overboard,* in which the bluegrass-inspired soundtrack signaled the comic comeuppance that the plot devises for a spoiled, rich ice queen (played by Hawn) who, under the influence of what the music stands for, loses first her memory and then her ice. (See the further discussion of *Overboard* in Chapter 6.)

## Ma and Pa Kettle

In some instructive ways, Ma and Pa Kettle (Fig. 2.19) descend directly from the Lovingood clan—Hoss and Mam and all the eighteen dirty kids (see "Hillbilly Archaeology" above). Several minutes into *The Egg and I* (Universal, 1947), the very first shot that introduces the Kettle concept into the movies also suggests the affront that Ma and Pa offer to middle-class American striving: we see a medium-close shot of Claudette Colbert's prettified garden plot, carefully tied off and precisely delineated by a decorative little string. Colbert plays the not entirely optimistic city bride of Fred MacMurray, the boundlessly optimistic but often bilked city boy with visions of idyllic country living based on "old-fashioned American" ideals of personal enterprise. He's practically an evangelist for capital entrepreneurship, and he has brought his sophisticated urban bride "high up in the mountains" to practice what he preaches. (Which mountains these are is not at all clear: the place seems sometimes vaguely western, with comic Indians;

Figure 2.19.
Marjorie Main and
Percy Kilbride as
Ma and Pa Kettle,
in a publicity shot
for *Ma and Pa Kettle
at Home* (Universal,
1954). (Courtesy of
Wisconsin Center
for Film and The-
ater Research)

sometimes vaguely southern, with the Kettles' ramshackle farm; and often vaguely New England, with Percy Kilbride's accent.)

Colbert, as MacMurray's doubting but dutiful wife, struggles to do the right rural thing and plants her little perfect garden. But intruding into this symbol of conventional effort come the legs of mules and then a wagon wheel, which rudely tromp on the rosy expectations of capital investment. Pa Kettle has arrived. After destroying the garden with great unconscious aplomb, he laconically begins to "borrow" from his new neighbor MacMurray—lumber, nails, hammer, saw, and green paint. Borrowing, to Pa Kettle, means appropriating without cash, but MacMurray is himself perfectly unconscious of the fact, in that Ronald Reagan way of his. If he were aware at all, he would recognize in Pa the bent reflection of his idealized hopes, the perfect cracked mirror image of his true rural potentiality. MacMurray is portrayed, after all, as not only inept but as dangerously inept at country subsistence.

*The Egg and I* ends after the city slickers are completely burned out by an act of nature, a savage lightning storm. But just as suddenly, the Kettles and all their neighbors shower the burned-out city newcomers with enough supplies to rebuild and start their egg-production business anew (blessed economic resurrection). In addition, Claudette Colbert discovers she's pregnant, finding herself, too, finally reflected in the distorted Ma Kettle mirror of country fertility. The music swells along with everything else.

The *real* Maw and Paw Kettle, the originals for the fiction, were launched in Betty MacDonald's nonfiction book *The Egg and I* (1945). The Kettles lived in the Olympic Mountains of Washington state—nowhere close to Appalachia, the Ozarks, or New England, but on the required rough edge of the economy nevertheless. MacDonald's book was far less lighthearted than the movie Hollywood made from it. The book is very long and often quite funny, but overall rather surprisingly mean. Betty MacDonald seems to have been a very supercilious person; she said nasty things about other people and meant them. However, it was not the Kettles—the unclean blasphemer Maw or the whining beggar Paw—who drew the full BTUs of MacDonald's contempt. *That* she saved for the American Indians of the Northwest coast: "It was a bitter blow when I learned that today's little red brother, or at least the Pacific Coast variety which I saw, is not a tall copper-colored brave. . . . Instead, our [real] Indian, squat and mud-colored, was more apt to be found slouched in a Model T, a toothpick clenched between his yellow teeth, a drunken leer on his flat face" (p. 22).

Hollywood moved MacDonald's story to its own vaguer Kettleland, which looks suspiciously like the Universal lot in southern California. (The Ozarks were featured as a place of distant kinship in *The Kettles in the Ozarks*, the very last of the series, with Arthur Hunnicut playing Pa after Percy Kilbride's death.) And Hollywood transmogrified MacDonald's vicious and debased Indians into the almost unnoticed Geoduck (pronounced *gooey-duck*) and Crowbar, Pa Kettle's occasional, all-but-silent Injun sidekicks.

After debuting as subsidiary characters in *The Egg and I*, the Kettles hit as stars of their own long-running foolshow in 1949 with the simply titled *Ma and Pa Kettle*. (Marjorie Main was nominated for an Oscar for this film but lost to Celeste Holm in *Gentleman's Agreement*.) The plot has Pa winning a tobacco-slogan contest, for which first prize is a "Home of the Future," something that the Kettles need beyond all measure but that, comically, they're just not able to handle. In other words, the Kettles on screen confirmed convenient urban pieties holding that rural poverty was noble for rural people. Ma and Pa are forever going into snooty society (*Ma and Pa Kettle Go to Town* [1950] and *Ma and Pa Kettle on Vacation* [1953]), or snooty society is forever seeking them out (for example, Alan Mowbray playing Alphonsus Mannering in *Ma and Pa Kettle at Home* [1954]), and through the very simple, poor, rural, unmodernized goodness in their hearts, the Kettles always stumble through to victory.

Universal produced these movies deliberately for the small-town market, for what *Variety* contemptuously called "the hicks in the sticks," and in that venue the flattering Kettle movies had an "astonishing commercial success." Sophisticated urban critics howled in disbelief—"Ma and Pa Kettle Open a Gaucherie Store"—while people in the pokey country symbolically thumbed their noses at the fast city in an illusion of rube persistence.

On TV the habitually bilked city slickers of *Green Acres* were the direct descendants of Fred MacMurray and Claudette Colbert in *The Egg and I*, just as the Clampetts of *The Beverly Hillbillies* hailed directly back to the Kettles, in a sort of sequel that might have been named *Ma and Pa Kettle Go to the Mall*. (*The Beverly Hillbillies* was lately trashed by Penelope Spheeris in a major motion picture.) The latter TV show's formidable popularity in nonurban parts of the country and in large sections of suburban America again suggests that for a time and for a particular audience, the hillbilly served as the bounce-back clown who mirrors an undeniable possibility in the majority and who violates the normal boundaries. The Clampetts are utterly naive and stupid about money, which they improbably have in great gobs, and they are naive and stupid about greed, which everyone else has in great gobs. Yet in their very stupidity, because it is pure and true in ways that can flatter *us*, they survive and in fact triumph in the fantasy of the show. Horace Newcomb writes: "I think it is possible to demonstrate that the larger [American] populace has historically used Appalachia for that *liminal* ground on which to criticize its own values, to challenge the 'acceptable' way of life with other attitudes. . . . The real thrust of condemnation in such a presentation is not against the Southern mountaineer, but against contemporary American culture."

The fool's hangout is "that liminal ground," a threshold into unacceptable but irresistible chaos.

## Andy Griffith as Clown

Our public hillbilly imagery swings between foolshow and horror show. The career of Andy Griffith illustrates that range very well. He has played both bounce-back hillbilly clown and the hillbilly male monster (see "Andy Griffith as Masculine Monster" in Chapter 6). They are actually the same character, but because the Griffith monster develops *motives*, the two hillbillies tip our reactions in very different directions.

Griffith started his showbiz career as clown. From his novelty record debut in late 1953 ("What It Was Was Football") to his first *Ed Sullivan Show* appearance in January 1954, to his 15 March 1955 live TV debut as Will Stockdale in *No Time for Sergeants*, to his September 1955 Broadway debut as the same character in the stage play version, to his featured role on a thirty-minute episode of *The Danny Thomas Show* as Sheriff Andy Taylor of Mayberry (15 February 1960), Andy Griffith struck it rich playing sweet country ignorance, angelic-but-wrong reasonableness. He was a magical rural scapegoat-fool, appearing—poof!—amid an obsessive urban waltz of split-level, two-car-garage, drip-dry, get-ahead Eisenhower Republicanism. In such a world, the Griffith clown's rural dumbness should stigmatize and doom him. But his fool's magic protects him.

In the early 1950s, *From Here to Eternity* pictured strong male aggressiveness as an American patriotic norm, and *Rebel without a Cause* portrayed a *lack* of strong male aggressiveness as pathetic. Both movies, and many, many more, presented ideal masculinity as street-smart, not rural, since rural—by definition in the prevailing comic hillbilly representations—meant subnormal and slow. One would never expect a city boy to be slow. (The movies that tended to idealize masculinity in a rural setting were Westerns, always set in the dismissible past. In the real world, contemporary rurality need not apply.) So here comes the bumpkin from Carolina, who doesn't know a rumpus from a rumpus room, crossing boundaries, going where he clearly should not be able to take care of himself, and surviving very well anyway and despite all odds.

Griffith began perfecting his country clown act in Goldsboro, North Carolina, about 1951. He and his wife Barbara developed a civic club act of dancing, singing, guitar playing, and humorous monologues (including Griffith's hillbilly description of football). Some might have thought he was making fun of country people, and that element certainly was present, but Griffith so clearly loved his character, embracing him not as Other but as himself, that his dumb act was not offensive. He benefited from what Steve Smith calls "the in-house factor," being connected to what he was ostensibly making fun of. Griffith in his clown guise gently stroked small-town and middle-class Carolina audiences—educational groups, conventions, association meetings—with a friendly sort of leveling. We're all hicks and hillbillies to *somebody*. Everyone has to look into this mirror and not be blinded or appalled.

Griffith had grown up not as a hillbilly but as a townie in Mt. Airy, North Carolina, where he attended Mt. Airy High School, but by his own admission he "was not sports-oriented or especially bright." He wasn't popular, and not playing sports shut him out of one of the normal routes to masculine achievement in small towns all across the land. Already outside the adolescent mainstream, Griffith's devout participation in the Moravian Church probably shut him out even more. For a time, influenced by a particularly strong minister, he set his goals on becoming a minister, too, and in high school he must have offered a very peculiar sort of provocation indeed.

It is interesting that when Griffith began to ease *inside* the American mainstream as a married high school teacher in Goldsboro, his acceptance by the parents of the kids who might have called him a hillbilly nerd was won by performing—by masquerading as the epitome of the dumb rural outsider who, by all logic, should not be in attendance at a banquet for the Jefferson Standard Life Insurance Company (where he first performed "What It Was Was Football"). Here was a super-serious and "cultured" young man who had "half-yearned to try opera," speaking in the exaggerated flap of someone so out of it he doesn't know beans:

Somebody had took and drawed white lines over this here cow pasture and Ah looked down there and, friends, Ah seen the awfullest fight Ah ever seen in mah life. They would throw one another down and stomp on one another and Ah don't know what-all. And quick as one of 'em'd get hurt, they'd tote him off and run another one on. It was that both bunches of them men wanted this funny-lookin' punkin to play with. They couldn't 'a eat it because they kicked it the whole time and it never bust.

This is ingratiatingly accurate ignorance. It appears before its betters with no offense intended and *insists* on presenting itself with no evident fear of derision. It turns the tables on its audience. And it's very sly.

In the movie version of *No Time for Sergeants* (1958), the U.S. army drafts the Griffith character and carts him off to basic training. With that, the hillbilly fool crosses the boundary into a special arena of masculine anxiety. To lose your identity in a cadre, to suffer physical pain and humiliation, and to find the gumption to train to face death is no male passage of little moment, yet the symbolic fool who can't do anything right (your own worst suspicion about yourself?) nevertheless survives induction into This Man's Army (Fig. 2.20).

There have been numerous movie fools for every war, going all the way back to Charlie Chaplin in *Shoulder Arms* (1918), followed by the likes of Bob Hope, Jerry Lewis, and the "Brit" Norman Wisdom or by the even more prevalent fool teams such as Wheeler and Woolsey (*Half Shot at Sunrise* [1930]); Laurel and Hardy (*Pack Up Your Troubles* [1932], *Blockheads* [1938], *Great Guns* [1941]); the Ritz Brothers (*We're In the Army Now* [1939]); Abbott and Costello (*Buck Privates* [1940]); Jimmy Durante and Phil Silvers (*You're In the Army Now* [1941]); and Dean Martin and Jerry Lewis (*At War with the Army* [1951]). More recently, Bill Murray played the fool in uniform in *Stripes* (1981), and Pauly Shore did the same in *In the Army Now* (1994). All of these movies are nervous essays on male competence, symbolically surviving the trial that ought to doom it. They make us feel better about our own potentialities.

In the movie version of *No Time for Sergeants*, Griffith is "a backwoods bonehead," assigned perpetually to wear "a look of friendly idiocy." The plot contrives to put him quickly under the strain of military training, but the comic reversal is prompt. Whereas every other man around him wrestles with duty, Griffith's Will Stockdale is blithe and unscathed, even though he's handcuffed, verbally abused, insulted, assaulted, and

Figure 2.20. Andy Griffith as Will Stockdale in *No Time for Sergeants*, with Myron McCormick (right) and Nick Adams (left). (Courtesy of Wisconsin Center for Film and Theater Research)

set to cleaning toilets. (He's made "permanent latrine orderly," to which he responds "GOH-a-AH-LEE!")

In the movie, Griffith's street-wise and wise-ass nemesis Irving (played by Murray Hamilton), along with three of his bully boys, decides to pick a fight. Irving taunts the Griffith fool, suggesting he sleeps with pigs. And the fool grins in response, genuinely amused by the idea. As traditional fool, Griffith does not seem to know he's been insulted. Irving then ups the ante and speculates out loud on what breed of hog the fool's father must have been ("Chester White or Poland China?"). Making jokes about the fool to his face is one thing; but making jokes about his father, in this instance, proves who the real fools in this piece are. Irving and his boys get their faces cracked. The Griffith fool soundly whomps them all. (In any other service comedy, the requisite barracks brawl might end differently, with the fool's head through the latrine wall. But either way, the message is the same: the male fool miraculously survives whatever physical/psychological punishment the army can deliver.)

As Will Stockdale, Griffith roused himself to defend certain eternal verities: the sacredness of family and home. He believes in the eternity of goodness. Here he is narrating his first day in boot camp:

> It sure was interesting when we got to the classification center. They took us around from one building to another'n, and they stuck needles into our arms and whumped us on the knees with a little rubber hammer and mashed down our tongues with an ice cream stick. And then after *a rail nice* supper—I never had such a fill of beans in my entire life!—we was all sittin around the barracks in our snappy new uniforms, learning how to salute?—everbody talking and joking and feeling the back of their necks, where they'd had these horse-clippers run over 'em?—when this *nice* fellow, this here *sergeant* come in.

Something as realistically ridiculous as *niceness* in this situation is for our hillbilly the improbable yet functional supreme ideal. Later, after he's been punished by Sergeant King and put to work cleaning the latrine ("You're the officer in charge"), Will takes it as a great honor and turns directly to the camera: "Well. It just goes to show ya how good things happen to ya when you're *least* expecting 'em!"

Griffith's launching on episodic television as Sheriff Andy Taylor in 1958 (in the episode of the *Danny Thomas Show* already noted above) was far goofier, in the Will Stockdale tradition, than his long-range character became on the hugely popular *Andy Griffith Show*. One reason for his toning down was that the show's writers gave the former hillbilly fool his *own* fool in Don Knotts's Barney Fife, so Sheriff Andy became progressively normative, while Barney took over the dumb-hick duties. Eventually the show might have been renamed *Andy Knows Best*.

## The Hillbilly as Priapus

Three hillbillies fall all over each other in pursuit of a female erotic dream who spends her time wagging her tail and fondling her breasts. Soon the men join her in this happy activity.
—*Soho News*, describing a performance of the avant-garde dance troupe Pilobolus, December 1981

Much of Sut Lovingood's energy was derived from sexual heat, and traditionally fools and clowns have often broached the obscene—frequently *the* boundary that is most taboo. Many of the movies offering hillbillies as stars of their own foolshows have been thinly veiled assaults on sexual respectability, perhaps even more than they are assaults on the assumptions of Pax Capitalismus. Some are attacks on both.

Sut was alive and well (under a variety of aliases) in those fast cars hauling 'shine that roared through the so-called "good-old-boy" movies of the 1960s and 1970s. These were essentially comedies that combined priapic male fantasies with car- and propriety-bashing high jinks. The good-old-boy moonshine-running movies were spit-in-your-eye foolshows that pretty directly mirrored the tied-down frustrations of large numbers of wage-earning men who were nothing without that cash (see Chapter 5).

The 1959 movie musical *Li'l Abner* was also a priapic tease, one long, late burlesque leer with songs. The central fool is that strapping mountain hunk, Li'l Abner, who as the clown must reverse all expectation. The reversal in this case is that Li'l Abner, as embodied by Leslie Parrish, is as erotically inert as a stump. One subplot, as a result, hinges on curing him of his sexual passivity. In fact, all the new husbands of Dogpatch—a whole chorus of muscle-beach boys newly bagged in the latest Sadie Hawkins Day race—are sumps of romantic lethargy. It seems that Mammy's Yokumberry tonic, her secret muscle-building-and-masculindizin' formula, has ironically robbed the men of all sex drive even while it pumped them up. It falls to ineffectual little henpecked Pappy Yokum to use psychology to reverse the effects of the Yokumberry, and masculinity is saved. General libidinal rejoicing follows and closes the show.

The hillbilly milieu as a paradise of unbridled lust is practically an industry standard in much soft-core porn, from *Child Bride of the Ozarks* (1937) to *Shotgun Wedding* (1963) to *Scum of the Earth* (1976) to *I Spit on Your Grave* (1978) and beyond. But these were not foolshows; laughter wasn't the primary thing they were meant to give rise to.

Russ Meyer sometimes used hillbilly eroticism in his grim jokes about uptight American morality during the decay of Eisenhower Republicanism. In movies like *Mudhoney* (1965), that phantasmagorically painful descent into the twilight zone of the Ozarks, sex is a bludgeon.

Figure 2.21. Albert T. Viola (center), as preacher Amos Huxley, preps the ignorant hillbilly's daughter for a visit from the Angel Leroy in *Preacherman*. (Courtesy of Wisconsin Center for Film and Theater Research)

But when the object *was* laughter and the subject was erotic tomfoolery, the result might be more like *God's Little Acre* (1958) or, even better, like *Preacherman* (Preacherman Corp., 1971). *Preacherman*, according to Jimmy McDonough and Bill Landis, cost $65,000 and was shot in sixteen days on location in the countryside around Charlotte, North Carolina. It featured a randy preacher, a dumb hillbilly moonshiner, and the hillbilly's very ripe daughter (Fig. 2.21). The movie benefited from "the bang-zoom direction of one Albert T. Viola, an obscure Texan," who under the name Amos Huxley also starred, improbably but convincingly, as the libidinous Preacherman of the title. Huxley boinged his characters into the frame and boinged them out, retelling the hilarious Miller's Tale of a traveling priapic fool—the Preacherman himself—who is focused unfailingly on forbidden fruit. The very first shot in the movie is a close-up of the tip of a hickory hoe handle. The camera slowly moves down the handle and onto naked female breasts, which are presently visited by a man's hands. Almost immediately Preacherman, the unhandsome owner of those hands, gets severely beaten by the sheriff, who happens to be the mean pappy of the gal Preacherman is caught fondling. On the run into the next county, Preacherman stumbles into a veritable nest of ignorant hillbillies, whose spirits and standing in the world he nevertheless manages to raise, whose group identity he inspires, whose self-interest he fosters, even while he adopts the hysterically funny nighttime identity of "the Angel Leroy" in order to crawl religiously into the comely daughter's bed each and every night "for prayers."

The movie grossed $5 million and spawned a sequel, *Preacherman Meets Widderwoman* (1972?), and then a formula (*Hot Summer in Barefoot County* (1974) and *Truckin' Man* (1975?), both done by Preacherman Corp.) — country foolshows for country audiences. But what happens when the indigenous foolshow falls into the hands of the not-native, the condo chic?

## Raising Arizona

The yuppies who make movies and the yuppies . . . who see them
have become so removed from the poky, traditional universe that used
to be called the backbone of America that life there suddenly seems a
mesmerizing novelty, at once incomprehensible and strangely familiar,
us and not us.
—Stephen Schiff, *Vanity Fair*, April 1987

*Raising Arizona* probably was, in fact, snide and contemptuous at its heart, because the Coen brothers who made it are snide and contemptuous at heart. But they also invented and entertained like no one else making movies in 1987. *Raising Arizona*, the ultimate in late-eighties urban hip, promoted the "postmodern," if that term means what I take it to mean: the exhilaration of universal mockery.

The specter of country subsistence haunts the urban memory in the form of the Coens' hillbilly protagonist H. I. ("Hi") McDunnough, the scapegoat fool who saves us all. McDunnough, played by Nicolas Cage, is a southwestern clod, a miserable failure at American acquisition. He lives resigned to robbing convenience stores, getting caught, and serving his time, over and over. He has become the dreaded recidivist, "a ree-peat O-fender," a backward evolver and, incidentally, a classic knock-down fool, a clown who gets to cross boundaries the rest of us

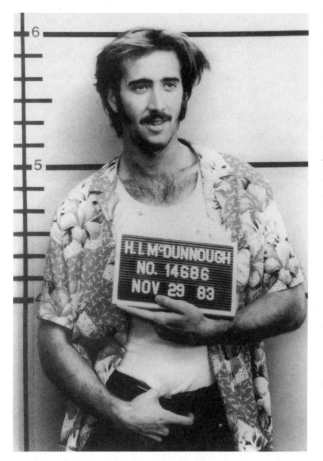

Figure 2.22. Nicolas Cage as the "ree-peat O-fender" in *Raising Arizona*. (Courtesy of the University of California at Los Angeles Arts Library, Special Collections)

dread to cross and who yet survives the multitudinous punishments he gets (Fig. 2.22).

With naive faith in the American dream, this hillbilly fool tries to go straight in the American way but blunders into more and worse crimes to achieve by irregular means "the basic family unit." Meanwhile, his physical pummeling goes from harsh to much harsher. Is he not a classic scapegoat/fool? And does he not mirror mid-eighties yuppie anxiety about nuclear families? When this movie was released in 1987, critic Stephen Schiff noted the highly devised contempt of its makers, the Coen brothers, and wisely observed that most of its paying audience would also probably fail the test of humility—they would laugh *at* the clod rather than see clearly into his mirror. Schiff said that rural America, "the cast-in-amber, never-never land of small town and countryside," had obviously become a foreign place to the city dwellers of our mainstream culture—people like the Coens themselves. Yet their text for this parable should have signaled humility and fellow-feeling: "Let no man deceive himself. If any man among you seemeth to be wise in this world, let him become a fool, that he may be wise" (I Cor. 3:18).

*Raising Arizona* employs a screamingly funny (and absolutely dead-pan) narration by Nicolas Cage as Hi, coupled with a cartoonish and highly entertaining visual style that we might call Hillbilly Reckless, invented by the Coens and photography director Barry Sonnenfeld. The story mocks the sentimental Yuppie desire to achieve the ideal American family. (*Raising Arizona* happened to coincide with the "family values" wave in Hollywood that produced such pictures as *Three Men and a Baby* and *Baby Boom*, both also released in 1987.) But the Coens' would-be model husband and father is the clown of Tempe rather than the prince of Wall Street. He stands outside the very possibility of success. In the classic way of fools, Hi is also the scapegoat, the butt of the joke, a sacrificial fool who must bear the humiliations of an absurd world but who also survives to bounce back eternally for the entertainment of his betters.

*Raising Arizona* is brilliantly composed to produce the experience of chaos. Its opening narration is underscored by the suggestive plunkings of a banjo, a harbinger of bluegrass Dionysiacs without the actual bluegrass. Although Hi's narration of his own story ostentatiously maintains a belief in logic, system, and order—Divine Order, in fact—the images the Coens and Sonnenfeld compose to go with that narration are more appropriate to a drunkard's dream or a fool's paradise. Hi thinks the world is orderly, but his world is absurd. In a film that mocks everything and everybody, Hi's dumb willingness to believe in orderliness is the greatest folly.

Early in the film, Hi describes prison life in terms of heroic masculinity: "There's a spirit of camaraderie that exists between the men that you find only in combat, maybe, or in a pro-ball club in the heat of the pennant drive." But while we listen to Hi's conventional rhetoric, we are seeing the bald-headed Mopping Convict, an intimidating behemoth played by the appropriately named Henry Tank, who growls at the camera as it moves past. When Hi is thrown into prison for the third time, he sentimentalizes the experience: "The flood of familiar sights, sounds, and faces almost made it feel like a homecoming," and the camera makes a repeat pass by the growling, floor-mopping convict.

"You're a flower, you are, just a little desert flower," Hi croons to the pint-sized tyrant Edwina ("Ed," played by Holly Hunter), the booking cop who takes his mug shot repeatedly and with whom he will form the matrimonial black hole that sucks everything into it. "I couldn't help thinking that a brighter future lay ahead, a future that was only eight to fourteen months away," Hi says, settling in to wait for his third parole and the opportunity to marry his little "desert flower." "Okay then," the parson says in pronouncing them man and wife, echoing the dithering idiots of the parole board. "Well, okay then" is the only philosophy necessary in a world where people think mere words can overcome the chaos of reality.

In his hopeless pursuit of middle-class heaven, Hi becomes a working stiff. Wonderfully surreal scenes of his workplace follow. On payday, Hi receives his piddling wages from a grotesquely made-up Payroll Cashier (the unforgettable Mary F. Glenn): "The guv-ment *do* take a bite, don't she?" But Hi's voice-over narration of these scenes never loses its fool's naïveté: "These were the happy days, the salad days, and Ed felt that having a critter was the next logical step. . . . Her point was that there was too much love and beauty for just the two of us, and every day we kept a child out of the world was a day he might later regret having missed."

Camaraderie, homecoming, beauty, hard work, and commitment to family—these are key and fixed terms for Hi, orderly concepts that he clings to ridiculously in a world designed to prove that words have no meaning. In fact, the Coens obviously see the very persistence of belief as premodern simple-mindedness. As he ends the movie, relating yet another of his dreams, Hi is still spinning the same fool's romance (and then unconsciously puncturing it himself): "I saw our home! If not Arizona, not too far away, where all parents were wise and strong and all children were happy and beloved. I don't know: maybe it was Utah."

Hi builds a kind of cartoon cathedral out of inappropriately sanctimonious language. His narration is littered with mangled Jesus quotes and hallowed Americana. For example, Hi and Ed strive to be "fruitful," but Ed proves "barren." "Her insides were a rocky place where my seed could find no purchase," he deadpans. Later, he becomes Jesus Christ transmigrating into Abraham Lincoln in justifying the kidnapping of

Nathan Arizona Jr., one of the much-publicized Arizona quintuplets: "Y'all without sin can cast the first stone, but we thought it was unfair that some should have so many while others should have so few." The Coens' script is otherwise studded with biblical debris. The baby-worshiping neighbor Dot chooses Bible names for all her several kids, and her husband Glen tells Hi to "heal thyself" through wife swapping. And Gale Snopes, the escaped con played by the incomparable John Goodman, invites Hi to a bank robbery with this opening: "I'd rather light a candle than curse your darkness."

Since Hi and Ed's lack of a baby amounts to a sin of omission, the kidnapped Arizona quint is "the answer to all our prayers," according to Hi's narration. They have failed at forming the "basic American family unit," and so having any baby will require supplication at a suitably high Throne of Grace. That is, it takes a long ladder for Hi to ascend to the Arizona nursery—the hillbilly enacting a climb into heaven to steal glory (Fig. 2.23). (My student Angel Rippy pointed out the curious wall-papered clouds in that nursery.) Glen's wife Dot, when she first sees Nathan Junior (alias "Hi Junior," a.k.a. "Ed Junior" and finally "Gale Junior"), shrieks, "He's an angel—an angel straight from heaven! . . . You just *got* to tell how you got this little angel. Just fly it straight down from heaven? . . . You're *going* to send him to Arizona State!"

In comic juxtaposition to all the pseudo-biblical rhetoric is the chaos of Hi's actual life, a chaos effectively suggested by the full-throated screaming of men. Gale and Evelle Snopes scream repeatedly; the "Hayseed in the Pickup" (as he's identified in the credits) screams as he is about to run down Hi during the central protracted chase sequence; Hi himself screams many times at full volume. Screaming signals the complete collapse of expectations, the touching of "the abyss," being possessed by chaos itself.

As a mirror image of yuppie anxiety, Hi is continually assaulted for his failed masculinity. Edwina bosses him around unmercifully. (Elaine Vann has pointed out that shortening Edwina's name to Ed bends her gender.) And she is the more dominant McDunnough. She makes Hi go through with kidnapping the baby when he wants to call the whole thing off. "Now you go up there and git me a toddler right now!" she orders, locking the car doors from the inside. Later she rescues him on the street after he returns briefly to convenience-store robbery and is

Figure 2.23. "The hillbilly enacting a climb into heaven to steal glory": the "adoption" of Nathan, from *Raising Arizona*. (Courtesy of the University of California at Los Angeles Arts Library, Special Collections)

being chased by a Doberman-led pack of snarling dogs, by cops with guns, and by an albino convenience-store clerk with a sawed-off shotgun. As soon as Hi is safely in the car with her, Ed gives him a stiff right to the jaw and chews him out: "You're supposed to be *an example!*" Hi hollowly defends himself: "I come from a long line of frontiersmen!" and then immediately confirms his true status as a henpecked joke of a man: "Oh, here it is, Dear. Turn here"—the obsequious husband back-seat-driving his more dominant wife.

Later, when Gale Snopes directly confronts Hi's weakness as a man— "Say, who wears the pants around here, H. I.?"—Hi reacts as if a hot poker had just touched his privates. So he backslides and plans armed robbery with his escaped-convict buddies, Gale and Evelle Snopes, who of course are named for Faulkner's notorious hillbillies.

Hi is not who he thinks he is, and he can't be who his wife thinks he ought to be. So who is he? My students pointed out a detail that had repeatedly escaped me through several viewings: Hi's tattoo of the Thrush Company logo, which looks very similar to Woody Woodpecker, is exactly duplicated on Leonard Smalls, "the Lone Biker of the Apocalypse," the scarifying vision of fire and death that Hi both conjures up in his dreams and must eventually fight for real. (The visual paralleling of the Thrush logo on both Hi and The Lone Biker is *not* in the movie's published script.) In planning to go off with Gale and Evelle on their crime spree, Hi is trying to draw the dark force away from his fledgling, illegal family: "If I leave, hopefully *it* will leave with me," he writes Edwina in his farewell letter. He understands, however dimly, that the reality of the Biker is an extension of himself, like an image in a cracked mirror.

Leonard Smalls may be a projection of Hi's own dark potentialities, the unloved human morsel gone rancid in the sunlight, but Smalls is not the only mirror for Hi in the movie. His very name, Smalls, points us in a concurrent direction to Nathan Junior, one of the many small and helpless things that Hi worries about. Besides the Thrush tattoo on his chest, Smalls sports another tattoo on his arm: a skull and crossbones with the legend "MAMA DIDN'T LOVE ME." This he perversely wears as a kind of coat of arms, along with the sinister trophy of a pair of baby shoes tied to his road-warrior belt. Smalls tells Nathan Junior's real father, the wealthy Unpainted Furniture King, "Why, as a pup I myself fetched $30,000 on the black market, and that was 1954 dollars." So *he* was a kidnapped baby, too.

The linking of Hi, Smalls, and Nathan Junior becomes even more pointed and clear: Hi, the chronic, maybe "genetic" outlaw, vows to leave his outlaw condition behind, but Leonard Smalls, the eternal outlaw with the duplicate Thrush tattoo, stalks him with uncanny instinct. Smalls explains: "You wanna *find* an outlaw, you *call* an outlaw." And the baby is a further mirror, reflecting *pure* potentiality. When Hi first holds him up in the McDunnough homestead (the "starter" trailer), he looks into that baby mirror and unconsciously recognizes himself: "He's a little outlaw. . . that twinkle in his eye." And later Evelle Snopes seconds it: "He's a little outlaw. You can see that, Hi." Angel Rippy has pointed out that Gale and Evelle also are mirrors. While Hi is trying to be someone he can't be—Edwina's notion of middle-class decency, ironically symbolized by the grotesque cartoon couple Glen and Dot—Gale and Evelle represent the hungry and self-indulgent fleshiness of the nature Hi can't escape. When Hi protests that he just can't go out and rob banks with the Snopeses any more, Gale sagely replies, "You ain't being true to your own nature, H. I."

So in the funhouse mirror of *Raising Arizona*, the dark Lone Biker is the kidnapped child is Hi McDunnough is outlaw and hillbilly by nature, trying with no possibility of success to steal himself back as a baby, to redeem with a forlorn and laughable fondness the dread summary, "Mama didn't love me."

The Picts were

apparently an

unconverted tribe

of indigenous

savages, still

tattooed and

woaded.

—Robert Southey,

*The Life of Wesley,*

1820

 **3** ## The Coonskin Cap Boys

The wildman has haunted European imagination for hundreds of years. The British, especially, have a tradition of depicting nearly naked, savage, shaggy, blue-dyed near-men who both threaten from the shadows and tingle the blood. Why should white European culture in America be any different? In our scenario, though, the clown and fool traditions of the previous chapter meld with a wildman tradition powerful enough that we feel the need for protection. But we can't always laugh this fearsome creature off in a foolshow—the Coonskin Capper, the man who penetrates the frontier and is intimate with natural chaos.

# The Long and Winding Woad

Rodger Cunningham single-handedly drove back the time line for modern Appalachian history several thousand years in *Apples on the Flood: The Southern Mountain Experience* (1987). Cunningham made the point that the pitied and reviled Southern Appalachian mountaineer of the 1960s and 1970s is culturally related to the fringe Celts of the Roman Empire, similarly pitied and reviled in their day. The Picts, for example, qualify as fringe Celts. Cunningham describes the northern frontier of the Roman Empire in England (what is now the Scottish border) during the time the Romans were losing their grip. By 400 A.D., the by then thoroughly Christianized Romans were gathering their legions and decamping for warmer climes, abandoning in the process some highly colonized and Romanized Celts, who lived like Romans in fortified settlements and who thought like Romans in their hatred of the painted, savage Picts who lived and slogged in blood north of Hadrian's Wall. The Picts were wildmen of the high ground who threatened civilization.

The Romanized natives farther south—ironically, cousins of the Picts—were justifiably terrified, for without the protection of the Roman legions, the Romanized Celts were indeed sitting ducks for the hungry and now resentful Picts. Thereby arose the negative racial stereotype applicable to one's actual cousins. Negative imaging was (and is) also partly an attempt at magic. We contain the wildman and ward off his evil by conjuring up a more comforting picture: "We are superior to you, and we will banish your rotten, stinking race."

The blue-smudged Picts did actually decorate their bodies in tattoolike designs with the blue dye painstakingly made from the leaves of *Isatis tinctoria*, the woad plant, a member of the mustard family that likes a cold climate. Woad, once established, is an aggressive plant, a pernicious and pestiferous weed, and in the Middle Ages its cultivation was commonly regulated by law. So in the view of their co-islanders to the south, the "woad-stained" Picts willfully chose to wallow in weeds outside the walls of Christianized civilization.

Hundreds of years after they ceased to be an actual threat, the Picts were still graphically depicted in the Elizabethan press. The publishing business in sixteenth-century London thrived on two-headed calves and Trojan kings. So the virtually naked and fantastically illuminated Picts were delectable surprises.

Since at least the twelfth century, when Geoffrey of Monmouth wrote his British history (his "Celtic fairy tales," said a later English critic, "a thriving garden of spurious history"), every educated English person believed that the island kingdom had been founded by refugees from the fall of Troy, and that one of that line of Homeric kings was Arthur, who married Guinevere and defended his people against the Pictish barbarians. For hundreds of years, the educated classes on the island imagined their earliest ancestors striking poses in togas and burnished armor. The Picts, offered as progenitors rather than opponents, challenged that myth.

The historian William Camden suggested in 1586 that the word *Britannia* had nothing whatsoever to do with the Trojan Brutus, as Geoffrey of Monmouth had proposed, but was a Celtic and Greek compound meaning "land of the painted people." Camden and others exploded the myth of Trojan ancestors and suggested that the pre-Roman Britons were all pretty much similar to the Picts. Elizabethans were both thrilled and repelled to discover that their ancestors were not classical heroes in period costume but "primitives": "They lived in caves and pit-dwellings; their dress was usually the hide of beasts and they were food gatherers, and they had as yet little skill in the chase and in fishing." The wildman turned out to be not an exterior threat at all but a mirror image of something disturbingly internal.

The intricate tattooing of ancient Picts reminded some Elizabethans of the Carolina Algonquins and the Iroquois of the New World, so lately encountered, who had been found to paint and tattoo their near-naked bodies, too. (Though in reality the more extravagant tattooing among native Americans was confined mainly to women. The men thought it painful—and it was). This recognition of similarities between the ancient Picts and contemporary Indians produced some outstanding cognitive dissonance. On the one hand, "greedy colonists intent on taking advantage of a simple folk," as British antiquities expert T. D. Kendrick put it, hid their own savage greed from themselves by defining "the simple folk" as subhuman primitives. The body painting could be made to prove it. Yet on the other hand, to see the savages *thriving*, like weeds, "amazed the [European] thinker into doubting the value of Western Civilization and of the Christian faith."

On this continent, no Hadrian's Wall delineated the frontier. We were never so neatly separated from savagery on these shores. So our mental pictures of frontiersmen, pathfinders, deerslayers, leatherstockings, and Daniel Boones are part terrifying memory, part flattering image of ourselves as masters of the nature we fear.

## The Thrill of Buckskin

Michael Mann's film *The Last of the Mohicans* (1992) rang me like a tuning fork, kept me up all night. (Michael Mann also invented *Miami Vice*, and clearly, to him both Miami and the early American backwoods signify the same electrifying wilderness.) In *Mohicans* the action takes place on foot, but it's motorized nevertheless—furious running, hand-to-hand fighting, killing, cutting out of human hearts, paddling down swift streams, going over and through waterfalls in both boats and buckskin—satisfying violence with clear necessity and solid resolution (Fig. 3.1). At the center of it is our American Pict, Daniel Day-Lewis as Hawkeye, enacting the dream of our competence, virility opening the frontier, and we will follow him through (never mind that Hawkeye has "the magical ability," as Randy Crutchfield put it, "to shoot accurately an extremely inaccurate round-bullet muzzleloader through dense hardwoods").

Surely at least part of the heightened charge of this *Mohicans* was the landscape in which the movie was filmed: the mountains of western North Carolina in parts of Burke and McDowell counties and on the shores of Lake James and at Chimney Rock and on the top of Table Rock Mountain and in the Linville Gorge. Mann's tracking shots and Steadicam work are marvels of technique, for example the extravaganza of making us move beside Hawkeye as he walks uphill with his band of survivors beside a dangerously signifying mountain river pouring in sheets like knife blades off sheer stone. Knifing nature meets elemental man (and woman, because the rest of Hawkeye's party does all right, too—even the ones who seem weak at first, like Cora's sister Alice and the British officer who loves Cora). All of them mount upstream

Figure 3.1. Daniel Day-Lewis (center) doing a little furious running in *The Last of the Mohicans*. (Courtesy of the University of California at Los Angeles Arts Library, Special Collections)

against this flashing water as though striving against relentless possibility. And they look *good* as they go, too. Some of them, three out of the six, actually make it. And the ones who don't make it demonstrate death as the ultimate opportunity, an affirmative act of willful courage. That's the rush of *Mohicans*, the illusion of human brilliance under the threat of extinction, and that rush is best induced where humans are symbolically woad-stained (notice, incidentally, the carefully authentic tattooing on the Native American extras in *Mohicans*). Also, the violence in this movie—a Michael Mann hallmark—turns out to represent the poetic side of our species after all, both necessary to our self-image (extolled by George Will in a glowing essay on *Mohicans*) and taboo. And how better to convey that complex propaganda than in these southern mountains.

## Fooling with Coonskin:
## The One and Only Original American Hillbilly

I was all set to roll up my sleeves and make some of my speeches and tell
hillbilly stories and help get my son elected to Congress.
—former senator Albert Gore Sr. (D-Tenn.) remembering when his son
    Al Gore Jr. first decided to run for Congress

The cover of *Davy Crockett's Almanac* for 1845 put the legendary
Davy back to back with another tall-tale character, Ben Harding (Fig.
3.2). Davy is the one on the right with the fool's grin and the fool's coxs-
comb, and is he not visually the descendant of the classic fool in Chapter 2 (see Fig. 2.1)?

This is not the way most twentieth-century Americans tend to remember Davy Crockett. Think of John Wayne playing the part in 1960
as an American Masculine Ideal. But in his own day, the political clout
Crockett wielded as a genuine backwoodsman became a threat to East
Coast power and had to be controlled. His social betters in the more civilized cities made him play the coonskin-capped clown for their political profit.

David Crockett was no fool, of course. He did belong to the frontier,
and he was a master at wilderness survival. Within living memory, members of his family had fought Indians in upper east Tennessee. And
when Crockett moved farther west to Lawrence and Hickman counties,
the land was still a hurricane-scarred wilderness full of downed timber
and big bears. But for all its dangers and discomforts, the frontier was a
right exhilarating place, and free.

One famous story about how David Crockett put down a snob in the
Tennessee legislature is supposedly true (unlike much of the other
freight, including that coonskin cap business). Crockett had been newly
elected by the inhabitants of Hickman and Lawrence counties to serve
in the Fourteenth General Assembly of that state's legislature, which
convened 17 September 1821 at Murfreesborough. In town David
Crockett represented two fringes, a geographic as well as an economic
one. He was regularly only a half-step ahead of his creditors. But by
the time he arrived at his first session of the Tennessee legislature, the
reality of life on the geographic fringe had made him a name as an all-
American specimen—a trailblazer, bear hunter, tracker, Indian-killer.

Figure 3.2. Cover of the 1845 *Davy Crockett's Almanac*, picturing Davy (right) with the equally legendary Ben Harding (left). (Courtesy of the American Antiquarian Society)

His fellow settlers of Hickman and Lawrence counties elected him magistrate, and Crockett himself claimed that his judgments "were never appealed from," that they "stuck like wax." "I relied on natural born sense, and not on law," he said, "for I had never read a page in a law book in all my life." But that proud ignorance was not necessarily an asset in the polite society of capital cities. In town, David Crockett was woad-stained.

But in the country they loved him. As the rube his political enemies said he was, and thought he was, and which in fact he was, he had a kinship with his fellow western settlers that was potent; as a clever rube, he swept them along with him. In one election in Carroll County, he had to run against Dr. William E. Butler, nephew-in-law of the super-popular Andrew Jackson. Butler was also "a man of education, refinement, and some wealth." Against such an accomplished and formidably connected opponent, Crockett hyped his own roughness, boasting publicly to Butler that he would finance his campaign by killing wolves and collecting three dollars a scalp in bounty. Crockett's "tactic was to present [Dr. Butler] as an aristocrat among backwoodsmen." And it worked brilliantly. He mimicked and mocked and played the scapegoat-fool, emphasizing his own (honest) poverty while he marveled at the (dishonest) wealth of his opponent: "Fellow citizens, my aristocratic competitor has a fine carpet, and every day he *walks* on truck finer than any gowns your wife or your daughter, in all their lives, ever *wore!*"

But when his neighbors picked him for the state legislature, Crockett's self-consciousness got the better of him, and he appeared in town wearing the best store-bought clothes he could afford, in the style then available (*not* in the buckskin of legend). The new clothes were a disguise, but it didn't work. In the legislature he was an open object of fun, of ridicule even, all the more so because he spoke up, ineffectually, for the dirt-poor and unrepresented squatters on the western lands of Tennessee.

One day in legislative session, James C. Mitchell, a gentleman from the great eastern valley of Tennessee, at that time the more established and economically dominant part of the state, publicly referred to Crockett as "the gentleman from the cane." "The cane" was the equivalent of Pictland. The legislative chamber erupted in laughter. Crockett was stung. At first he quite sensibly intended to beat the living hell out of the man; not for nothing had he lived on the frontier. Where *he* came from, direct action was called for. Genteel forbearance, "*manners*," were unknown. Social pretensions were a joke told with whiskey. But in the more aristocratic Tennessee legislature, men spoke ironically and wore lace. When Crockett squared his shoulders, meaning to level the field, Mitchell wisely apologized. Crockett was left humiliated and frustrated.

The gentleman from the cane was, as a matter of fact, very unsure of himself in this setting — awkward, uneducated, and in some ways exactly the thing itself that the fine gentleman of the legislature implied he was. But walking in the streets of Murfreesborough soon after the incident, Crockett happened to discover in the dust a cambric ruffle of precisely the sort affected by Mitchell, and this piece of lacy work Crockett facetiously pinned to his own shirt front "like a light on a locomotive" and appeared in the legislature thus attired. It was a brilliant stroke of comeuppance, for suddenly the humor of the performance dawned upon all the members, and without a word being uttered they burst out laughing at Mitchell's expense.

Crockett as frontier wildman played the fool. He gave Mitchell the chaos-inducing jolt of seeing himself in a cracked mirror. In acting so daringly, Crockett achieved the fool's special status with the state: the legislators' laughter embraced him, appreciated his ingenuity, and seemed to empower him with recognition. But it did not empower him; it limited him. He was thereafter allowed to tell a joke but not much else. He could argue all day for his poor squatters and later for the Indians, even to prolonged laughter and applause, but nothing he ever said or did had any serious influence on any legislature he ever served in. Crockett finally began to realize that, and he despaired. When he decided to break with the United States altogether and left for Texas in November 1835, he was pretty much a burnt-out case.

Eventually this great hillbilly soul made it to Washington as a U.S. congressman, but there again he collided with the confounded limits of entertaining one's betters by playing the country fool: he ended up as a prisoner of the role of subordinated hillbilly and, worse, an outrageously manipulated tool of repressive politics. The antidemocratic Whigs deliberately groomed him as the genial backwoods antidote to the irresistible rise of Crockett's fellow Tennessean, Andrew Jackson. Jackson was himself a kind of hillbilly yahoo who would become a powerful small-*d* democrat president and whom, incidentally, Crockett had come to hate (see the sources for this chapter). The Whigs wrote Crockett's anti-Jackson speeches for him and put his name to burlesque versions of backwoods wisdom; they paraded him in the cities of the East and said, "See, here is one of Andrew Jackson's own kind, and even he despises him." But Crockett was slow to understand that being a public low-Other—one of Jackson's own kind—did not free him. He was on stage, and stage freedom is an illusion. Crockett didn't get it. He really believed for a time that the Whig party might actually run him for president.

After his death he became, through the *Crockett Almanacs* series, a country joke serving a ruling urban elite. The almanacs, which appeared annually through the 1840s and the 1850s, were essentially joke books with yearly planners. The jokes mainly took the form of outrageous tales in which Davy Crockett was often both main actor and butt of the joke. John Seelye says that the Crockett of the almanacs was "half horse, half horse's ass," and according to Richard Boyd Hauck, the stories were "riddled with nastiness"—jingoism, gross violence, and scatology. The almanacs were mass produced and proved wildly profitable (much like the Sut Lovingood tales in the 1850s and 1860s). They fed an urban audience the picture of Davy Crockett as a country bounceback trickster, a scapegoat fool who was made to survive so he could go on suffering humiliation.

## King of the Wild Frontier

Frank Thompson attributes Crockett's transformation into a nonfoolish American image of ideal masculinity to the movies, which first made his death at the Alamo a widely shared visual experience in *The Immortal Alamo* (1911). But the mutation of Crockett from complex fool to one-dimensional hero had been underway a lot longer. The joke-book almanacs had faded from the market by the time of the Civil War, and his death at the Alamo was being rediscovered as a topic for the popular press. Dead, he was a useful symbol of male sacrifice for a right cause, useful especially to the folks who determine causes.

By the time he first appeared in the movies in 1909—in a non-Alamo, Crockett-as-Lochinvar romance called *Davy Crockett, in Hearts United*—the American public was already used to thinking of him as a principled defender of sacred virtues, an ideal American nature-man. The Alamo movies in particular made him into a symbol of masculine democracy: he was not afraid to fight, not afraid to die, yet he was a peacemaker, fence mender, and veritable theorizer of group solidarity. In *The Martyrs of the Alamo* (1916) and in most subsequent Alamo movies, he makes peace between cocommanders Jim Bowie and William Travis ("We're all fighting for one cause—Texas"). This symbolic higher love in the man made him an icon—and also a good-natured and convenient-ly fatalistic foot soldier in the acquisition of territory. The Crockett movies seldom allowed the old backwoods fool of the almanacs to co-exist with the Alamo man. But one depiction came close and was the best of the Crockett shows for doing so.

I was ten years old when the Walt Disney people made their first Crockett episode for the brand-new *Disneyland* on ABC-TV, and I got into the thick of the coonskin-cap concept along with all my cousins, boys and girls alike. Something in the television show released a flood of rank wild juice in all our systems, and we got downright hard to han-dle. We went native with Davy Crockett and rose up, in our play, against what for us was unjust power, the domination of adults, and I am per-suaded that from one end of this too-quiet Eisenhower country to the other, there were thousands of others who did likewise, from us country rubes to rich kids in mansions, all chorusing together, "Da-vy, Da-vy Crockett, king of the wild frontier!" "Like a bunch of little heathens," my great-aunt Beulah said, and that was precisely the point. We were woaded.

Compared especially to John Wayne's Davy Crockett in *The Alamo*, which would make its bloated appearance six years later in 1960, the Davy played by Fess Parker was downright subversive, jokey, askew; he was more a trickster than an overwhelmingly testosteronized fighter. Fess Parker's bravery seemed offhand and nothing special, not so much the product of hormones as the product of a respectful and resilient ac-commodation to the world. Like a classic fool, this Davy assumed a dem-ocratic equality and acted on it, and he expected every other man to do the same. He was hard to order around, though he was willing and able to collaborate as an equal.

I remember how the very first show of that series opened in Decem-ber 1954. The scene is a military camp: General Andrew Jackson, a pompous, portly, but formidable authority in uniform (played brilliant-ly by Basil Ruysdael), thunders, "Where's that scout?" and a fancy-pants major with gold epaulettes, a high Napoleonic hat, and a whining face answers, "He's gone hunting." The general sends the major in the fancy uniform to fetch "that scout" immediately. Cut to a different kind of face, Buddy Ebsen's comic sidekick mug squinting into the distance. He's standing on a riverbank watching the bushes beyond, and down the river in a little boat comes the fancy major calling, "Davy Crockett, Davy Crockett!" And Buddy Ebsen tries to shush the major, because Davy is *in those very bushes.* Why? asks the major. "He's trying to grin down a bear," Buddy replies. And the major scoffs, "You backwoods buffoons think we'll believe *anything*!"

But indeed the buffoon *is* in those bushes grinning down a bear, and the major's noisy interruption spoils the effect. Growling and bush-shaking ensue, and Davy gets thrown out a couple of times, comically. Buffoon, for sure, but he kills the bear "the hard way," with his trusty knife (albeit off-camera). All of this is to the amazement and consternation of the very proper, very answerable-to-authority major, who could not have done what Davy did and knows it.

In this version, imposed authority, especially military authority, is the real joke. Without this frontier buffoon as scout, Jackson's army would be stymied and also, clearly, hungry. Davy doesn't jump when the major shouts. He doesn't even jump when the general shouts, though he does let the general use him at times. In that first TV episode, the army has several large bands of Creek Indians surrounded, and Jackson plans an ambush. He orders Crockett's buckskin boys to go in and "stir up those red varmints." When he hears this order, Crockett looks at Jackson for a very revealing long take. His face says he understands the general's ruthlessness: his group of frontier volunteers will be sacrificed in the first shock of battle, while the real army waits. Crockett is *willing* to do it for a high ideal, not because this particular general orders him.

After the ambush fails and the most feared chief, Red Stick, escapes, Crockett pokes his head into General Jackson's tent and says, "Dropped in to say goodbye," a natural but impudent violation of military protocol.

Jackson: "Where do you think you're going?"

Crockett: "Home."

The major from scene 1 interrupts: "You're going after Red Stick with the rest of my command."

But Crockett firmly and reasonably explains that he and his neighbors signed up for sixty days, which have long since come and gone, and they can't embark on any further service without seeing to their families and their farms. So they leave. But not before the major makes one final, impotent attempt to hold them. He threatens to fire a cannon into their ranks if they don't fall back, but they simply brush him aside.

Under Crockett's leadership, the buckskin boys assume their freedom, and the major and General Jackson have to accept the leveling. After Davy's crew has left the camp, Jackson snorts: "Damnedest bunch of volunteers I ever saw! When they volunteer to fight, they fight. And when they volunteer to go home, they *go home!*"

Disney's Davy is as good a man as any and better than most, because he doesn't *think* of himself as better than most. Though he kills Indians, he can also talk to them as equals, and when he goes to the national Congress (strolling solemnly into the Capitol in his buckskins—something the real David Crockett most certainly never did), he's shown defending the hopeless cause of protecting the Indians from greed and deceit ("Indians got rights"). The Disney version makes his personal power huge and inspirational. In fact, this version claims that Crockett's grand eastern speaking tour, arranged by the Whigs, was really a ruse to get him out of Washington so they could ram through an unfair and exploitative "Indian Bill."

The thoroughly unhistorical assumption is that Crockett's formidable presence could have stopped the bill, that Crockett had real power for shaping public policy. But never mind: the illusion is an indictment of ruthless power. Davy doesn't get back to the House in time to stop the Whigs, but he does get to deliver a speech to stir the hearts of ten-year-olds: "Sure we've got to grow, but not at the expense of the things this country was founded to protect. . . . Expansion ain't no excuse for persecuting a whole part of our people because their skins are red and they're uneducated to our ways." In the Disney version, this speech was a great cause célèbre and supposedly ended Crockett's public career (whereas in fact the real David Crockett took steps to keep his speeches on behalf of Indians a secret from his Tennessee constituents).

Many of those kids drinking in the Disney Crockett would grow up to be colossal pains in the backside about what constituted proper Americanism in the 1960s. Maybe Fess Parker's Davy was our first intimation of who the hippies would be, of how slouching in the face of authority might look, and of how dressing inappropriately in the marble halls might feel. It was the Disneyfication of an entire generation. Ironically, "Uncle Walt" was viewed by many conservative people as the most benign of entertainers, a reinforcer of traditional values, a teacher of "good Americanism." So his Crockett was given an official stamp of approval. It was shown in many a classroom, and no less a right-wing arbiter of imagery than Max Rafferty, afterward the superintendent of public instruction for all of California, called Disney "the greatest educator of this century." Rafferty may have been even more right than he thought.

## The Race Heroes: Boone, Jackson, Houston

Except for the occasional Davy, most coonskin-cap boys in the movies have rarely been funny, except when they're sidekicks (and then they're almost always funny), but I'm not talking sidekicks here. I'm talking leading men, embodiments of frontier virility who have been scrubbed up and housebroken to the politics of national expansion — the Daniel Boones, Andy Jacksons, Sam Houstons. They make savage warfare on the frontier seem patriotic, and on average they're an embarrassing lot. That is, they were until Daniel Day-Lewis's turn as Hawkeye in *The Last of the Mohicans*.

In the Daniel Boone movies, the coonskin-wearing heroes aren't so much *of* the mountains as they are temporarily *in* them, passing through on their first step to conquering the continent. The pelts and skins they wear are trophies that they have taken by force. For the typical Daniel Boone, the mountains are purely a barrier to western expansion. The only people who actually live there are either wild Indians, whose humanity is rarely hinted at, or viciously malevolent white renegades, who have reverted to bestiality (like the character Simon Girty in both *Daniel Boone* [RKO, 1936] and *Daniel Boone, Trailblazer* [Republic Pictures, 1937]).

The race doctrine in these movies is transparent: extermination of savages may be messy and even occasionally regrettable, but it is oh so necessary. The coonskin-capper is the spearpoint of light driving a wedge into darkness. *Daniel Boone, Trailblazer* even made Boone a blond, in symbolic contrast to all the dusky dark and black-haired Others (Fig. 3.3).

The movie Boone typically mouths a lot of equal-men platitudes, but what he really stands stalwartly for is the profit motive; nothing is more sacred than getting more settlers onto this or that parcel of real estate. Nothing frosts his coontail faster than someone trying to stop the nat-

Figure 3.3. Lon Chaney as Chingachgook and the blond Bruce Bennett as Daniel Boone in *Daniel Boone, Trailblazer.* (Courtesy of Wisconsin Center for Film and Theater Research)

ural acquisitiveness of white people, though that blatant motive is usually masked by patriotic babble. A convenient abstraction—the government itself, a vague "we the people"—is usually Boone's "employer" or guiding light, as though he didn't work for speculators and developers and land combines (although in *Daniel Boone, Trailblazer,* a company *is* behind the exploration of new land, and it doesn't come off too well, either). But usually the hypocrisy is both obtuse and transparent, as the bottom line tries to stay carefully out of sight.

In 1923 Elmer Grandin as Daniel Boone was perpetually posing for Mount Rushmore. Grandin was cast in the fourth feature-length installment of Pathé's Chronicles of America series, conceived and produced by Yale University. A Pathé publicity release to promote the series' market potential ironically also identified its greatest commercial weakness: "It offers substantial entertainment to those who do not depend upon sensationalism and exaggeration for thrills."

In other words, in the process of denying the politics of force, the Chronicles of America were sanitized into an excruciating bore. After showing the Daniel Boone episode, theater owner A. L. Middleton of DeQueen, Arkansas, wrote to *Moving Picture World*: "Wonderful what college professors and club women think 'high class' pictures should be! No entertainment." As a matter of fact, Americans did then and still do glory in seeing themselves, in the mirror of the movie, commit what the Yale professors denied—exaggerated and sensational displays of violence for the purpose of Americanizing this continent (or any other continent, for that matter). The thrill in Michael Mann's *The Last of the Mohicans* is precisely that shock of recognition.

Though Yale's Boone bombed, Universal's *In the Days of Daniel Boone* became a successful serial that same year (1923). Universal's cliffhanger had plenty of what the Yale series lacked—spectacular violence. But then, most of the weekly episodes did not actually feature Daniel Boone at all, but other male specimens who were not handicapped by Boone's schoolhouse respectability. A lot of Indians died.

George O'Brien, in the 1936 *Daniel Boone* (RKO), is stiff and self-consciously all-American, virile by virtue of his pouter-pigeon chest and the animal skins he wears; but with the Great Depression in full blossom, O'Brien's Boone confines his masculinity to a kind of Rooseveltian care for the underdog: he is resolutely for fair play, and woe to those who don't play fair (that is, British snobs, most Indians, and Simon Girty). There's even a black man among the settlers going to Kaintuck— a piece of history usually ignored; and Stephen Marlowe (played by British actor Ralph Forbes) is a parody of the antidemocrat, both pompous and effeminate. He thinks he should be exempt from work. When Boone finally gets his wagon train safely to the Kentucky plain, the scenes of group devotion and group labor are strongly reminiscent of *Our Daily Bread* (United Artists), King Vidor's stunning piece of Rooseveltian mythology that had been released only two years before this *Daniel Boone*.

Andrew Jackson in the movies has most often been a supporting player in someone else's story, frequently Davy Crockett's or Sam Houston's. But occasionally he gets the leading role and sometimes fits the part of coonskin-capper. But Jackson was encumbered with a problematic backwoods virility. In real life, his manliness was notorious: he killed Indians, he killed the British, and he stole away another man's wife, Mrs. Robards. Although he was the hero of frontier settlers in Tennessee and elsewhere, his constituents were just a crowd of frontier yahoos to those who occupied the centers of power on the eastern seaboard. As long as there were wars to engage him, he was no threat. But when he wanted to run the country, Jackson became in the eyes of the urban press a dangerous frontier boob and fanatic, a backwoods wrecker-of-civilization.

In *The Gorgeous Hussy* (MGM, 1936), Lionel Barrymore played a bit part as Andy Jackson in a starring vehicle for Joan Crawford. The best sequence shows Jackson—now President Jackson—appearing on the White House balcony for his maiden speech to Washingtonians. A nameless, well-dressed heckler in the crowd calls out some provocative comment about Jackson's wife, the former Mrs. Robards (played by grandmotherly Beulah Bondi). Instantly upon hearing the insult, like the dominant male of American politics, Jackson climbs down off the balcony of the White House and punches the man in the nose, thereby starting a general brawl.

Much less vigorously, Charlton Heston essayed the Jackson part twice, as a solo starring role in *The President's Lady* (Twentieth Century–Fox, 1953), a kryptonite bomb, and again in Cecil B. DeMille's "slow, slack, and stolid" remake of *The Buccaneer* (Paramount, 1958), which was crowded with other stars. In the first movie, Heston is inert, trying to bend his Easter Island facade around Susan Hayward, who is very prim as Mrs. Robards. In the second, he is ludicrous in a bad wig.

In *Allegheny Uprising* (RKO, 1939) John Wayne, in the first of many coonskin-cap roles, leads fellow pre-Revolutionary American back-woodsmen in an uprising against the ineptitude of bureaucratic government (British in this case) and begins killing Indians by preemptive strike. The plot calls for Wayne and his fellow frontiersmen to put on Indian paint and Indian garb (Fig. 3.4) and to ambush Indians—all to general applause and also well before Wayne's apotheosis as a right-wing natural man guarding us against unnatural Communists in the 1950s and 1960s. Wayne played another such coonskin-cap character in *The Fighting Kentuckian* (Republic Pictures, 1949). In that movie he is the leader of a band of rough mountain men who have been down in New Orleans fighting with Andy Jackson against the British. On his way back to the Kentucky hills, the Wayne character gets involved with a super-sophisticated French countess and a whole settlement of French aristocrats (go figure), whose effeminate and corrupt European practices are quickly contrasted with Wayne's patented American virility. But the movie was a dud: too much drawing-room intrigue, not enough Oliver Hardy (who's watchable as Wayne's comic coonskin-cap sidekick), and not enough brawling.

It may be significant that the decade of the 1950s, itself full of anxiety about the massification of men into emasculating office work, offered at least six depictions of Davy Crockett as the free but doomed man of the frontier (see the sources to this chapter). In fact, the fifties saw coonskin-cap boys proliferating like crazy, including a character named Eli Wakefield in *The Kentuckian* (United Artists, 1955), the only movie Burt Lancaster ever directed.

## Buckskin Doubt in the Age of Eisenhower

Although the great majority of movie-made coonskin-cap boys were projections of the national male purpose and its intent to take this continent and hold it and make it turn a profit, the fifties also offered occasional glimpses of doubt. *The Kentuckian*, starring Burt Lancaster, is a pretty straightforward story about the loss of American virility due to an obsession with business and money and the spreading cancer of cities. Here is a movie that took very seriously the proposition that men on the frontier could be natural only when they were free from the entanglements of working for wages; once virility had sold itself into town bondage, all desire failed and manhood was finished.

Burt Lancaster plays Elias Wakefield. He is the single parent of a young boy, Little Eli. Big Eli and Little Eli, with their dog Pharaoh, come down out of the Kentucky hills and head for *TEXAS*, a word they always speak with awe; it is their code for Male Freedom, "the hunting life, never-ending" (Fig. 3.5).

But Big Eli is weak. We get our first intimation of that in the opening moments of the movie, after we've discovered father and son "traipsing along like natural men," as Big Eli calls it, on their way to paradise/Texas. The son says suddenly, "We're not really *runnin'* from them, are we, Pa?" No, we're not running, the father reassures his son, but events seem to suggest they are. *They* are the Fromes brothers, black-hatted and black-bearded hillbillies evidently supplied by Central Casting. The

Figure 3.4. John Wayne, disguised in Indian warpaint, during a break in shooting on the set of *Allegheny Uprising*. (Courtesy of Wisconsin Center for Film and Theater Research)

Fromeses have been anachronistically injected from a Hatfield-McCoy style feud parody into this dramatization of the 1820s frontier. But the Fromeses are there only as the ultimate test of Eli Wakefield's manhood: can he match their danger with his own power, defend himself against them, and defeat them?

As the movie progresses, Big Eli's vibrant dream of Texas fades and so does his manly resolve, his ability to act correctly, his ability to act at all. He hits bottom when he is publicly horsewhipped and humiliated by the local saloonkeeper (played by Walter Matthau in an early role). The reason he must go through this punishment is clear: he has left the mountains, the wilderness, and entered town society, which worships money and the civilization it provides. Just as soon as Wakefield and his son reach their first flatland Kentucky settlement a few minutes into the film, they are surrounded by corporate evil, a corrupt sheriff, mean dogs, prejudiced citizens, and double-dealing on every hand. Off the

Figure 3.5. Publicity still from *The Kentuckian*, with Burt Lancaster as Big Eli and Donald MacDonald as Little Eli, who is here shown holding the Gabriel Horn. (Courtesy of Wisconsin Center for Film and Theater Research)

frontier and out of his natural element, Big Eli is clearly no match for any of it.

He carries a hunter's horn, which he has endowed with special significance. He calls it his Gabriel Horn, and he tells Little Eli that when the boy can blow it, "it'll prove you're growed up," that he will have become a man. Little Eli tries to blow the horn several times during the movie, the more intensely as he sees his father literally mired in a symbolic projection of urban America—grasping men, compromise, defeat, humiliation, and the perversion of natural virility into passive obedience to the power of money.

In the very first settlement, Big Eli gets himself clapped into jail. Enter Hannah, a "bound girl" who befriends Little Eli (now by himself in a friendless town). *Texas* means freedom to her, too: "I was free once. I've heard the hounds makin' music and the horn to bring 'em in," she says, in a poetic female torch song to that ideal virility symbolized by the hunter's horn (*pace* Freud). A natural woman knows it takes a natural man to set her free. Hannah springs Big Eli from jail and asks him,

"Could a woman go to Texas?" Big Eli replies, "If she was man enough to stand it." This is an unintentionally ironic answer because, as a matter of fact, Hannah is more resourceful, more observant, more astute than he is—more virile, in fact, after the town begins to sap him. But she'll be one of the instruments to save his manhood.

Big Eli's loving brother Zack (played by John McIntyre) becomes the chief entrapper. Behind Big Eli's back, the brother says, "I'll work the buckskin off him," meaning he'll civilize him to the town, tie him down, and make him like it. "I'll make a businessman out of him," Zack chortles. And when Big Eli's horn-blowing vitality has indeed turned to the getting of money, the buckskin does wilt and disappear. Little Eli soon complains to Hannah, "Pa won't talk Texas no more."

Not only that, but Big Eli's head is turned by Miss Susie the schoolteacher, another symbolic agent of imprisonment, and soon Little Eli finds himself enrolled in the cruel jail of the local school system, where he is taunted by the other children for his woodsiness. A major crisis comes when Big Eli tells Little Eli that he's decided they're going to settle in this place permanently and forget about Texas. Big Eli gives his son the Gabriel Horn and tells him to throw it away where it can't be found again, in a ridiculously obvious self-castration.

Little Eli rebels. First he does as his father tells him: he takes the horn into the woods and covers it with leaves. But he marks the spot so he can return to it later. He can't bring himself to leave it, however. He rushes back, retrieves it, and—we cut to the schoolteacher, Miss Susie, in earnest conversation with Big Eli. Even she has realized he's *slumping*, and she knows furthermore that the former bound girl Hannah is worthier of the man Big Eli used to be—and which he can be again if he'll just get to Texas. Miss Susie's lecture is interrupted by the sound of the Gabriel Horn blowing in the woods, and Big Eli knows immediately it's his son: "He's growed up." More than that, he has reclaimed the manhood that his father abdicated. Big Eli perks up, and in close succession, the movie cuts from the face of Big Eli, animated again, to the boy blowing triumphantly on the horn, to the boy's dog Pharaoh, who has been tethered in town (another symbol of imprisonment), breaking the rope that holds him and bounding off to freedom.

This is all it takes for Big Eli to come to his senses. He reasserts his virility, standing and facing his enemies the Fromeses (killing one of them himself, while Hannah picks off the other) and then taking Hannah and the boy and striking out again for his old freedom: "We're going to Texas, and we're going to live it bold!" Near the end of the movie, the Texas man Babson, who has arrived on the riverboat that will take the trio to their dreamland destination, speaks to Big Eli the lines that sum up the propaganda of *The Kentuckian*: "Men like your brother [Zack] build businesses. But men like you build *countries*, if you only will."

Gonads like these just don't grow in towns or work in offices.

## Crockett-dile Dundee, the Last Great Davy

Gonads like those in *The Kentuckian* may not, in fact, even be native to America anymore. That at least was the implication behind 1986's *Crocodile Dundee* (Rimfire Films/Paramount), the Australian import that may have captured the full, transgressively woaded spirit of the coonskin-cap hero/fool better than any American movie has ever done. As the Australian version of Davy Crockett (with croc-teeth replacing coonskin), Paul Hogan plays the backwoods scapegoat for the purpose of criticizing modern mainstream American culture. He comes to New York City, where by urban logic he shouldn't survive a night. But he lives *for* the moment and totally *in* the moment; no other reality exists. So that although he is oblivious to urban practices, he is never surprised by anything. He conquers New York, handling every situation beautifully, from street crime to restaurants with foreign menus (Fig. 3.6). He doesn't follow timepieces or even calenders, and he is impatient with "causes" or useless opinions on "global issues": "It's none of *my* business."

What *is* his business is a casual domination of the moment in whatever landscape he happens to find himself. He does not brook direct challenge or insult. He fights a bully in the Walkabout Creek pub in his very first scene in the movie. Later he pops the woman reporter's smug boyfriend in the mouth. But the natural violence in him is always tempered by a democrat's ease of taking in the world and accommodating it largely, like Fess Parker's Davy.

That Hogan had Davy Crockett in mind is clearly evident in the script. Linda Kozlowski, who plays the Big Apple reporter Crocodile

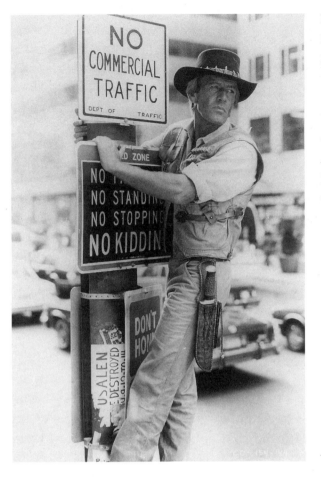

Figure 3.6. Paul Hogan takes Manhattan in *Crocodile Dundee*. (Courtesy of the University of California at Los Angeles Arts Library, Special Collections)

Dundee rescues and loves, says at one point about her excursion with him into the Australian outback, "Christ! It's like living with Davy Crockett." That is, there are constant scrapes, which are encountered with a just-as-constant (and rather good-natured) capability of dealing with scrapes.

Crocodile Dundee is ideal in his ability to adapt to the natural world, whatever that may constitute, and in response the world buoys him up. He strikes a special human chord not only with Australian aborigines but also with New York black chauffeurs, white hotel doormen, cops, transvestites, and hookers, all of whom assist or ease his passage. In the Australian scenes we even see him charm a water buffalo, à la Davy Crockett grinning down a bear (Fig. 3.7). His miraculous link with his surroundings is demonstrated in the movie's brilliant climax: Dundee

Figure 3.7. Crockett-dile Dundee grins down a water buffalo. (Courtesy of the University of California at Los Angeles Arts Library, Special Collections)

and the woman he now loves are separated from each other down a long New York subway platform, so packed and jammed with people that even though *he must get to her* (because the soundtrack is beginning to swell portentously), there is no passage through. With the crowd participating and cheering him on, all to the pounding of Peter Best's music, Dundee mounts aloft and walks over the top of the people—their shoulders, their heads—a daring blend of the comic/heroic that actually works.

The Paul Hogan character "puts down the 'tall poppies,' pompous people and anyone else in high position," explained Don Morris, the ad-agency man who was there at the birth of Hogan's marketability on Australian TV. "It's the essential convict spirit *in all Australians*," Morris added, invoking the myth of the Australian convict the way Whigs liked to invoke the myth of the American backwoods buffoon in David Crockett's day. According to Steve Smith, who lived and worked extensively in Australia, the convict image is deeply resented among ordinary Australians, much as hillbilly imagery can be deeply resented among ordinary mountain people. Interestingly, Paul Hogan got his start in the Crocodile Dundee role on a "Gong"-type television show that lampooned Australian media and advertising types who were exploiting the convict imagery in their marketing. And it was this very self-consciousness on the part of the Outback fool that allowed him his symbolic triumph over the more dominant Yank culture in *Crocodile Dundee*.

> [B]anditry is a rather
> primitive form of
> organized social protest.
> . . . The characteristic
> victims of the bandit
> are the quintessential
> enemies of the poor.
> —Eric Hobsbawm,
> *Primitive Rebels*

> Jesse James was a man,
> and a friend of the poor.
> —"The Ballad of Jesse
> James"

# The Hillbilly as Social Bandit
## Jesse James

Jesse James is "mountain," just as Davy Crockett is. Both men have a vital subliminal connection to the rocky parts of human experience, though not to real mountains. Davy came from the valley, and Jesse did, too: Clay County, Missouri, is nowhere near the Ozarks. But in our imaginations—and in the visual imagery of several powerful movies—his imaginary terrain is hilly.

There's a surviving photograph, probably from 1864, of Frank and Jesse James and a man named Fletcher Taylor, who was a guerrilla lieutenant for the Confederacy (Fig. 4.1). It's one of only a handful of authentic pictures of Jesse James. I have no doubt that the seventeen-year-

old beardless boy on the right in this photograph is the forerunner of the bearded and dead outlaw in the official police morgue shot (Fig. 4.2).

In the earlier photograph, elder brother Frank James is seated in the center. Like Jesse, he is also smooth-faced (he was all of twenty-one at the time). On the left, stubby Fletcher Taylor has the beginnings of his beard, but it's clear that these were essentially three older boys just beginning to take themselves seriously as men, dressed up and gone into town to have their group photograph made. And well they might take themselves seriously: Fletcher Taylor and Frank James, at least, had already been blooded in Missouri's guerrilla war. Taylor rode with William F. Anderson's bunch; Frank had joined up with William C. Quantrill's raiders and had been present at the notorious massacre of Yankee

Figure 4.2. Jesse James in death, 1882. (Courtesy of Western History Collections, University of Oklahoma Library)

civilians in Lawrence, Kansas in August 1863. And depending on precisely when this photograph was made, Jesse James himself was also probably riding with "Bloody Bill" Anderson. Of the two brothers, Jesse was apparently the readier pupil of the tactics of lightning raids and midnight rides and, yes, shooting unarmed people, willingly taking part in what historian Michael Fellman has called "a war of ten thousand nasty incidents."

In the photograph, Frank James is wearing a blousy, dashing, military sort of tunic much favored among the image-conscious guerrillas of Missouri. Frank is flop-eared, large-lipped, ascetic, almost slight—the most unlikely sort of egghead to be bushwhacking his neighbors. Now look at Jesse: he is slim, too, and seems to slouch into the picture in classic rube style, as though he fears the crown of his hat might brush the ceiling. But his mouth is small, precise, and humorous. (Figure 4.2 proves that this expression belonged to his soul: even in death he's still amused.) His eyes communicate a lively intelligence—in fact, a devilment. His left hand is jammed down so hard into his coat pocket that the material is straining, and he lets his thumb poke out in an unconscious obscene gesture. Is this not the half-clown, half–ax murderer from the economic fringe and our rural past?

## Rube-in-Hoods

In his indispensable study *Primitive Rebels*, Eric Hobsbawm uses European sources (largely Italian) to prove how remarkably consistent and similar are the legendary bandit heroes of Western cultures, the folk-glorifications, the Robin Hoods. Hobsbawm calls them "social bandits" because their criminal acts are perceived to be committed on behalf of their own peasant societies and against an invading or oppressive power from outside. The bandit is always bred in a rural culture. He is typically young, frequently unmarried, and totally unremarkable until circumstances—specifically, some injustice—forces him into acts that the state or other dominating power regards as criminal but that the bandit's local community, vaguely defined, does not. Some element of that community always protects the bandit, helps him escape, and spreads outrageous rumors to encourage the impression that he is superhuman or magical, that he can be everywhere and simultaneously nowhere (what Hobsbawm calls "the ubiquity amounting to invisibility"). His supporters' desire is to make the bandit immortal and thereby render the oppressor impotent, whether that oppressor be landlord, law, government, or whatever. Only betrayal by someone within the trusted circle can bring the bandit down—and such a betrayal, incidentally, is inevitable.

Though their legends have lived long, Hobsbawm found that, on average, the careers of most European bandits lasted only about two years. In this country, Jesse James did much better for much longer—more than sixteen years—but he, too, was eventually shot in the back by "family." All bandits die; their resistance always fails. *That's why*, Hobsbawm implies, the bandit hero lives on in folklore, where through formulaic ballads and stories he can transcend his inevitable real failure. This transformation from real-life loser to legendary hero is at root the people's doing, or that of some portion of the people. Hobsbawm says the bandit is "the poor boy who has made good," but he is also merely "a *surrogate* for the failure of the mass to lift itself out of its own poverty, helplessness and meekness." From a hopeless situation, the real man is conveniently transported into an illusion that can live forever. The illusion, like all stories perhaps, both energizes and ironically controls.

Hobsbawm mentions Jesse James as an American example of the European social bandit but carries the analogy no further. And although folklorist Kent L. Steckmesser has amply demonstrated a Hobsbawmian, Robin Hood–type glorification at work in the Jesse James legend, we should not rush too quickly to embrace Hobsbawm's theory in explaining how our slouching, wry hillbilly boy became such a powerful hero in American pop culture. For one thing, Hobsbawm drew all his examples from what he terms "peasant societies." As a somewhat doctrinaire Marxist, Hobsbawm had an "ideological motivation for examining bandits" that, according to Billy Jaynes Chandler, caused him to assume that a "primitive" form of working-class rebellion—that is, rural banditry—must be ultimately superseded by a more mature form of industrialist-Marxist Leninism. But however far we stretch the romance of the nineteenth-century American countryside, we cannot make peasants of Missouri farm people.

Other critics of Hobsbawm say he exaggerated the "element of protest" in social banditry; that is, they contend that some bandits used violence mainly in defense of their own selfish interests and even formed alliances with those same dominant outside forces that were oppressing "the people." Some hardnoses have stuck to Carleton Beals's opinion, first published in 1930: "Despite popular sentiment, the true nature of the bandit is not that of the social reformer. He is essentially selfish and has no fundamental interest in rectifying social ills."

Jesse James was the hero of a well-defined underclass in Missouri, composed of migrated southerners known as "pukes." As of 1850 an estimated 75 percent of Missourians fit this profile: recently arrived rural southerners who were said to be dirty, backward, slow, and dangerous. Non-pukes—the ones who controlled or had access to the image-building press—tended to be clustered away from the rural landscape in big cities, especially in St. Louis but also in nearby Chicago or

Cincinnati. That's where the big banks were, and that's where fat fingers traced routes on maps for the new railroads, which were by nature oligarchic. The popular press that served those powers obliged their fantasies: If you're going to take people's land and make them kowtow, it's easier done if they're just pukes. Michael Fellman explains the process:

> [T]he popular press . . . attacked traditional smallholders for their supposed backwardness. Racing toward progress—defined as industrialization, urbanization, education, and personal orderliness and accumulation—would-be cultural trendsetters disparaged the antiquated ways of folks like rural Missourians who, if they would not jump on the modernizing bandwagon, would be left behind as quaint relics of a passing and inferior culture.

This process of creating an image and using it to channel acceptable thought is called *ordination*; in essence, it promotes group solidarity by defining "what is high, what is low; what is us, what is them." Jesse and Frank James—and their associates the Youngers—were part of *them*, and they knew it.

To fight back against ordination is to be insubordinate. One way to do this is to play the hillbilly fool. Another is to rob banks. Really talented country people do both. Consider the James gang's robbery of the Ocobock Brothers Bank in Corydon, Iowa, on June 3, 1871. On that day nearly every man in town was at the Methodist Church to hear the famous traveling orator Henry Clay Dean praise the merits of a proposed railroad line through that section. The bandits timed their arrival so there was only a lone cashier in the bank. They got all the money without hurting the teller and then rode to the meeting at the church, where "their leader"—Jesse—interrupted Henry Clay Dean to announce that the bank had just been robbed. But his news was delivered with such a smirk that the crowd didn't believe him. They thought it was a prank to discombobulate the orator, which in one way of thinking it was, so Jesse and his gang rode unchallenged out of town after confessing publicly to their crime. A similar, grand element of jokesterism runs throughout much of the Jesse James folklore.

For the first few years of Jesse's career as a bandit, his identity, his very name, was shrouded in mystery among the social elite. Four years after he and his brother presumably began robbing banks, the James boys were still living at their mother's home back in Clay County, and according to scholar William Settle, they came and went as they pleased. In plain sight of God and witnesses, Jesse joined the Baptist Church in Kearney and was baptized. His effective invisibility to officialdom testifies to his connection to large segments of the population who applauded him, for whom his acts of violence had political meaning and could be championed and abstracted into stories and songs. Homer Croy, who wrote *Jesse James Was My Neighbor*, remarked:

> There was a lot to be said for the Clay County Boy; the banks were unregulated and could charge any old rate of interest they wanted; the railroads likewise were unregulated and could shake the contents of a farmer's pocketbook into their own private grain-sacks. So the people of Missouri didn't toss around in their sleep when Jesse and his boys robbed a bank. In fact some said that the people of Missouri turned over and slept like babies.

According to Kent Steckmesser, the Jesse James ballad was especially well known among "the poor whites and Southern Negroes" and may have been composed by a black convict. Evidently, in fact, the more powerless the beholder, the more potent the illusion surrounding the bandit.

It is perversely heartening to note how strongly the James gang was opposed by local boosters and government officials and the whole structure of capital investment. Governor Thomas Crittenden and Senator Carl Schurz of Missouri both defended Jesse's cold-blooded assassination in 1882 (and the $10,000 reward that was necessary to induce Robert Ford to perform the deed). The governor said Jesse's death rid the state of "a great hindrance to its prosperity and [is] likely to give an important stimulus to real estate speculation, railroad enterprise, and foreign immigration"—all the ties that bind. It is also heartening to note that the improbable egghead Frank James was talking radical politics late in his life, long after he had put banditry behind him: "If there is ever another war in this country, which may happen, it will be between capital and labor, I mean between greed and manhood, and I'm as ready to march now in defense of American manhood as I was when a boy in the defense of the South."

*Greed* versus *manhood*—what a startling conflation from the Clay

County thinker! According to historian Richard White, the real cultural power of the Jesse James myth is not its appeal to a bandit impulse — heroically principled opposition to dominant power — but a stronger appeal to a traditional version of American masculinity. In Frank James's estimation, real men were selling out to the unnatural pursuit of money. (Whereas, of course, robbing banks is the *natural* pursuit of money!) Corporate structures, including enabling beliefs and the politics to impose them, were even then being created and promoted by American mass culture. And White says that the spread of the Jesse James legend happened to coincide with a spreading, mainstream male anxiety that capital dominance and the mechanisms of industrialization were quickly reducing men to commodities, to office-and-cog eunuchs.

A definite dynamic seems to have been at work in the early years of the Jesse James legend. Homer Croy said that around the turn of the century he counted no fewer than 450 copyrighted dime novels about the James gang. And the most avid consumers of this pulp happened to be middle-class urban boys, adolescents whose own fathers may have already lost the battle between greed and manhood, boys who may have been feeling what Robert Bly calls the pangs of "father hunger."

There were, of course, those who deplored this merchandizing of the bandit. The dime-novel Jesse James was often ruled evil precisely because he did appeal to boys. Consider the *New York Daily Graphic*'s 11 April 1882 front page, which announced (or rather celebrated) Jesse James's death (Fig. 4.3). Hordes of little boys crowd around an ironic tombstone bearing the epitaph: "Hic jacet [here lies] Jesse James. . . . His exploits excited the emulation of the small *boy* of the period." At the base of the tombstone, the proper inscription "Of such is the Kingdom of Heaven" has been defaced to read "Of such is the State of Missouri." All the little boys strike poses of amazement and alarm or posture obliviously as baby outlaws. The joke is supposed to be on Jesse James: who *is* this fake, admired exclusively by nonadults? But the real joke may more obviously be on those very adults, then and since, who thought they would train manhood exclusively to the good of the corporation.

Figure 4.3. Front page of the *New York Daily Graphic*, 11 April 1882. (Courtesy of the Library of Congress)

## Social Bandit Meets the Silver Screen

Hillbilly revolts against the system are promoted in several Jesse James movies. Almost all of these portrayed Jesse as initially being a good sort of Missouri hill lad, clever with a gun and full of pluck. Then the banks and the railroads and the corrupt officials in bed with the banks and the railroads make his naive country scrappiness by definition a crime against the state. Jesse James massified in the movies is an interesting spectacle to contemplate, because what he celebrates is so often antithetical to the system that finds him entertaining.

The first movie about the bandit was *The James Boys in Missouri* (1907), a production of the Essanay Company of Chicago, which may have sent its camera and crew into nearby Missouri to film on location.

This movie was evidently based on a stage play that, according to William Settle, very successfully toured the country during the first decade of this century. (There were other popular Jesse James plays as well.) The movie does not survive, but *Moving Picture World* said it was "a thriller from beginning to end and cannot fail to please," partly because it used "some excellent work by genuine cowboys who know how to ride." If the movie plot followed the stage play, we can assume it "emphasized the daring and bravery of the Jameses and the treachery of the Fords."

Though it does not survive either, the next known movie about Jesse James starred Jesse James Jr., or Jesse Edwards James, the bandit's only son, who had become a practicing attorney in Kansas City. He and other Kansas City "capitalists" formed the Mesco Pictures Corporation in 1920 expressly to make "a superfeature" (eight reels) called *Jesse James under the Black Flag*, which premiered in Kansas City in March 1921 and presented the son's sanitized version of his father's heroic blamelessness. It pictured, according to William Settle, "a young man from the East as having fallen in love with the granddaughter of Jesse James. To help the suitor decide whether her family was acceptable, the girl's father had him read an account of the career of Jesse James which, of course, was enacted on the screen. The story stressed the persecution that drove the young Jesse into guerrilla warfare and prevented his settling down after the war." This was a weirdly ironic (and safe) scenario: the former capitalist enemies of Jesse James were investing their capital to help the bandit's now respectable son romanticize his father's legend in order to certify his own class acceptability to the fine families of the East.

By the time *Jesse James under the Black Flag* was shot, all the big-time movie companies had settled in California, and the look of the Western had come to dominate action pictures. So instead of sensibly crossing the Missouri River from Kansas City and filming their exteriors on location in Jesse's home country, the Mesco crew went west to a ranch near Albuquerque and reportedly later filmed in four other states just "this side of the Rockies," which gave the film's exteriors all the wrong look (dry mesas and buttes, cattle roundups, Mexicans as extras, Indians wrapped in blankets, and cowboys in Western hats). The interiors were filmed in the Rothacker Studios in Chicago. According to Settle, the finished movie was a commercial flop.

The Western cowboyizing of Jesse James continued apace in 1927 with Fred Thomson's portrayal for Paramount. Thomson had been a famous college athlete, winning the all-around AAU championship an unprecedented three times, and he was already a very popular Western star for F.B.O. Pictures when he was lured away to Paramount by Adolph Zukor. *Jesse James* was Thomson's first Paramount feature, and Zukor spared no expense to make it spectacular (though it must have looked all wrong, too, since it was filmed in the California Sierras). It was a conventional Western, featuring Thomson's established costar, his horse Silver King. The film showcased "one of the most spectacular 'stunts' ever tried," an attack on a train moving at 35 mph by thirty-nine horsemen who simultaneously climbed in the train's windows. (This stunt was later one-upped by Henry King's rolling take of a bandit running the entire length of a moving train, jumping from car roof to car roof, in the 1939 *Jesse James*, discussed below.) In the Fred Thomson version, "Jesse James, returning from Quantrell's [*sic*] campaign, finds his mother maimed through the villainy of Slade, guardian of the girl he loves. Arrested for attempting to enforce the Mosaic law, he escapes and turns bandit, but wins the girl in spite of his proscription." As a matter of fact, Jesse's mother did have her right arm blown off in an 1875 bomb attack on her home by those durn Pinkertons, but the rest of this plot is as phony as a banker's religion.

Thomson's version was also controversial because some thought it "whitewashed" the outlaw at the very time another Kansas City attorney was trying to raise money to erect a memorial to Jesse in the Kearney, Missouri, cemetery where the outlaw's body had finally been interred in 1902. The respectable press howled in protest. How dared *anyone* propose to honor the memory of such a "scoundrel, a thief, train-robber, Wild West border thug, and murderer," declared the *Boston Globe*. But this respectable outrage naturally only excited the male adolescents of that day to flock even more eagerly to see Thomson's movie, and his Jesse James was a big hit.

Meanwhile, Jesse James Jr., whose own earlier venture had flopped, served as an adviser to Thomson on the new film, and he also loaned the actor memorabilia that had belonged to his father. In 1928 *Variety* reported that Jesse Jr. was broke, his law practice shut down, and that he himself had gone belly up from a nervous breakdown. In 1929 both he and his daughter Jessie Edwards, the bandit's granddaughter, sued Paramount for $35,000 (later amended to $75,000) that they said they were owed, including money for "personal objects" that Thomson never returned to the family. The main point of the daughter's suit was the alleged damages she suffered by not having a role in Thomson's movie and hence, in her mind, a Hollywood career.

The *Jesse James* of 1939 (Twentieth Century–Fox) was Darryl F. Zanuck's big-budget homage to the rural rebel. Zanuck chose one of his favorite directors, Henry King, to make the movie, and King was an inspired choice. He had grown up in the Shenandoah Valley, and he knew farm people. He had made the early masterpiece *Tol'able David* (1921) on location in the Shenandoah; in its day, *Tol'able David* reintroduced a mass urban audience (jaded, jazzed up, and drop-dead sophisticated) to the re-vision of rural America as the haven for national identity (see Chapter 7).

King was a location genius. For the exteriors of his *Jesse James*, King took his cast and crew on location to Pineville, Missouri, and its environs, a much truer approximation of the real landscape of Jesse James than anything Hollywood had ever heretofore tried. King convinced the city fathers of Pineville, who were very proud of their freshly-paved town square, to let Twentieth Century–Fox truck in tons of dirt to cover the new paving and to antique the storefronts and set up hitching posts—generally, to return Pineville to the 1870s.

This movie was one of the early films made using the new Technicolor process, introduced in 1936, so the countryside in which Jesse James is found working is an insistent green and gold—mothering, settled and stable, not wilderness, not dark and threatening but with fields and faces open to the sun (Fig. 4.4). The sequence that introduces Tyrone Power in the role of Jesse moves from long shots of him working a field with a scythe—the very image, John H. Lenihan suggests, of the depression's romanticized farm boy—to an arresting close-up of the actor's open and boyish grin, broadcasting a natural warmth and friendliness. This very vision of ordinary rural innocence is what the movie puts under assault.

Figure 4.4. Publicity still from *Jesse James* (1939), with Tyrone Power as Jesse and Henry Fonda as Frank. (Courtesy of Wisconsin Center for Film and Theater Research)

One could also call country innocence by its cousin's name, *ignorance*. Jesse and his neighbors stand in the path of the Iron Horse, the territorial imperative, western expansion, greed. And the community is proving ridiculously easy to eliminate—there's not a real man among them except for the Jameses. The railroad's unscrupulous agent Barshee (played by professional heavy Brian Donleavy) has been alotted two dollars an acre to buy the farmers out, but instead he is strong-arming them into accepting a dollar an acre and pocketing the rest himself. His task is easy because the farmers are ignorant and meek; at least it's easy until Barshee encounters the James boys and their stubborn mom (played by the mother-of-us-all, Jane Darwell).

For all his shining innocence, Tyrone Power as Jesse is no weakling, plus he knows how to use a gun. When Barshee tries to strong-arm brother Frank (Henry Fonda), Frank knocks him down first. Barshee tries to retaliate by siccing his whole gang of thugs on Frank. But Jesse arrives, wholesome and strong from fieldwork, and uses his gun to hold the gang at bay while Frank gives Barshee a frank thrashing to teach him a lesson. We think the confrontation is over, but Barshee, being the pusilanimous villain he is, grabs a scythe and runs at Frank from behind (Fig. 4.5). Jesse shoots the blade out of Barshee's hand, and the company's men are sent packing, temporarily bested.

The movie wants us to see this opening as a just and manly act against an evil and corrupt invading greed. An agrarian instrument used for harvest is turned by Barshee into a weapon of ambush. But having started out by so forcefully identifying Jesse James as an ordinary man transformed by extraordinary circumstances into the social bandit, a symbol of justice pursued and of ideal masculinity embattled, this film can't bring itself to face the political implications of its own opening. To keep from being labeled as a fiction that advocates violent rebellion against monolithic power, the script halfway through begins to withdraw its support from Jesse; it darkens his personality, increasingly isolates him from his fellows and from love itself, and essentially renders irrelevant the initial justice of his cause and the consummate evil of his adversaries. Even though some men are corrupt, it seems to say, the system they serve is above corruption and is inherently right. So our innocent rural angel is transformed into a cold-blooded wolf that has to be destroyed. He can have our support only when he is innocent, and he cannot remain innocent and still fight back.

Jesse's wife Zee, his true love of yore, *defines* Jesse's very rebellion out of existence and judges it harshly as unacceptable for home and family life, when ironically it's the very preservation of home and family that launched Jesse as an outlaw in the first place. In Zee the script has also embodied a chief psychic hindrance for Jesse. She is no cheerleader but a nervous Nellie, a worrier, a frail reed who delivers the eviction notice on Jesse's farm-boy virtue:

> *Zee*: Right now you're a hero, to yourself and to a lot of other people too. It's a FIGHT you're in . . . and it was the railroad that started it. But that won't last, Jesse. The more luck you have, the worse you'll get. Shooting and robbing, it'll get in your blood—and you'll be like a wolf, just doing it because it'll be your nature. That'll be your *appetite* —for shooting and robbing—until . . . until something . . . happens

Figure 4.5. Barshee (Brian Donleavy) with the scythe in a publicity still from the 1939 *Jesse James*. (Courtesy of Wisconsin Center for Film and Theater Research)

. . . to you. . . . There's only one way out of it, darling—come in . . . give up.

Later, in desperation because Jesse refuses to surrender, she tells another character: "He's wild. . . . He's like a horse you can't break. He's crazy with wildness. . . . All last night I wanted to die. I prayed and prayed . . . that I'd die. And my baby—I prayed that he'd die, too, and end it all." Theodore Roosevelt celebrated the wolf blood in American men, which he said made them first in war and first in business. But to Zee, Jesse's Roosevelt Man is a lycanthrope, and the movie begins to agree with her (Fig. 4.6).

Near the end of Nunnally Johnson's screenplay, Henry Fonda's Frank joins in the chorus of condemnation: "You're mean, Jesse, and you're getting meaner every day. I don't know if you're going crazy or not, but sometimes it looks like it." Then the purely fictitious character Marshall

Figure 4.6. "Innocent rural angel is transformed into a cold-blooded wolf": Tyrone Power in a studio shot emphasizing the dark side of Jesse James. (Courtesy of Wisconsin Center for Film and Theater Research)

Wright (played by Randolph Scott), the symbolic, stabilizing Mr. Right of the American System, delivers the final formulation of this film's conservative doctrine on banditry: "He's no good! . . . Once you let yourself go the way he did, you can't stop. He ain't a—a KNIGHT any more, fighting a bad railroad. He's a wild animal. You can't love him. Nobody can. . . . He ain't got a friend left—not a friend in the world!" The indisputable message of this *Jesse James* is that it's noble to suffer economic injustice. But fight back, and you lose. Cruelly, you lose either way.

## Saving Jesse's Face

The best of all Jesse James movies, and the most uncompromising, is the one that the Keaches, the Carradines, the Quaids, and the Guests made in 1980 (Fig. 4.7). More than any movie before it, *The Long Riders* (United Artists), directed by action expert Walter Hill, located Jesse

Figure 4.7. From *The Long Riders* (left to right): David Carradine as Cole Younger, Randy Quaid as Clell Miller, Stacy Keach as Frank James, James Keach as Jesse James, and Keith Carradine as Jim Younger. (Courtesy of the University of California at Los Angeles Arts Library, Special Collections)

in a definite and definable rural (and mountain) culture. The film was made on location in the north Georgia hills. This location gave Jesse's banditry the resonance of believable social context that has been missing from most cowboyized film depictions (with the possible exception of Henry King's version, just discussed).

Several scenes in *The Long Riders* were designed to offer a full impression of a working, breathing, sustaining mountain culture that produced the Jameses, the Youngers, the Millers, and the Fords too. One example is the sequence at the wedding dance that celebrates the nuptials of Jesse and Zerelda Mimms (Zee), his cousin. Director Hill crowds the frame with dozens of country extras in the butternut-dark clothes of rural working people and stages a community dance that seems thumpingly right. (Randy Crutchfield mentions especially the visual impact of *hair* in these scenes, "particularly the women's, which has the flat, shiny quality which is the result of natural oils.") The circling of the dancers on the bare wood floors of an old frame schoolhouse delivers a powerful image of the community's collective strength and cohesion, the encircling ring of any legendary bandit's native magic.

Another even more indelible sequence suggests both the power and the fragility of community: the funeral for Jesse's half-brother Archie, who has been killed in the Pinkerton bomb attack on the family homestead (a mountain cabin that is more stereotypically hillbilly than any James homestead in any other movie version). Walter Hill framed the outdoor scene as though he had studied period photographs of eastern Kentucky funerals: we look down a long mountain slope to see the funeral procession winding up to the cemetery at the top of the hill, the black of the mourners a powerful etching on the lush green of the mountain landscape. (Here and elsewhere, the cinematography of Ric Waite seems soaked in damp emerald.) A single horse-drawn wagon carries the now maimed Mrs. Samuel, Jesse's mother, and the casket. Behind walk the men and women and children of the community, and every man in the procession is casually carrying a rifle, as farm people might tote hoes or rakes. The guns of the James gang, seen in this context, are organic and natural, common and essential tools.

At the close of the funeral, it is Jesse's new bride, Zee, who turns to her husband and asks what he plans to do about Archie's death: "Are you gonna make 'em *pay*, Jesse?" Zee and the wives of the other bandits are as strong and forceful as the men, not the back-of-the-hand-to-the-pale-forehead women of earlier versions. It's a welcome development, this incitement to action and fierceness in Zee, the cinematic admission of women to the ranks of rural resistance (Fig. 4.8).

James Keach as Jesse shows no trace of the country-rebel-as-clown. The scapegoat humor is left to others, particularly Clell Miller, played by Randy Quaid, and Cole Younger, played by David Carradine. And in a movie with a fair amount of humor (but without much fun, granted), Jesse is basically humorless. He's as grim and cold as March rain. He never smiles. He's a sour parson. Why? Because he is also chief of sinners, as most parsons are, and he wears his guilt like a heavy coat. He will not sleep with a whore after he's married, but repentance in his particular case seems to produce only rage and hurt. This country boundary-crosser kills with the wrath of a vengeful god, the rural god of strict and mathematical retribution, and he scares some of my students to death.

Figure 4.8. "The cinematic admission of women to the ranks of rural resistance": Savannah Smith as Zee James (center), flanked by the wives of Jim Younger and Frank James, in *The Long Riders*. (Courtesy of the University of California at Los Angeles Arts Library, Special Collections)

The Cole Younger character is closer to the traditional fool, the deep jokester no one understands, the truth-speaker who actively wants to hurt no one but whose truth often stings. He tells Belle Starr, played by the astonishing Pamela Reed, that she wasn't invited to the wedding of Jesse and Zee because "you're a whore." She fires back, "Well, at least I'm not a cheap one!" Cole alone seems to know that the kind of life Jesse has been living as a free-range rooster doesn't sort well with marriage. Later he jokes he'll write a book some day and put his exploits on stage for the world to buy. All of this denotes a self-consciousness that often goes with the role of magical clown. Cole even seems to watch himself with amused resignation as Belle corners him into a knife fight with her pneumatic husband Sam Starr, the half-breed.

The gang's southern allegiance in the Civil War becomes a key issue. In the first whorehouse scene, when we meet Belle Starr, a man singing in the saloon mentions a liberated slave in a song, and Clell Miller good-naturedly offers to blow the singer's knuckles off. But Cole's only comment on the war— "I fought four years in the Army, eleven trying to

*The Hillbilly as Social Bandit* 117

get out"—kills the issue of dumb southern allegiance. (Compare his little brother Jim's much blinder loyalty, even though he was too young to fight: "No, but my brothers fought in it, and we all go the same direction.") Had the movie fully explored the inherent racism in these former Confederates, our sympathies would not have been so engaged on their side. Randy Crutchfield points out that not one single black face is seen in *The Long Riders*, surely its most serious historical flaw, but because of this absence of African American characters, Crutchfield writes, "we forget the racial part of the Civil War and focus on the part that pits rich Yankee squareheads against us."

David Reynolds sees the squarehead culture, symbolized in the movie by Northfield, Minnesota, as the triumph of greed, better known to us as progress. Instead of the cataclysmic battle between capitalism and manhood that Frank James foretold, a slower war of attrition has been fought, not with guns but with lawyers, technology, and mass culture. When the James/Younger gang arrives in Northfield, the "burgeoning middle-border town they intend to rob," writes Reynolds, "they see confident citizens going about the business of creating the new American capitalism that will exclude these rural rebels. Northfield represents the American future, and our heroes are impotent in its presence. They are unable even to open the bank's vault, stymied by a new technology."

*The Long Riders* resisted any impulse to soften or ennoble or otherwise sentimentalize violence, one of Walter Hill's specialities, although of course the violence does carry a propagandizing point, best seen in the contrast the film draws between the violence of the Pinkertons and the violence of the James-Younger gang. The film opens in the middle of a bank robbery. Gang member Ed Miller (played excellently by the explosive Dennis Quaid) loses his head and shoots a bank employee, which forces more firing, the wounding of Jesse, and a mad dash out of town, action that the Jameses would obviously prefer to avoid. For his mistake, Ed is kicked out of the gang, but the important point of the sequence is what it shows about these men's intimate relationship with violence. The connection is not glamorous; it is achingly human.

In contrast, the Pinkerton detectives are detached from any human community. They and their many hired guns ambush the boys in Mr. MacCorkindale's barn with an almost comic hail of bullets. The Pinkertons are unseen and impersonal agents of violence. From a distance

Figure 4.9. Action scene during the disastrous Northfield, Minnesota, bank raid in *The Long Riders*. (Courtesy of the University of California at Los Angeles Arts Library, Special Collections)

they kill MacCorkindale and several pigs and leave the barn an absurd sieve of light holes. The Pinkertons' violence seems mechanical, inorganic, and unnatural.

The inhuman violence of the outside invaders and the human consequences for the inside resisters come together in the film's vivid and appalling climax, the Northfield bank raid (Fig. 4.9). The gang is trapped, perhaps set up, and again the source of official violence is hidden. We see only shadowy figures with rifles and anonymous puffs of gunsmoke. But the devastating effects on our human heroes are shown in intimate close-ups. Bullets strike almost every member of the gang, some of them repeatedly. Direct hits explode all over their bodies. Blood spurts from shoulders, thighs, faces. Gestures of struggle and pain and expressions of despair choreograph a slow-motion, cathartic ballet of defeat.

The doctrine of *The Long Riders* holds that, as long as the rural rebels are encircled in the dance of their community, they are safe and nurtured. But when they leave their home turf for Minnesota to pull off one more big robbery, they symbolically travel away from their culture and their strength. Ironically, they go by train—the old mechanical enemy, the Iron Horse so expressive of an inhuman power, the irresistible rise of capital. After the gang has been shot all to hell-and-gone, some of them dying, almost all of them hurt, Frank (Stacy Keach) delivers the obvious message: "We never should have left Missouri."


Probably the most historically accurate rendering of the Jesse James story was 1986's made-for-TV movie *The Last Days of Frank and Jesse James* (Joe Cates Productions/NBC-TV), starring Johnny Cash as big brother Frank and Kris Kristopherson as Jesse. Although this movie has the right look (it was filmed in Tennessee), and although it is far truer to the facts than any of its predecessors (Frank James curses his mules with Shakespearean quotations) it unfortunately is all exposition—talk, talk, talk, explain, explain, explain—with a large, bewildering parade of named subsidiary characters.

Country music bad-boy stars pepper the film's cast: besides Cash and Kristopherson in the title roles, Willie Nelson and David Allan Coe both have parts. (June Carter Cash, Johnny's real-life wife, plays his mother in a most startling piece of casting.) These country stars add a certain resonance that may be the movie's best idea. After all, commercialized country music is the direct descendant of that cultural rebellion by southern pukes against the big-city swells.

Though obviously well researched and unsensationalized, William Stratton's script is so stuffed with genealogical information that it hardly has time for a story. (This script knows, for example, that Frank's and Jesse's nicknames were "Buck" and "Dingus.") At one point, one of the many young men who hang out around Jesse gets shot dead by another hanger-on in a contest for the affections of Martha Bolton, one of Jesse's distant relations, and Martha gloats to the killer, "You just killed Jesse's *favorite* cousin!" (What was so special about this one?) The issues of consanguinity are clearly supposed to mean something, but exactly what is only dimly understood and never dramatized. And a potentially rich antagonism between Jesse and his big brother comes to a head in a fistfight—they want different things and they resent each other, as real brothers sometimes do—but instead of a brother-against-brother fight that might have advanced our understanding of the psychology of these men, we get unintentionally hilarious fisticuffs, with the two actors talking all the way through it, panting between blows to keep up with the still-yammering script. One socks the other and says there's a rumor that we got different daddies, and the other socks him back and says *my* daddy was a good man and he went to California, and so on. The script also puts its cast through tongue-twisters of archaic and awkward speech. Johnny Cash, for example, just can't quite pull off Frank's learned literary allusions: mule-cursing can be Shakespearean, God wot, but it's got to flow fast. Cash recites his Shakespeare like a man reading words for the first, and the last, time. Otherwise, he has a great face for underclass hurt and fury, which is much of what the Jameses are all about.

You're the only

natural man I've

ever known.

—Francie to Luke

Doolin in *Thunder*

*Road*

 **The Good Old Boys**

Some hillbilly movies frankly suppress any sense of ambiguity about our dark potential, allowing us to see ourselves unambiguously as Roosevelt Man, the romanticized American frontier primitive. Such movies are peopled with characters like the moonshine-running good old boys of the 1960s and 1970s. Hollywood overtly acknowledged the connection to social banditry: In Burt Reynolds's Johnny-come-lately but highly successful *Smokey and the Bandit* (Universal, 1977), sidekick Jerry Reed's big eighteen-wheeler (in which the fun-loving duo haul many cases of bootlegged Coors) is painted with a mural of Jesse James holding up a stagecoach.

## The Fountainhead: *Thunder Road*

In the history of celluloid hillbillies, *Thunder Road* (DRM Productions, 1958) was a landmark, the first film since Biograph's *The Moonshiner* in 1904 to look at the moonshining outlaw from squarely inside the culture. The old Biograph silent accomplished that aim with a nonjudgmental and documentary frankness. Unfortunately, the many, many moonshining shoot-'em-ups that followed it throughout the silent era—I've counted literally hundreds—were mainly done from an outsider's viewpoint. That is, the moonshiners were almost invariably exotics, conjured up for one or two reels to menace a hero (usually a lawman) and then vanquished completely in the end. Another popular plot focused on the moonshiner's daughter, who predictably fell in love with an outsider lawman and left the mountains with him at the movie's close.

*Thunder Road* changed all that. From its insider's perspective, moonshining is hardly exotic or glamorous; it is matter-of-fact to the point of drabness, filmed in an unemphatic black-and-white (Fig. 5.1). But the movie nevertheless constructs a full-fledged tragedy and introduces a hero, Luke Doolin, who must die for his people.

Doolin the moonshine runner helps his father, respects his mother, protects his younger brother, and is chivalrous to women and hard on cads. Luke's people are not the hurting poor, though they are poor by any comparison to late-fifties urban standards. They live on the economic periphery in Harlan County, Kentucky (which in this movie is strangely free of any vestige of coal mining). But as the movie takes pains to dramatize, though Luke's people inhabit the urban fringe, they nevertheless constitute a rural community. They are relatively untouched by the city's evils and do not live by the city's cash alone, depending also on the rural barter-borrow tradition and on self-sufficiency. But city cash has invaded the garden in a destructive way, and with it come some rules and some arrangements and some corruptions that ironically make the mountain people poor indeed. The new cash makes them dependent as well as peripheral.

It was not from greed that they first started selling moonshine. Rather, they make whiskey by training or by talent or by habit, and when trading it is proscribed and then becomes competitively dangerous be-

Figure 5.1. The Doolin home in a publicity still from *Thunder Road,* with Robert Mitchum, James Mitchum (left) as the brother, and Frances Koon (center) as Mother Doolin. (Courtesy of Wisconsin Center for Film and Theater Research)

cause of the contaminating greed from the city, one of them at least considers it an important exercise of ideal American freedom to continue. Luke Doolin explains the politics of his position: "I knew . . . that what my old man was doing was against the law, as the government saw it. But my family held, and had held all the way back to Ireland, that making whiskey on your own land was one of the basic rights of free men."

These mountain people have not willfully isolated themselves from participation in the rest of the American social contract. Luke, after all, has done his duty: "I didn't ask for anything except to grow up in these hills, but the government fetched me out of Rillow Valley and into a uniform." He fought honorably in Korea and has come home to traditional pursuits, only to find the old ways branded as outlawry. He has done right by the State, but the State has not done right by him. The movie points up that irony in a scene that puzzles many contemporary audiences. When Luke comes into his mountain home after a night of running liquor into Memphis, he unbuttons his shirt and then turns and looks at a flag on the bedroom wall. The movie never explains what kind of flag it is, but the shooting script identifies it as "a battle pennon of the 32nd Regiment, 7th Army Division." And suddenly Luke's gaze at the symbol of his faithful service has a darker resonance. Where has that service gotten him? Though his people look up to him and even fear him a little as "a machine-gunner," the state now calls him criminal and "bush ape."

The money to be made running moonshine has been good, good enough to attract the interest of organized crime. But money does not transform the Harlan County moonshiners the way greed has obviously transformed American capitalism, symbolized adequately by the Mafia-like mob, the very image of arbitrage. Early in the movie, when Luke scolds his slaving mother for not spending a little money on herself, she "pushes a lock of gray hair with the back of one hand" (shooting script) and replies, "This money you make might as well be counterfeit. You know if I buy anything I'd like to, the news will be all around and somebody will ask me where I got it." Before, without so much illicit cash, they had been getting by all right (with the men generally driving the cars—that is, having all the fun—while the women stayed at home). Now, with so much money, they're downright deprived, ironic prisoners of it. *Thunder Road* is not about the dangerous acquisition of illegal cash but about the tragic erosion of liberty as a result of other people's greed. Subsistence is replaced by subservience, only Luke Doolin is too much the "natural man" to bend. His story is a fable about resistance, bound to fail but brilliantly romanticized.

The Doolin family and the rest of their community have lived in Rillow Valley for generations. Their homeplace is described as "long-weathered," its other contents calculated to suggest old ways: "a big stone fireplace," "a large hand loom," "faded family portraits." But the script also says the Doolins have a new electric refrigerator standing "in a place of honor." Everyone goes to church, and everyone believes in the rightness of the old rural gods. Even the preacher, played by Barter Theater founder Robert Porterfield, prays for the Lord's keeping of the embattled cultural imperative: "We ask Your blessings on these sinful sheep who are gathered under Your roof today, to worship Thee, but also on all the men of this congregation who were unable to attend because of pressing business." The movie cuts from the preacher's prayer to the "business" meeting of the moonshiners, all of them in overalls and caps. Some are ready to give up and go to work for Mr. Big, Carl Kogan, the boss of the mob. Kogan wants to employ the country people, he says, in a pipeline business. That is, he wants to buy them out and then make wage slaves of them.

Kogan is not the only force drawn up against their freedom and, by implication, against the very longevity of their culture. The law also opposes them, also with no sense of fair play. It is the law's job to enforce the morality of an even bigger pipeline than the mob's—that of federal dependency. In other words, both the mob and the law are different expressions of the same force, the assigning and control of value by way of domination. And by their outside evaluation, moonshining mountaineers have been ruled expendable. To the mob, they are peripheral obstructions to expansion and domination of the market. And to the pious law, they are untaxed purveyors.

But for actual, moviegoing country people in 1958, how *Thunder Road* mythologized the country outsider! As Luke Doolin, Robert Mitchum lights a cigarette like a rattlesnake buzzing itself into a coil. His don't-tread-on-me potency is all the more powerful seen through the eyes of men in the audience who feel they've been trod upon. In the closing minutes of the movie, driving tight but cool and pursued by Lucky, the big-city henchman, Luke is overtaken on a winding mountain road. Lucky the hired gun pulls even with Luke and tries to muscle him off. Luke glares and Lucky glares back. Then Doolin, like a striking snake, flicks the cigarette he's been smoking through his open window and through the open window of the other car and into the face of Lucky, who flinches, who therefore loses, who presently dies. This is the clear, clean gesture of defiance in a dying fall, for Luke Doolin won't survive this auto race either.

There is one other force arrayed against Luke Doolin that we must not overlook and cannot discount: women. (This female-as-enemy subtext in *Thunder Road* became the main pretext in the good-old-boy movies that followed and imitated it.) The women around Luke Doolin are, without exception, stereotypes of the old entrappers and "civilizers." Luke's girlfriend in Memphis, Francie the cabaret singer, wants him off the road and settled down: "Can't we ever get married?" "Don't push," he says, and he means it. Their scenes together have as much comfortable intimacy as prickly heat. "I'm just naturally otherwise-minded," Doolin tells Francie. "If we're to stay together, bear it in mind."

Meanwhile, back home in Rillow Valley, a second woman in Luke's life, the young Roxanna, boldly flirts with him, climbs into his hot rod beside him, openly idolizes his roadrunner image, and tries to lure him to her with schoolgirl perfume, but Luke knows this mere foolish child is jailbait. He gently rebuffs her, and like the mythic conserver of culture he is, he steers her toward more suitable mates in the community: "Roxanna, Roxanna . . . find yourself somebody who's content to bang a time clock and have a mess of kids." "I would if they looked like you," she moons back. "Oh, Lord. You ain't got any sense," Luke replies. And she doesn't. It is the lovelorn and clinging Roxanna, in fact, who finally goes to the law and gives her hero away because she wants to save him from himself: "He won't ever stop, unless somebody stops him." In gratitude, naturally, the law lays a vicious ambush, an oil slick with tire-puncturing spikes, and kills him in a crash. This movie's hidden agenda: death and betrayal are what women can bring you.

*Thunder Road* was Robert Mitchum's movie, and the movie was him. He thought up the story, produced the film, starred in it, even wrote the title song ("The Ballad of Thunder Road") and the sad love theme ("Whippoorwill"), and by all reports the movie made him rich. In some sense the film was autobiographical. Mitchum had been scandalous, a notorious bad boy—a former fugitive from a Chatham County, Georgia, prison gang, busted for dope in 1948 long before most Americans had heard of marijuana. And that was just one of many other scrapes. According to an article in the *Saturday Evening Post,*

> In 1951, he floored a soldier . . . in the bar of a Colorado Springs hotel and, according to a Military Police sergeant, kicked [him] "in the head." In 1953 he outraced a Los Angeles motorcycle cop in his sports car at seventy miles an hour, and was charged with "evading arrest" and "resisting and obstructing an officer." . . . In 1956 he flattened two U.S. Navy sailors in a barroom brawl on the Caribbean island of Tobago and became involved with the Navy Shore Patrol.

And so on.

He had grown up hard. Essentially orphaned as a boy, he was early forced to depend on his own wits to survive, taking to the road during the depression along with thousands of other homeless "wild boys." He knew hobo jungles and rail yards and jails. He worked every job there was to work. In other words, he found out what it meant to be a hillbilly, the dangerous natural who bounces back, but not forever. Out of the experience he created a rebel self who knows he must perish yet acts as though he never will.

Later in life, Mitchum enjoyed exaggerating his hillbilly background for impressionable reporters, putting them on with ever ranker tales that mocked their gullibility. Mitchum's own weakness, which he was willing enough to flaunt like the fool, was the poet in him, the great big sensitive lug who sees the beauty of hopeless gestures and who surprisingly revels in thought as much as in action, who once wrote an oratorio and saw it performed in the Hollywood Bowl at a benefit for European refugees. *Thunder Road* is Mitchum's soft side mythologizing his roughneck side in a poem.

Every good poem has a symbol, and the chief symbol of *Thunder Road* is the ominous bird of freedom, the whippoorwill (which was also the film's original title). The song "Whippoorwill," which Mitchum helped write and which Keely Smith, as Francie, sings in the movie two or three times, is addressed to the Mitchum character:

While all alone beneath the tree,
Where once you pledged your love to me,
My lonely heart cries out for you—
The whippoorwill is crying too.

The wild blood that runs the roads is faithless in love only because it cannot be untrue to itself.

The bird symbolism comes in handy. In one scene, Luke Doolin pays a visit to Kogan, whose thugs have already shot at Luke and tried to run him off the road. Kogan has made him a do-or-die offer—join the mob or get rubbed out—and Luke comes to the gangster's Memphis hideout not to accept the offer but to knock Kogan down.

He finds Mr. Big listening to classical music and watching a bird build a nest on the ledge outside his office. Kogan explains that he's been experimenting with Pavlovian stimulus and response. "That bird won't interrupt his work for trashy stuff," he says, "but slam him full volume with something real good—Wagner, Bach, or Beethoven—and he really takes off. I'm sorta interested in stuff like that." And he gives Luke a smug up-and-down appraisal, the implication being that he knows how to condition this bird, too. But we know better. Luke says, "I don't like being shot at," and when Kogan replies, "Just how rough do you want it?" Luke floors him. No further discussion required. Then to underline his status as the free (though doomed) bird of folklore, Mitchum ends the scene by flying out Kogan's window into the bed of a dump truck in the street (Fig. 5.2).

In the closing scene of the movie, after Luke has been killed and the lawman has pronounced that mountain people are hopelessly "wild-blooded and death foolish," we see Luke's brother Robin (played by Mitchum's son James) taking young Roxanna's hand, while in the distance a long trail of car lights wind up the mountain, bringing Luke's body back to Rillow Valley. The "Whippoorwill" song is reprised on the soundtrack. The distant moving string of headlights are votive candles, for is not Luke Doolin a ritual sacrifice, the last admirable, real man in America, willing to go to battle in what Frank James predicted would be the next war—the struggle between manhood and greed? He knew the measure of freedom and would, in a more honest time, have preserved himself and the ways of his people. But he has been unfairly cornered by profit and its regulators.

In romanticizing this doomed masculinity, *Thunder Road* also energized an entire generation of adolescent males, especially in the South, to tempt death. The movie was an incredible hit in the drive-in trade all across this more rural land. It freed some of those same rank wild juices that old raccoon skin had stimulated three years earlier with the debut of Walt Disney's Davy Crockett, only by this time the former Disney audience had grown out of frontier costume and into four wheels and eight pistons. In addition, *Thunder Road* had the power of revelation. Robert Mitchum fueled empty egos. Rollovers proliferated as many a teenage hellraiser tried to duplicate the bootleg turn. Most of the ones who survived the squealing tires eventually knuckled under to the world of work and wages in the button-down, drip-dry Eisenhower years, settling their dreams of economic freedom—or rather the freedom from economics—into job, home, and kids. This is what happens

Figure 5.2. Robert Mitchum, as the doomed "whippoorwill," takes a flyer out of Kogan's window in *Thunder Road*. (Courtesy of Wisconsin Center for Film and Theater Research)

to rural rebels, if they survive. And mythic tragedy has a way of reasserting the status quo.

## The Sons of Doolin

Everything comes down to going 75 miles an hour in your truck with a fifth of Jack Daniel's between your legs because NOBODY'S GONNA TELL ME WHAT TO DO! NO GODDAMN GOVERNMENT OR ANYBODY ELSE! That's just the simple hillbilly truth of it all.
—Roseanne Arnold, in *Vanity Fair*

*Thunder Road* was the first moonshiner film to link the "devil's thirst" to fast automobiles, a combination that had been achieved in reality considerably earlier than 1958. But until *Thunder Road*, mountain moonshiners in the movies always rode horses.

Although *Thunder Road* was the direct inspiration for the car-crash-ing "good-old-boy" movies of the 1960s and 1970s, the formula that ultimately developed was curiously unlike *Thunder Road* in a couple of important ways. In later films, the good old boys are not tragic; they're bounce-back country clowns. And they are not rooted in a believably cohesive rural culture as Luke Doolin was. Their fast cars detach them from any community. Rather, the landscape is populated only by symbolic types, because the landscape is symbolic, too, a fool's paradise where everyone is silly and nobody ultimately gets hurt. The *noir*ish threats to men's freedom that shadow *Thunder Road* are here lightened into comedy.

The irony is that the good-old-boy movies were as angry at heart as *Thunder Road*. In them, *something* is threatening the freedom of men, and all these movies trotted out the usual suspects first: (1) the law (which represents state, church, and middle-class respectability); (2) the mob (which represents advanced capital); and (3) uppity women. But the dark lecture on the first two in *Thunder Road* is rendered irrelevant. In the fantasy of the good-old-boy movies, the law and the mob are usually characterized as silly fat guys who are easy to escape. But the women! They are now not only entrappers of male freedom but assertive to boot. Put another way, the first two enemies of free males, big government and big business, are nothing compared to the big ideas of modern women.

It seems tiresome yet necessary to point out that these movies proved most profitable at the box office from the late sixties and straight through the seventies—in other words, during the most recent rise of feminism. This far-more-than-coincidental fulmination of male anger, masquerading as good-natured high spirits, reveals how truly mainstream these movies were politically, even though they were made for and pushed into the peripheral movie market: drive-ins and small-town theaters, especially in the South and the West. (*Thunder Road* had also played strictly on the entertainment periphery. It was not shown in mainstream urban theaters, nor was it reviewed in mainstream periodicals—*not one.*) These movies reveled in a rough dominance over women and simultaneously laid that retrograde attitude off on rural low-others.

The demonstrable powerlessness of real good old boys in the face of economics is transcended in good-old-boy movies by car chases and overturning beer trucks, fistfights and vulgar high jinks. If these movies were angry at independent women—and they certainly were—their anger may have come only from the dumb, self-sustaining desire to feel powerful and confident about *something*, a desire that's fulfilled partly by demolishing the wrong enemy. So the Sons of Doolin became strutting Petruchios taming their shrews. Sadly, the question "Will she or won't she?" is just no substitute for "who's in charge here?"

*Moonrunners* (United Artists, 1974) was notable for two things: it co-starred James Mitchum, who had played second fiddle to his dad in *Thunder Road*; and it was based—at some wee distant level—on the real exploits of a Taylorsville, North Carolina, moonshine runner named Jerry Rushing, who became a fairly successful professional hillbilly himself. A filmmaker stumbled on Rushing "through a friend of a friend," and Rushing wound up telling his stories to a tape recorder. The result became first *Moonrunners*, for which Rushing received a "based on" screen credit, and then, without Rushing's consent or knowledge and certainly without his receiving any compensation, *The Dukes of Hazzard* TV series. One day he turned on the TV and found his 1958 Chrysler 300D, which he had named Traveller in honor of southern rebel saint General Robert E. Lee's horse, transmogrified into a miraculously undentable Dodge named the General Lee, being driven acrobatically by two blow-dried California stud-muffins, Tom Wopat and Jon Schneider. Rushing sued and won, got paid his cut, and then consented to appear in episodes of *The Dukes* in bit parts. He also took other roles in several movies (especially in the *oeuvres* of "redneck auteur" Earl Owensby) and on TV, including the part of the blacksmith in *Young Daniel Boone*.

In *Moonrunners*, Kiel Martin (best known for the character J. D. Larue on TV's *Hill Street Blues*) plays Bobby Lee Hogg, our rebel fool, our symbolic male piglet. (James Mitchum took the lesser role of Bobby Lee's sidekick.) Where Luke Doolin was uptight, Bobby Lee is about as loose as they come. For example, after he has a run-in with a motorcycle gang, he gets back at them by gunning his car through the wall of a saloon where they're drinking and then falls out of the car laughing (Fig. 5.3). That's our boy.

The great glory of *Moonrunners* is the wonderful Arthur Hunnicut as Uncle Jesse, the master distiller (a composite of Rushing's father and his uncle). Uncle Jesse will sell no 'shine before its time. He stands for

Figure 5.3. Kiel Martin, playing Bobby Lee Hogg, at the wheel in *Moon-runners*, demolishing a bikers' den. (Courtesy of Wisconsin Center for Film and Theater Research)

old-fashioned virtues, quality and service. He considers the stuff the northern mob is peddling to be nothing but poison, and the mob wants him to mass-produce this "garbage" for them. It's a classic confrontation between what venture capital has indeed become and what precapitalist American enterprise is naively believed to have been.

John Saxon, as a roadrunner in *Moonshine County Express* (Universal, 1976), is up against not one but three willful gals (a sister act). The requisite Mr. Big is played poisonously by veteran fat man William Conrad. The three sisters' pa, a master distiller, has been murdered by Mr. Big, but the spunky women decide in true feminist style to carry on the family business without him, come hell or high water. After serious reverses, the two younger sisters admit they need a man. But the eldest sister, stubbornly independent Dottie (Susan Howard), balks: absolutely not. The available natural man, played by Saxon, is, in her opinion, a no-good smiling skunk. But that's an opinion this movie will force her to retract: "I can't do it by myself," she finally wails, and the no-good smiling skunk chooses to accept her apology.

The funniest and most outrageously inventive of all the good-old-boy movies was Roger Corman's *Thunder and Lightning* (Twentieth Century–Fox, 1977), directed by Corey Allen. It takes place in the same weird "South" that *The Dukes of Hazzard* brought to TV, the one in which the people are often our classic hillbillies, yet the landscape includes swamps and alligators. David Carradine, who was Cole Younger in *The Long Riders*, here plays Kung-Fu Hillbilly. Carradine is the only movie moonshine transporter I know of who sports an earring. The movie also has the other usual characters, inept thugs and more inept lawmen and also a backwoods Jimmy Swaggart who wrestles an alligator in church while preaching against "the serpent." And there's a long sequence in which every single bottle of pop on a big Honey Dew soft-drink truck gets broken, the ultimate in preadolescent wet dreams. *Thunder and Lightning* fulfills what Bob Snyder calls every moviegoer's reasonable expectation: that a car chase will end in an overturned truck of live chickens. And true to the formula, there's a pretty and willful woman (Kate Jackson) who needs overwhelming. The Kate Jackson character is also the daughter of the corrupt Mr. Big, and it's a useful conflation. By sticking it to the usual independent woman, our fast-driving hero can stick it to the corporation too.

Burt Reynolds made several of these films, though his hillbilly was more often located in the swamps of the Deep South (*White Lightning*, its sequel *Gator*, and the long *Smokey and the Bandit* series). Reynolds was more like a Ken doll dressed for a moonshine theme park, which seems to have given his movies a crossover appeal to large numbers of female fans. In many ways his good old boys were a cultural harbinger of the long night of the Reagan Revolution.

## Bad Georgia Road

The most offensive of all the good-old-boy movies, and the most interesting for the way it subsumed the economic issue in sexual politics, was *Bad Georgia Road* (Producers Group Inc., 1977). The story went like this:

Lovely Molly Golden (she's a blond, natch) is a New York fashion-magazine flunkie with distant north Georgia roots. She is haughty, arrogant, and a snob—her last name is a shimmering irony. One day at work she gets a call that her uncle has died in the Georgia hills and left her everything, supposedly a hundred-thousand-dollar fortune. She lights out immediately, giving up her career and the city both.

Molly can shuck her conventional urban success so readily because it is shown to be unpleasantly neurotic and destructive. Hers is a symbolic world filled with aggressive women only, a high-rise compost heap of gender-specific spite, lies, accusations, lesbian innuendo, and bizarre psycho-corporate rituals. Before she gets her call from Georgia, Molly is obliged to take part in stress-reduction therapy, during which all the women wield big padded orange phalluses and whack each other in a mutual basting. *Where are the men?* this movie asks. Well, they ain't in New York, though parts of them have been fabricated in foam rubber.

Naturally, there's no fortune in Georgia, though there is another kind of redemption. Molly drives to the southern hills in a spiffy foreign convertible, trailing a stream of pompous opinions about southerners and accompanied by a new character, the simpering Darryl. He's a male model—not a model male—who can pass for straight. And now we know what's become of urban men. The script refers to Darryl contemptuously as "gay" or "queer" no less than three times. Molly and Darryl have an "arrangement": he's her pretend boyfriend and her protection in fact against any possibility of real male advances. So with Molly in the driver's seat in more ways than one, she and Darryl motor on down South for Molly's comeuppance.

On the way, she lectures Darryl about Tennessee Williams's *A Streetcar Named Desire*, about how the Stanley-brute ended up raping the Blanche-belle, "savagely and without a care," because "Blanche wanted it all the time." Ironically, Molly Golden is unconsciously choosing her own poison: she will come to desire to be raped savagely and without a care. That's the politics of this movie; that's how bad it is.

Leroy Hastings, played blisteringly well by Gary Lockwood, is the designated fornicator, the Masculine Primitive ideal who is going to restore Molly to nature. Leroy seems perpetually covered with a patina of tallow and soot. He's a butter melter and a ring-tailed roarer, a wide-bore, honky-tonking, quadruple-barreled hillbilly. "Damn sonovabitch is crazy," says one of his rivals. And to Molly, he's potently ambiguous: he is both her worst nightmare and precisely what she must have to get well.

Molly's inherited Georgia estate turns out to be a squalid moonshiner's farmhouse with adjacent sheds, shacks, and barns in a junk-strewn landscape. Her uncle, naturally, was the county's biggest moonshiner, though she doesn't know that at first, and naturally there's no money left in the uncle's estate. The lawyers got it all, what little there was. All that remains is the farm where the uncle's two loyal employees live: Leroy, the prize transporter, and old Pennyrich, the preacher-distiller.

From the beginning of their acquaintance, Leroy's very physical presence offends Molly, affronts and assaults her self-possession. She calls him "an ape" to his face and later a "hillbilly" and "sonovabitch" and other names. She's a duchess, and he's supposed to be a footman, like the accommodating Darryl, but Leroy won't play his assigned role. During Molly's first morning on the farm, she walks in on Leroy uninvited and catches him in his underwear cooking his breakfast, with a Confederate flag on the wall and cool hostility on his face. It's her shack, she insists, because she owns everything, including his sorry ass. He eats his breakfast eggs like an animal, eyeing her sullenly. Later he says to old Pennyrich, "That city bitch! I'd kill her for pure pleasure." It's what she stands for that he wants to kill—the tyranny of economic domination, the full implications of her name, Golden. She represents the rule of money, the blond flowering of greed.

Leroy's loyalty and service to her dead uncle's moonshine business has earned him nothing tangible, not even the car he drives, which technically now also belongs to Molly. But the script has designated him to take back his economic independence from her and incidentally to redeem her soul in the process. "Ain't no woman gonna be this child's boss," Leroy vows.

Molly doesn't want the farm any more than Leroy wants her on the farm. At first she says she'll sell the place, but there are no buyers. She's stuck, and Darryl whines: "This is the end of the earth, Timbucktu, where time stands still." But then Molly discovers Leroy loading plastic jugs of corn liquor into his car, and she quickly asserts her ownership of that enterprise, too, giving Leroy and his Bible-spouting preacherman-assistant only 30 percent of the profit to split between them. And she demands that they buy the ingredients for the mash out of their cut.

Molly stereotypes Leroy as a southern Stanley-brute, speculating smugly that he lusts after her body. That's because Molly has begun secretly to lust after his. She spies longingly on him. Leroy comes back from an all-night haul, tosses the proceeds on the ground, and disappears into his shack with a giggling, jiggling, and compliant Moonbeam McSwine look-alike. Molly observes this joyous carnality, and it both infuriates and arouses her. She raises her bedroom window so that she can hear even better the sound effects of Leroy's mating, and then, in response to that stimulus, she climbs on Darryl, who is surprised and humiliated. Later Molly sunbathes provocatively in front of Leroy and orders him to rub suntan oil on her back. He won't, but he substitutes car grease for her bottle of suntan oil, and while she is obliviously smearing black hundred-weight all over her lily-white self, she haughtily reviews his love life, calling him "a sexual ghoul." "*Where* do you find those Barbie dolls?" she asks. "At least they know what they want and how to find it," he replies. As the scene ends, she's a blackened ice maiden on the hard rural dirt, and he walks away from her.

Molly rationalizes that a man is not what she wants, that she's found what she wants: her own lucrative business, independence, and, only coincidentally, domination over every man in sight. But she's perfectly miserable. She looks for ways to get in Leroy's face. She insists that she be allowed to accompany him on one of his runs. He just as forcefully insists that "*nobody* rides with me when I'm hauling." But it's *her* car, *her* investment! Finally, she steps directly in front of him as he tries to drive away. The camera sees the moving car as a projectile aimed squarely at her groin. He stops, she gets in, and Leroy grimly drives off with her.

On the haul, she yammers the whole time:

> *She*: Do you have to drive so fast? . . . You're a prime example of castration anxiety, inadequate psycho-sexual development, and a need to act out absurd fantasies.
> *He*: You're full of shit!

She primly announces that she's got to stop for a bathroom. He tells her he doesn't stop for nothing. She threatens, she yells, she beats on his arm. He offers her a fruit jar, which she hotly declines. He warns her: "Don't you wet my seat!" Then, *in* rapid order, they're trapped in a roadblock by the local Mafia types and shot at, and Leroy guns off down a ditch and across a field to escape. As they regain the highway we hear Leroy's disgusted voice-over: "Goddamn! You did it! You pissed on my seat!"

That incontinence is partly also an explicit suggestion of sexual longing, which reaches absurd lengths in the next sequence, when Molly and Leroy reach Birmingham. Leroy goes off by himself to visit his favorite dive, and Molly follows him to spy. What she sees is truly remarkable, even for the cog-dragging that characterizes this movie genre. In this fistarian bar, Leroy is a willing sex object for the local women. He accosts one, the luscious Lu Ann, at the bar:

> *She*: Comin' back for more, boy?
> *He*: I thought I wore you out the last time.
> *She*: Shit! Bring your lovin' ass over here and find out.

At which invitation Leroy shouts at the country-western band, "Put that gittar in low gear. I'm carrying a *heavy* load!" and begins a lascivious, pelvis-thrusting strut in Lu Ann's direction. They perform a raunchy dance, ending up locked in a French kiss and down on the floor together, fairly grubbing. Then Lu Ann's boyfriend Jesse appears and pulls Leroy up by his hair. There follows an eye-gouging, ear-biting, chair-flinging fight, and while this melee is progressing, another woman who has been eyeing Leroy says to Lu Ann: "Leroy is *purty*!" To which Lu Ann dryly replies, "Don't mess with him, darlin'. He's got a dick from here to the door." The important thing is that Molly sees and overhears all of this, her eyes very big now for Leroy of the heavy load—the real thing to replace those enormous fake phalluses that the women were using on one another in New York City.

Molly needs to be mastered by this man, and she wants it but doesn't know she wants it, so she must be shown her own reflection. She will be Blanche to Leroy's Stanley. His taking of her will also be a convenient confirmation of her social superiority. But there's a twist that keeps the film from veering into Molly's fantasy; instead we get a table-turning epiphany.

Leroy has proposed that his cut of the business should by rights be greater than the 15 percent Molly is giving him, especially considering the personal danger he is in (of which Molly now shares firsthand knowledge). She brays back at him—"No-o-o!"—but this time she goes too far. She throws something and yells, "Do you hear me, *boy*?" He replies with a frightening resolve, "The shit has hit the fan."

She grabs a butcher knife and tries to fend him off. He smiles. This is going to be better than he had imagined. He backs her into a corner, the knife going limp in her hand. He has developed a plan. "I've seen your kind before," he sneers, "sleeping with queers, always dry-humpin'"; Molly shrieks and bolts. The chase is not comic but realistically violent and not a little unnerving, because the audience is now implicated in wishing these just desserts on her. He grabs her, rips her bodice, and grasps her by the hair as she wrecks the place throwing dishes at him, knees him in the groin, pummels him with her fists. He gets verbally nastier, playing vividly on her expectations: "I'm gonna poke you so deep you're gonna flop like a fish outta water. I'm gonna make your eyes bulge and your mouth hang open. I'm going to give you a fuckin' you won't soon forget."

The floor of the kitchen is covered with spilled milk and broken dishes. She's down flat on her back in the mess. Still fully clothed, he lies on top of her. "Do you feel it?" he asks her, pressing his pelvis into hers. "*You* feel it," he answers his own question, looking at her face. "You *want* it!" Her outraged screams and threats have now become more satisfied cries and whispers, and before we know it, just the weight of him and the excitement of him on her has made her achieve orgasm. Yes. Leroy, by now differently satisfied, asks, "How does the animal look to you now?" and he gets up, laughing at her. With her own nature dawning on her for the first time, Molly must now listen to him: "You thought you had me all figgered out. You ain't got the slightest idea. You are *nowhere*!" He goes off jeering aloud at the spectacle she has become.

Ever a bundle of confusion, Molly runs after him, grabbing his double-barreled shotgun. She bursts into his shack and levels the gun at him. Leroy says, "Girl, either you admit to yourself that you wanted me and drop that gun, or you lie to yourself and pull the trigger." Molly chooses the lie. She pulls both triggers. Click, click. But the gun isn't loaded. And then, in the final reversal we've been waiting for, she throws down the gun and pitches herself into his arms, begging "please, please." And Leroy pleases.

Immediately after Leroy has made a real woman out of her, she's still trying to maintain domination: "I want you to know that what you did to me was illegal. . . . Let me put it another way: I've had *better*." But he has restored her to sexual balance and himself to economic independence. They make one final haul together before the final credits, and he spells out the facts of life: "You're not the center of the world, honey. You're just a face in the crowd." He tells her there's going to be a new deal, a sixty-forty split "with me on top." She counters with fifty-fifty. He says, "Okay, but I get to lay you any time I get the urge." "Same for me too," Molly replies, and with that altogether logical melding of business and sex, male power is supposedly reasserted.

In your dreams, buddy! It's not the women who've got you by the balls.

## The Biopix

You get people who have been poor that have seen things get better, and nothing scares them like being poor again.
—Race car driver Tim Flock

The economic subtext for the Sons of Doolin is explored more soberly in two movie tributes to stock-car legends Wendell Scott and Junior Johnson, both of whom, in real life, learned to drive like maniacs out of economic need and cultural habit, running moonshine out of the Virginia and the North Carolina Blue Ridge, respectively. They, like many another NASCAR legend such as Bobby Isaac and Tim Flock, did for real what Burt Reynolds pretended to do.

The Wendell Scott story, *Greased Lightning* (Warner Brothers, 1977), starred Richard Pryor in a sanitized and basically hopeful narrative that tried to deny the harsher truth that the real Wendell Scott, as a lone black man in a frankly racist environment, never gained much of anything tangible from his efforts to race competitively with the white boys. He did clearly win a Grand National race in Jacksonville in 1964, but track officials took first place away from him and gave it to Buck Baker, presumably because the reigning Miss Florida was at the track that day to kiss the winner.

The movie version, on the other hand, chose to fade out on a come-from-behind victory that seemed to suggest black Americans can make it into the winner's circle if they just keep trying. In other words, the movie expressed a late-seventies civil rights optimism, unaware of any irony in its validation of a system of economic rewards and punishments that would very soon begin to put blacks "back in their place" again in the Reagan eighties.

The actual truth was that Scott was not only nearly killed but also economically busted by his gruesome wreck in 1973 at Talladega. He never did recover financially to race competitively again. There was no come-from-behind victory. The economic truth of his career in racing was aptly dubbed by Sylvia Wilkinson "From Rags to Rags." But the movie version puts the Talladega crash in the middle of the narrative and allows Scott to struggle back from it triumphantly, even though nobody thinks he can do it, including his devoted wife (played by Pam Grier). She speaks discouragingly to him as he lies in his hospital bed, all mummified by bandages and plaster of Paris: "Please stop. . . . You're forty-two years old. You got fifteen years on half the men you race against. They got the sponsors, the big oil companies, and the car companies. They got the best cars, and the best mechanics. What you got?"

"Heart," he answers, and in *Greased Lightning* heart is supposed to be enough.

Not only did Scott's actual racing career feature no Cinderella reversals, but Scott himself also naively signed away his movie rights, agreeing to a percentage of "profits after expenses" instead of sensible up-front cash. Under those contingencies, Hollywood bookkeeping rarely declares a profit. Several years later, a much wiser Scott told Wilkinson, "You wouldn't think it was a best selling movie, the way they did me. . . . They claim they are [still, in the early 1980s] $4,600,000 in the red."

Meanwhile, some of the white guys who had made things tough for Scott on the southern dirt-track circuit ironically pulled down good salaries working as stunt drivers on *Greased Lightning*. And at least one of them—Soapy Castles, a middle-of-the-pack NASCAR racer with hillbilly bona fides who had himself never made it into the big money—managed to cling to his perfect contempt for Scott. Castles was stunt coordinator and technical assistant on the movie, and he told Wilkinson, "If Wendell didn't get something out of it, it's his own fault. . . . I remember when he first started racing. . . . He was just more or less a joke. Wendell's life wasn't that rough. A nigger couldn't make no money back then to amount to nothing. . . . [But] the reason he stayed in it, he was making more money than the average nigger. . . . He stayed in his place. If he got out of his place, somebody put him back in his place."

From such poor soil, irony blossoms like stinkweed. First, Soapy Castles was uttering his estimations on the set of the very movie meant to ennoble the subject of his pronouncements. Second, Wendell's "place" in the scheme of Castles's whites-first universe did not have so much to do with his black skin as with an economic system that had also ground away at Soapy Castles. After all, Castles realistically had been only slightly better off in the racing world than Scott. He had never been able to afford the best or the latest rolling stock, so he, like Wendell Scott, was shut out of the NASCAR chips. But he could feel infinitely better because at least he wasn't a black man. (Not surprisingly, Scott expressed bitterness that Soapy Castles "got rich" coordinating the driving stunts while Scott himself got so little out of *Greased Lightning*.)

While the movie soft-pedaled racism (Richard Pryor's best buddy in the movie is Beau Bridges, a soft-core redneck whose rough exterior turns out to conceal the heart of Jimmy Carter), Pryor's low-key performance also stayed well clear of the kind of bug-eyed caricature for which the comedian was even then making himself famous on stage. Instead, Pryor established what Richard Schickel called "a sort of quizzical intelligence" in the role, which makes Scott's dogged determination to compete with the good old boys seem reasonable and even noble.

Much tougher minded on the issue of economics was the Junior Johnson story, *The Last American Hero* (Twentieth Century–Fox, 1973), based on Tom Wolfe's *Esquire* magazine profile, which was prominently reprinted in *The Kandy-Kolored Tangerine-Flake Streamline Baby* in 1965. Free of any necessity to put a pious face on race relations, *The Last American Hero* took the theme of good old boys versus economic necessity and burrowed into it like a hookworm into muscle.

The Junior Johnson character in the movie (inexplicably renamed Junior Jackson) stands for and represents a distinct community of people, much as Luke Doolin did in *Thunder Road*—a cohesive rural culture that understands all the rules have been written to keep the big guys big and the little guys little. So Junior quickly becomes his neighborhood's cultural hero/rebel when he charges through the sheriff's roadblock and when he begins to bend the fenders of the big guys in stock-car races. In his first legitimate competition, he's all bull-shouldered push and drive, so that one of his better-equipped rivals screams at him, "What kind of racing's that, you dirty corn-running hick!" (Fig. 5.4).

As played by Jeff Bridges, Junior seems explosively compressed even in repose, an impudent rural covenanter charging the obstacles to freedom, especially the dominating power of the money men who rule the world of professional stock-car racing. "All they gotta do is stay outta my way," he says, and that line is not just macho posturing but a version of rough egalitarianism: staying out of each other's way is another definition of democracy. But in fact the world does not work that way, and the movie is surprisingly brutal with the truth. To stay in racing, to achieve and maintain a competitive credibility, Junior has to subordinate himself to economic power, specifically to a man named Colt (played by Ed Lauter), who, according to Pauline Kael, "suggests a personification of the power of money. . . . Colt is almost lascivious about winning, and his winning is evil." "Corruption seems to be inescapable," Kael said in summing up the theme of *The Last American Hero*. "You can't win, and everybody's a sellout."

Well, not quite everybody. Junior's father, renamed Roy "Wildcat" Jackson for the movie and played as "a mule-headed man of principle" by Art Lund, is a veritable pillar of male country virtue and a sort of economic revelator to his son. Early in the movie, after the father is busted at his still and incarcerated, he rails against the system of "laws and official values"—the corruption, in other words—that defines as illegal his cultural practice of making whiskey. In his estimation, the courthouse is populated by "the country-club boys," and "City Hall is so full of crooks, they're falling out of the windows—boys with their payoffs and kickbacks. Where do you go to find a little justice?" His hypocritical lawyer replies, "You get what you pay for." For the big guys, staying clear of the law is a matter of what they can afford, so if you're a little guy, better not get on their wrong side.

But old man Jackson spits in power's eye, and he expects his son to do likewise. This is the old man's second stint in prison. After he had served his first sentence, he hired on at a local sawmill to please Junior's ma. "But that paycheck wasn't money—it was a bill of sale! Three

Figure 5.4. Jeff
Bridges in *The Last
American Hero*.
(Courtesy of the
University of
California at Los
Angeles Arts
Library, Special
Collections)

months of that—back to whiskey." And what is whiskey making but "giving folks a little pleasure at a dollar a pint"? "There's only two grades of everything: the best and all the rest," he tells his son from behind bars, effectively reversing the valuation that put him there.

Junior may be the best at wild charging, but in the world of stock-car racing he has to run with all the rest, and in such a world he adopts the protective coloring of the sellout: "I only do it for the cash." It's a lie, of course. He doesn't only do it for the cash, but it seems to be a tradition among former hillbilly bad boys turned NASCAR racers always to claim that cash alone explains why they run wide open into curves, boxed in on all sides by other cars running wide open into curves, too. If not for cash, then for what? For fun? "Why, that's crazy, boy!" Why not for affirmation of self? Because the economics of the run compromise the men even before they put the pedal to the metal, and what affirmation is there in compromise?

So Junior buys into the prevailing rationalization: "I only do it for the cash." "Is that all it is, the money?" his father replies, eyeing his son as though he might have become one of those country-club boys. "If that's all it is, then I have to agree with your ma [that you should stop it]." At that, Junior caves in: "No, that ain't all there is." He doesn't actually say what else it is that fuels him around those tracks. He doesn't have to. His father says it for him: "Damn foolishness to one person is the breath of life to another." And a little craziness is maybe the only antidote to greed.

An unexpected counterpoint to all Junior's crazy rebel roughness produces the best scene in the movie. Away from his rural home, now on the stock-car circuit and far removed from any cultural context where people have friendly eyes, surrounded by "phony hired jockeys" and "gut-sprung millionaires," Junior happens on one of those make-a-record booths in a shopping mall. He pauses, then pumps in his quarters and stammers his way through a lame message home, whose subtext is a cry for reunion; but, as it turns out, he can't deal with his own naked need for country cousins and their own need for him as hero, so he tosses the recording into the trash.

These astringent themes both put *The Last American Hero* head-and-shoulders above the other good-old-boy movies it competed with at the box office and ironically made it a lead-pipe cinch to fail at finding an audience. Twentieth Century–Fox gave up on it from the beginning. They torpedoed its chances of being taken seriously as an essay on the corrosive union of money and American rural community by advertising the movie primarily as a slam-bang actioner and releasing it widely only in the South. Naturally, audiences misled into looking for typical roadrunner high jinks were disappointed, and the Fox executives, according to Kael, "decided [the movie] was a dog that wouldn't go in the big cities, because they knew that sophisticated people don't go to racing pictures. It opened in New York for a week . . . as a 'Showcase' presentation — that is to say, it got a second run without a first run — and its failure was the movie company's self-fulfilling prophecy."

Urban America's snobbery toward the cultural heroics of Junior Johnson had been at the heart of Tom Wolfe's original *Esquire* magazine article. In his introduction to *The Kandy-Kolored Tangerine-Flake Streamline Baby*, Wolfe complains about the biases of eastern-establishment prudery, which could not see the artistry in a country boy like Junior: "He had starved, suffered—the whole thing—so he could sit inside a garage and create these cars which more than 99 per cent of the American people would consider ridiculous, vulgar and lower-class-awful, beyond comment almost."

It is a good

thing to make

the wolf rise in

a man's heart.

—Theodore

Roosevelt

# **More than Dogpatch**
## **The Mountains as Monstrous**

Through one stream of our culture there obviously runs a deep current of fear toward nature. Consider some modern movies that made money:

1. *Deliverance* (Warner Brothers, 1972). On location on the Chattooga River in north Georgia, Burt Reynolds says, "Sometimes you have to lose yourself to find yourself," and Ned Beatty promptly gets turned around in the woods, which also happen to be the perfect lost, rotting place to bury a guilty secret. This basic plot has been imitated many times over: a group of urban invaders push arrogantly

into a mountain landscape and find they must take the dread with the exhilaration. Nature is taboo, and they have crossed the boundary into electric possibility. They encounter alien creatures, the symbolic spawn of mountain chaos, but the real story and the central irony is that they themselves are also the aliens, and the heart of darkness is their own secret, too. (*Deliverance* is discussed more fully below.)

2. *The Evil Dead* (Renaissance Pictures Ltd., 1983). On location in east Tennessee near Morristown and in studio sets in Detroit, this movie imagined the southern mountains as supercharged with an active human-hating evil. The very air itself, especially the mountain fog, contains a suspirating malevolence that never quite materializes as a specific It. Horrible, unreasonable, nature itself is *awe*-ful, evil, the ambiguous Other. Trees and vines reach out to grab and violate a young woman, one of several urban invaders. Infected with the evil, she becomes a flesh-chomping ghoul and in turn infects others of her group. Their sin is the sin of Burt Reynolds's party in *Deliverance*: they have touched raw Nature without respect or caution, have arrogantly gone where they shouldn't go, and have heedlessly done what they shouldn't do. Nature is taboo. So they end up hacking, stabbing, lacerating, chewing, and chainsawing one another to death during a single night in a mountain cabin. The evil is also them, and it is eternal.

3. *The Evil Dead II* (Renaissance Pictures Ltd., 1986). Pretty much ditto, but with much more hilarity at the idea of it all, shot on location partly in Anson County, North Carolina (represented to be in the mountains, though it really isn't).

4. *Pumpkinhead* (Lion Films/United Artists, 1988). Using dry Nevada hills and machine-fogged studio sets, this movie, too, portrayed the southern mountains as seething with a potent evil. Once again, a set of urban invaders—this time, surfer boys and their dates—swagger into a mountain landscape, where they ride motorbikes up hill and down holler until one of them accidentally kills a mountain boy. This action provokes the revenge of Pumpkinhead, in this case an exterior It, an *Aliens*-style monster conjured out of a mountain cemetery by a hissing mountain witch. The monster's sole reason for rising is to destroy fresh whitebread who (again) have gone where they

shouldn't go and done what they shouldn't do—touched the hidden heart of Nature without respect or caution.

These movies don't just reflect our fear of nature; they actively teach that fear with the subverting thought that nature can easily have us for supper, and that we might even *submit* to it in a kind of ecstasy. So don't dare go beyond where the pavement ends. *Stay where you are!* Touch nature only with a blade.

## Ferociousness without the Monstrousness: Or, All Balls, No Strikes

Going beyond where the pavement ends is exactly what ideal American manhood has been told it ought to do since at least the time of Theodore Roosevelt's presidency. The natural world is there to be engaged and made to submit. So although the hillbilly monster movies can nicely terrify us, they can also mobilize group identity: *us* against *it*. That is to say, the irresistible ferociousness of hillbillyland is horrifying, but one's own ferociousness is glorious and good—and luckily it is still present in our national core (and in our Corps).

How well the movies have showed us this aspect of our character, using hillbillyland as the stage. For example, two imaginary white guys go ferocious in *The Mountain Men* (Columbia), which celebrated the violent expansion of America in the age of Jim Bridger. In it, mountains are the pretext, the explanation, for the antics of Charlton Heston and Brian Keith as they chew rawhide, shoot Indians, fight with bare fists, shoot more Indians, live on fresh meat, and survive exceptionally well while joyously drinking whiskey and carousing with abandon at endless fraternity parties called *rendezvous* and wearing numerous animal hides as trophies. The more *these* guys get to know the horrible heart of nature, the better Americans they become—not monster-bashed at all, but empire builders.

Released in the fateful year 1980, *The Mountain Men* reflected a growing political frustration. Male politicians were carping that the United States wasn't kicking enough butt around the world. *The Mountain Men* opened during the last months of the Carter presidency, hard on the heels of the Tehran hostage taking and the subsequent failed rescue attempt. Roger Ebert denounced the movie as a racist embarrassment. I loved it. It had punch and the exhilaration of seeing ourselves wild and competent without the nagging doubts of ambiguity. Ebert found it dangerous, and it was. (With similar materials, it's true, Michael Mann's *The Last of the Mohicans* achieved even greater exhilaration and left the ambiguity intact.)

Two years later, *The Man from Snowy River* (Cambridge Films, 1982) offered a jaunt among Australian hillbillies. A mountain boy loses his strong, heroic father, a simple man of the mountains, and because of this accident he is exiled to the lowlands to prove himself a man. The boy's secret, which even he does not at first suspect, is that he is already imbued with a ferociousness that guarantees in advance his triumph as a fully initiated man. Because he is *from* and *of* the mountains already, there's never any doubt of his competence. He gets the girl and also all the horses.

In *Overboard* (MGM–United Artists, 1988), stereotyped rich bitch Goldie Hawn finds what she really needs when she meets an Oregon coast hillbilly, a master carpenter (a "manual laborer" in her eyes) who essentially abducts her to his Dogpatch spread to take care of his rowdy brood of kids (okay, she has amnesia). This is her penance for being a stereotyped rich bitch, but it's also her salvation: hard physical work closer to the heart of nature, but more importantly, subservience to a man—which means going to bed with Nature himself, known to us as Kurt Russell—makes a real woman out of her. Goldie immediately begins to do laundry and cook and clean, all willingly. At the end, when she has gotten her memory back and can return to urban idleness, she chooses not to. Her fulfillment has come through exposure to untamed masculinity, which just isn't found among the yachting set.

In *The Winter People* (Nelson Entertainment, 1989) a weak city man (Kurt Russell again), a clockmaker, comes to the southern mountains and is forced to reassert his virility, saving himself and others. But first we see him stand still and do nothing as a tribe of hillbilly yahoos, looking like the cast of some improbable ethnic production of *Die Walküre* (all in bear furs, with uncut hair), wreck and steal his worldly possessions. The man's own daughter indicts him: "You didn't say anything, Papa. You didn't *do* anything. You just *stood there*." "He's not much of a man, is he?" says the beautiful and mysterious mountain woman who has watched his passivity. She and what she stands for will be part of his renewal. In touching her, the logical clockmaker touches his necessary madness. Soon he leaps onto the back of a giant bear and blows its brains out, and then he is victorious in mortal combat with a wildman rival for the woman. Lesson: it's good medicine for the virtuous man (or woman—see *The Silence of the Lambs* below) to touch the heart of chaos.

In *Next of Kin* (Warner Brothers, 1989) a macho mountain man from eastern Kentucky has become a Chicago cop. His younger brother follows him to the city to find work. There he crosses some Mafia-like hoodlums, but it takes four gangsters to bring him down. Just before the bad guys kill the younger brother, the mob capo says with contempt, "You're a fuckin' hillbilly, aren't you?" But the contempt is edged in respect: "I've got to hand it to you. You've got balls. . . . Stupid as shit but major balls." The testicular doctrine of the hillbilly is crucial. The older brother, the city cop who has successfully transferred his life to urban streets, has in a sense lost his balls and must refind them to avenge his brother's death, and he accomplishes this by first revisiting the mountains of his childhood. The movie went on location to Perry County in eastern Kentucky, where the moviemakers photographed a curious array of hatchets and bows and arrows (Fig. 6.1) and pet snakes, which stirred together make this doctrine: "an eye for an eye and a tooth for a tooth." Masculine violence, raised to holiness by solemn necessity, is proposed as a vital gene in the seed of the heart of the country. But *Next of Kin* made the doctrine look contrived and silly. When it was released, reviewer Rita Kempley wittily asked, "Whither testosterone?"

The male characters in *The Mountain Men, The Man from Snowy River, Overboard, The Winter People, Next of Kin,* and many other movies cater to the expectation that displays and contests of masculine dominance are right. The alpha males in these movies offer clear lessons about virtue: they seem to be saying that to be worth anything to the race, which also means being good for women (though not necessarily for furniture), an American man might do well to be a hillbilly.

In these instances the hillbilly mirror purely flatters. Historian Bruce Curtis has recently pointed out that the real reactions of ordinary American men to crises are complex, "involving confusion, resentment, resistance, and grudging acquiescence" (the unscripted George Bush, for example—and Bill Clinton too, as it turns out). But the impulse

Figure 6.1. "A curious array of hatchets and bows and arrows": Patrick Swayze in *Next of Kin*. (Courtesy of *Now and Then*, Center for Appalachian Studies and Services, East Tennessee State University)

of these same ordinary men is to deny any feeling of ambiguity and assert the show of stable control, even dominance (George Bush again, scripted for his Gulf War mode, and Bill Clinton in his bluff, naive, new-president assumption that Congress *would* do his bidding). But the steadily erupting chaos of the real world, the uncontrollability of events, continues to produce in great abundance what Curtis calls "masculine anxiety," the gender-specific experience of ambiguity.

Curtis sees a clear connection between inordinate American concern about proper masculinity and "the birth and growth of American politics" as we now know it. Our president at the turn of the century, Theodore Roosevelt, mythologized in the most public and visible way an image of big-stick national male dominance. Casting doubt on a rival's manhood—his little stick by comparison—became "a venerable U.S. tradition."

Another clear forerunner of obsessive male anxiety was the birth and growth of the American economic system. Industrialization reduced men to cogs in wheels and also brought women into the work force.

Ironically, once there, women began to get dangerous ideas about their own economic freedom, bolstered by the paychecks that allowed them to taste it. Responding to that threat, according to Curtis, men intensified their traditional gender-distinctive pursuits—hunting, fighting, risking death, "the manly arts." These activities expressed a willful belief in dominance over chaos, over nature, and this assumption of dominance became a hallmark of American male self-esteem. Any doubt or ambiguity was suppressed for the comfort of a mass illusion, however blood-covered it might be, for American men prove their competence through violence when necessary—and it is often necessary, against *whatever* comes along to threaten the status quo. Missing from this fantasy self-image is any functional appreciation for how it might feel to be devoured or of what devouring ourselves might entail.

Numerous recent films have delivered images of overpowering masculinity—Sylvester Stallone as Rambo, Arnold Schwarzenegger as anyone, the Bruce Willis of *Die Hard*, the Tom Cruise of *Top Gun*. Meanwhile, our individual uncertainties and hesitancies are rendered irrelevant by corporate and national power brokering and aggressiveness, from leveraged buyouts to making Nicaragua cry uncle, from the Grenada invasion to the strafing of Gadhafi, from the stomping of Panama to 100,000 dead Iraqis. There has been great exhilaration in all this, with little of the dread of seeing ourselves as male monsters capable of killing and/or raping animal, vegetable, and mineral.

But sometimes the possibility of seeing ourselves in that mirror, of discovering the consequences along with the exhilaration, can subvert our smugness and scare the bejesus out of us. Horrible nature is also the green fuse that through the flower grows.

## Ed and Lewis and Bobby and Drew: The Monster in the Mirror

I'm just what I am and I ain't no different. You can find me today just like you'd find me tomorrow. I ain't no high son of a gun. I guess you think we're the biggest fools there ever is. If these people that's a-growing up now had to go through with what I have they wouldn't be here.
—Mrs. Andy Webb, an extra in *Deliverance*

In *The Silence of the Lambs* (Strong Heart–Demme/Orion, 1991), a talented young novice FBI agent (played by Jodie Foster), the daughter of a West Virginia cop, has struggled against great odds to establish herself in a world dominated by men. Her further struggle during the course of the movie is partly against her own West Virginia mountain heritage, which both defines her and limits her. For her great climactic trial of courage, she must revisit her uneven ground psychologically and physically. Psychologically, she is stripped bare by Dr. Hannibal Lecter and then revealed again, to herself and to us, in one of the most creepily intimate mental strip searches in movie history. Safely behind his bars, Lecter paws her mind:

> You know what you look like to me, with your good bag and your cheap shoes? You look like a rube, a well-scrubbed, hustling rube with a little taste. Good nutrition has given you some length of bone, but you're not more than one generation from poor white trash, are you? And that accent you've tried so desperately to shed—pure West Virginia. What does your father do? Is he a coal miner, does he stink of the land? You know how quickly the boys found you, all those tedious, sticky fumblings in the back seats of cars, while you could only dream of getting out, getting anywhere, getting all the way to the FBI.

The camera is riveted on Jodie Foster's face. Lecter has ripped away her carefully composed disguise, and now she must face her dragon naked, as she must face herself.

In *Cape Fear* (Amblin Entertainment/Universal, 1991), an apparently strong urban man, a lawyer played by macho Nick Nolte, is made weak by a guilty secret: he sent a violent psychopath to prison when he could have saved him. When the psychopath (played by Robert De Niro as a crazy, scripture-spouting hillbilly) is released from prison, he embarks on a program of remedial education, tormenting the lawyer with the bitter knowledge of self revealed in the monstrousness of survival. At the end of the movie, as the crazed hillbilly slowly sinks to his doom in a maelstrom of churning water that only Hollywood could imagine or devise, his baleful eyes stare straight into the hidden soul of the guilty lawyer and straight into the camera's eye. We are invited to look into this hillbilly face of horror as into a mirror.

The *invasion* of mountains by city folk in the monster films, the pattern that began this chapter and then metamorphosed into an Americanized and sanctified macho in the "All Balls, No Strikes" films, is revealed by this last group as a *return* to psychological origins. We are afraid of what mountains hide because we are afraid of our own hidden potentialities. Our basic natures are not what we want to believe.

*Deliverance* was one such notorious jaunt to the hills concocted by two city-despising romantics, James Dickey (who wrote the novel and collaborated on the screenplay) and John Boorman (who directed the movie and put his agenda indelibly into the script). Perhaps no other movie has been as influential as this one in shaping what people think they understand about the southern mountains, and also what they think they understand about themselves and the way they confront such threats as the southern mountains are supposed to be.

But Rodger Cunningham suggests that the hillbillies in *Deliverance* are really urban America's projections of its own worst knowledge of its own worst impulses. The assault at the core of the movie's plot, in other words, is properly understood as a confrontation between mainstream America and its own hidden potentialities. The masculine power-rape is the film's central shocking image, and obviously Boorman wanted his audience to squirm. But what happens to the Ned Beatty character, Bobby, in the rhododendron hell on the banks of the river (called the "Cahulawassee" in Dickey's novel and in the movie) is not the only rape. There is a larger one that in Boorman's eyes ought to make us just as queasy: the first images we see in *Deliverance* are those of a mountain landscape being blasted, bulldozed, and hauled away.

The raping of the mountain landscape to clear the way for a new dam to supply power to Atlanta is the proximate cause for the canoe trip that will deliver Bobby into the hands of his tormentors and his companions to their fates as well. Lewis (played by Burt Reynolds) has been telling his softer urban friends, "Look, we've got to get up there and *do* this river before they get that dam finished." Their trip is a sexual metaphor, a display of penetration driven by the terror of inadequacy. *Doing* the river would be one proof of their worthiness of survival.

In other words, *Deliverance* is not about mountain people; it is rather a critique of city people—a scalding depiction, in fact, of their inchoate needs brought face to face with their most loathsome fears. One mirrors the other, but Ed and Lewis and Bobby and Drew do not recognize themselves in that reflection when they set out for the wilderness of their choosing.

Several of my students thought it especially appropriate that Bobby (the Ned Beatty character) is the particular urban invader who suffers the rape. David Reynolds pointed out that Bobby is, after all, the one who is most condescending to the natives, the one most assured of his superiority. He smirks about the junk at the Oree gas station: "Christ, Drew! Drew, look at the junk. I think this is where everything finishes up. We just may be at the end of the line." Bobby is the first to encounter the old man who pumps their gas at Oree, but instead of greeting him civilly, Bobby turns his back and addresses Lewis: "You've got a live one here." When he finally does condescend to speak to the old man—"I like that hat"—the comment is a form of ridicule, and the old man knows it. In hindsight, his response is chillingly accurate: "You don't know nothin'!" Nancy Collins said that Bobby in a sense *invites* his fate with a steady patter of sexual innuendo:

All my youth and passion spent in that back seat, all gone.

Is this the way you get your rocks off, Lewis?

That's the second-best sensation I ever felt.

I'm gonna go be mean to my air mattress.

I had my first wet dream in a sleeping bag.

Bobby's fear of his own impotence draws cosmic irony like cold temperatures draw wind.

But most audiences in 1972 probably did not recognize the urban mirror in *Deliverance*, the critique of the city; certainly mountain educators and intellectuals didn't. The movie was angrily denounced in mountain institutions and at regional professional conferences as an impious return to hillbilly stereotypes, which had been used by past generations of corporate exploiters to justify land theft and wage slavery. And certainly it was true that images from the movie were used that same way again in the seventies, particularly by self-serving tourists, developers, and second-home buyers who needed to feel superior to the people whose land they were buying up and transforming.

An early version of the *Deliverance* script ("second draft," dated 12 January 1971) made the urban criticism much more explicit. That draft opens in Atlanta (as did the novel) and has no fewer than thirteen scenes set in the city before the four "joy-riders," as Dickey himself called them, ever get to the hillbilly wilderness. In these opening scenes, the symbolic import of the city is established as a prelude and counterpoint to the symbolic import of the monster hillbillies.

After two opening helicopter shots of an unidentified dam being built, the second draft cuts to a tight two-shot of the faces of Ed and Lewis, concentrating, it turns out, on Ed's attempt to aim and shoot a bow and arrow. The setting is a field-archery range, and the fact to be established is the considerable strength that shooting an arrow requires. Ed (played by Jon Voight), is described as "an indoor desk man . . . early middle age, flesh a little soft." But as he's pulling back the arrow to let fly, the script says, "the nice, open, suburban American face contorts in the act of concentration, becoming animal and a little frightening."

Ed is the nascent masculine primitive ideal hidden under office flab, an unlikely specimen for Cahulawassee heroics. Although this scene was dropped, Voight got to do a different version of it in the finished movie. Camped on the river, in the early morning light, Ed goes hunting. He sights down a deer, but can't hold the bow steady and shoots wild. During these moments the camera concentrates on his face, which resembles more choirboy-in-extremis than the "animal" the second draft had called for. Ed thinks he has discovered that he can't kill, in Lewis's philosophy a clear indictment of his male worthlessness. The reason Ed can't kill the deer is what Lewis calls "buck fever," the failure of nerve. Ed will eventually have to overcome that failure before he can get to know his own ferociousness and become our hero.

After the archery opener in the second draft, the camera was to pull back to reveal Ed and Lewis isolated in an urbanized landscape, "hemmed in on one side by an elevated freeway, on the others, by railway sidings and indeterminate industrial buildings." Three scenes later, Ed and Lewis, along with Bobby and Drew, are now talking up the canoe trip on Peachtree Street after lunch, and the urban critique is again explicit in the script: "The black glass circular tower of the Regency Hyatt House Hotel dominates the street. Drab typists and flabby businessmen thread their way back to the office blocks over the hot sidewalks. The street is snarled with traffic, choked with exhaust fumes. . . . Ed watches all this, the dead faces of the crowd, the moan of the traffic." The next few scenes, the most claustrophobic, are set in Ed's advertising agency: "Two or three men are bustling about under the lights. They clear away newspapers from the place where the model will stand to be photographed. They are incredibly serious and intense as *only men doing something fundamentally trivial can be*" (emphasis added).

The photography session involves a partially nude woman, and the script now suggests that what is lacking in the city is (no surprise) equal to sex. There is a moment of "private giving" as the nude model smiles enigmatically at Ed, and he in return gives her what would have been one of those Jon-Voight-as-Saint-Sebastian looks. Then the scene was to climax with physical contact: "Ed stretches out an arm and touches her shoulder with his fingertips." Cut immediately to Ed in bed with his wife; he requests anal intercourse and she complies—a howler of a scene considering where this script is headed.

That the "deliverance" of *Deliverance* was clearly meant to be a liberation from the city is a point hammered again in the second draft's scene 13, in which Lewis, Ed's manly ideal, rounds up the three other guys for the trip. The draft script included this exchange:

> *Lewis*: I never thought getting four guys out of this city could be so tough.
> *Ed*: Maybe the city doesn't want to lose us.
> *Lewis*: . . . the old whore.

Little of this explicit urban angst made it into the finished film. Ed is still established as the central character, the improbable nascent hero who will relive the folktale pattern, becoming Saint George to slay the dragon (or David to bring down Goliath), whereas Lewis, as the putative he-man, is set up for a fall. Rodger Cunningham is right: this movie is at least half satire of the empty urban swagger that Lewis embodies. Lewis is hollow. He may have "an awesome bicep" and seem to Ed "confident, calm, and mystical," but he can't deliver them from evil. He preaches primitivism, but in the second draft version he telegraphs his phoniness by showing up at lunch dressed in "an expensive sports shirt." The other guys have mainly bought the line that Lewis is indeed the natural man, perhaps because individually they feel so weak and beaten. They hear Lewis brag: "The machines are going to fail and the political systems are going to fail. . . . Then it's going to come down to who can survive and who can't, when the lights go out and the taps are dry. Survival." And then it turns out that he can't survive, not without Ed.

In the screen version, very early in the movie when Lewis is driving like Jehu to find the river and takes the wrong track, he says, "I've never been lost in my life." Later he claims he's never been insured, either — "no risk." But halfway through the trip he's a washout, and Ed must take over. In fact, Lewis becomes not only incapacitated but essentially mute, a wounded, urban dead weight, his deliverance entirely in the hands of formerly gentle and now wolf-fierce Ed. Lewis "can't hack it," which is what Drew had predicted early on. But neither can Drew and neither can Bobby and neither can Ed, at first.

While half of this movie conspires to bring down the braggart Lewis, the other half conspires to raise up the improbable Ed against the mountain monsters. The camera dotes on Voight even as his character dotes on Lewis. Ed and Lewis are each other's own best image (Fig. 6.2). The multitude of male-on-male glances in the second draft of the script opens the narrative to all sorts of speculation. But suffice it to say that the man that Lewis thinks he is is the man that Ed already is, though he doesn't know it yet. Lewis says to Ed: "City life is killing you. It's *boring* you to death. You're rotting." The script then notes: "Ed is shaken, penetrated." Yes, well, isn't everybody?

Despite his evident disgust with urban culture, Boorman clearly sees the Voight character in a romantic light, as someone who bears the dark seed of savage nature even in the heart of the city. Ed is the blond avatar who can rise to scale the cliff, kill the monster, save the race, and affirm the right to survival.

In a sense, Boorman remade *Deliverance* in his 1985 film *The Emerald Forest* (Embassy Pictures). A comparison of the two is revealing. In both films, arrogant city invaders are raping a previously savage landscape. In both films, a dam is being built. In both films, primitive "natives" menace the city intruders. (The hillbillies of *Deliverance* became cannibals in *The Emerald Forest.*) In both films, a blond avatar climbs an intimi-

Figure 6.2. Burt Reynolds as Lewis and Jon Voight as Ed in *Deliverance*. (Courtesy of Wisconsin Center for Film and Theater Research)

dating height to prove his worthiness symbolically. *The Emerald Forest*'s blond hero is young Charlie, son of the chief dam builder. Amazon Indians kidnap Charlie, and ten years later he climbs, not a jungle cliff, but a city skyscraper to refind his father. In both films, Boorman is clearly guilt-tripping the men in suits for raping the natural world. Simultaneously Boorman is romanticizing the primitive masculinity that must prove itself by violent domination. He's having his cake and eating it, too.

*Deliverance* had a profound significance for many urban males who saw it. To them, Boorman's movie constituted a dare, and soon real joyriders flocked to the real Chattooga River and chanced the same rapids in rubber rafts and often wrecked like Ed and Lewis and Bobby and Drew. Within a year of the movie's release, no fewer than eleven people had drowned in the Chattooga, all but one of them with significant blood-alcohol levels (revealed by autopsy). This irresistible urge among flocks and hordes of mainly suburban and college males to *do* the river—the "Deliverance syndrome"—became a topic in the mainstream press, made the network news, and put a severe strain on the thirty-two-man Rabun County rescue squad and the local sheriff's department. One of the more interesting manifestations of the Deliverance syndrome was that rafters would squeal like a pig, especially on that part of the river where the rape scene was filmed. The squealing was both a mockery of the weakness of the Bobby character and a direct invitation to cosmic irony.

The Chattooga joyriders were doing more than imitating the plot line of *Deliverance*, to their peril. They were also illustrating the underlying theme of this movie, as stated at the beginning of this chapter: arrogant urban adventurers touch raw nature without respect or caution and suffer the consequences.

### *Deliverance* on Location

To menace their urban men and to call out the lone wolf in Ed, Boorman and Dickey needed authentic monsters. The second draft included these descriptions of various speaking parts and extras:

He is almost ridiculous country, almost like a caricature, with an absurdly cocked straw hat. [The old man who pumps gas at the Oree gas station]

He is probably a half-wit, likely from a family inbred to the point of imbecility and Albinism. [The boy with the banjo]

THREE or FOUR WEIRD LOOKING HILLBILLIES have materialized out of the weeds. [At the Oree gas station]

He is an enormous country brutal-looking man, with no humor in him. He suggests nothing but brutality and stupidity. [Griner, the man who agrees to drive their cars down to Aintry]

If there were ever any degenerate red-necks, they are these two. [The two rapists in the woods]

Boorman's Gothic realism in picturing these characters on screen drove the mountain middle class nuts when the movie was released and didn't exactly please the local people of Rabun County, Georgia, once they got a look at themselves in Boorman's story. In retaliation *Foxfire* magazine, also headquartered in Rabun County, set out to humanize

Boorman's monsters by interviewing some of the locals who were in the movie. Although some clearly wanted to put some distance between themselves and a screen rape that had stirred up a hornets' nest, in the main they said they enjoyed their brush with Hollywood. (Compare the positive vibes among Graham Countians over the highly negative images in *Stark Love*, discussed in the next chapter.)

One of the most useful of the *Foxfire* interviews was that with Rabun County native Frank Rickman, whom Boorman hired to help find locations and the "mountain types" called for in the script. It was Rickman who located Mrs. Andy Webb and her tin-roofed shack on a Rabun County dirt road—the end of the trail, the jumping-off place for the heart of American darkness.

Mrs. Webb's place was transformed into Oree, a backwoods service station and cluster of sheds where the urban adventurers plan to hire drivers to take their cars back down to Aintry. Rickman was responsible for hauling in junked cars and tons of assorted salvage so that Bobby could make reference to his teen sex life. The filmmakers also bulldozed Mrs. Webb's potato patch and put in a road so Burt Reynolds could drive the few feet to Griner's garage. Mrs. Webb told the *Foxfire* interviewers: "Yes, they paid me for [the potatoes], but not what they ought to. You know a patch of taters like that is worth something." And they photographed Mrs. Webb and her retarded fourteen-year-old granddaughter for horror—the brief glimpse that Voight catches of them through a window, causing him to suffer "the acute discomfort of suburban dwellers when confronted with the unseemly" (second draft).

According to Rickman, Boorman casually and matter-of-factly used the word *hillbilly* on the set and in front of the extras and got away with it, perhaps because as an Englishman he was theoretically not a party to the power relations the word usually signifies. For example, Boorman would say to Rickman, "You know more about you hillbillies than we do." Boorman wanted easily recognizable types, and Rickman obliged by rounding up a collection of people who fit the profile, including especially Edward Ramey, whose character (the old man who pumps gas) is described in the script as "ridiculous country . . . a caricature." Boorman got Ramey to flatfoot dance a little during "Dueling Banjos," and Ramey spoke one of the film's important lines in his prophesy to Ned Beatty: "You don't know nothin'!"

Behind the scenes, Ramey was as direct and impertinent as he was on-screen with Beatty. Rickman remembered that when a particular quiet scene was ruined by the "awfullest racket" made by a tree frog up a dogwood tree, and Reynolds, Voight, and Boorman all said they'd never heard of tree frogs, "Well, it insulted Ed Ramey that they didn't know what a tree frog was. . . . [So] he . . . came stomping over there . . . [and] said, 'Don't you know nothing?'"

In his own interview, Ramey said he told some of the crew what he thought of the rape scene: "You may not like what I say, but I won't go around your back about it. I think it ought to be a violation of the law to show pictures like that of the act." When it came time for Ramey to do his flatfoot dancing, he noticed production assistants oiling down the ground, and he felt he understood why: "I believe they thought I'd slide down that hillside. . . . They had it awful greasy, and I had to dance on that oil there on a sloping hill . . . but I didn't [fall]. They was just having their fun, I reckon." Ramey's assumption of malice on the part of the film crew is interesting. David Reynolds wrote: "His theory on why the crew oiled the ground approaches paranoia. Surely the production assistants oiled the ground to prevent the kicking up of dust. Had Mr. Ramey fallen, the scene would have been reshot, as slapstick comedy was not the desired tone."

Most of the local people, if they felt resentful of the way they were used in the film—"They didn't tell me *nothing*," said Nell Norton, who is seen in the boarding house scene near the end, telling about her giant cucumber—were not usually offended by how they were treated but by the fact that they were on-screen in the same movie that contained the awful rape, something they were embarrassed to witness with their families. (Some also felt queasy about the filming of Mrs. Webb's retarded granddaughter and the use of Billy Redden, who played the inbred banjoist in the "Dueling Banjos" sequence. Redden was in fact retarded, and some of the *Foxfire* informants felt his use in the movie was unseemly in the extreme.)

Rickman had no luck finding a local to play the main Griner brother, the "enormous country brutal-looking man" to whom Lewis pays forty dollars for driving their vehicles down to Aintry. According to Rickman, Boorman and his wife, Chris, both began to suggest that Rickman himself could play the part. Chris Boorman, especially, seemed convinced that Rickman was right for the part. But Rickman wasn't about to be seduced by Hollywood to that degree: "I wasn't nothing but a little toad you know." Boorman finally flew in California actor Seamon Glass at the last minute. Rickman understandably felt some curiosity about this expensive talent flown in from the West Coast: "[He was] this big old monster of a man. He's so big I can't hardly see his head a way up in the car. . . . [He] had a big old hard face and a big rough old mop of hair and a big old nose—just one of the worst looking men you ever did see."

But according to Rickman, Glass's physical appearance was a case of false advertising, because he turned out to be "a California fairy" with a high voice that Rickman described as sounding like Zsa Zsa Gabor's. In desperation, Boorman gave Rickman the assignment of coaching Glass into some acceptable version of hillbilly masculine menace. The script called for Lewis and Ed to approach the darkened door of Griner's garage, through which the Griner character suddenly erupts. (He has hit himself with a hammer, though the city boys don't know it.) Ed in particular is worried that the locals may think he and Lewis are snooping deputies or other unwelcome company. The first time Glass played the scene, according to Rickman, he came out of the door "fighting in the air with his fists—fighting up in front of his face sort of like he was mad . . . what I call more or less acting." Rickman advised Boorman that this looked silly, and Boorman agreed. Then he asked his trusted native adviser to play the scene and show the assembled company how it ought to look:

> I go in there and I hit my thumb. And I come out over the top of Burt Reynolds and Jon Voight, and I draw back with my right foot and I kick [a car] door shut . . . so hard, it breaks and all the glass flies out of it, and then I spin around and I kick that barrel out down through the field. Then I got up in Burt Reynolds' face and I said, "What did you say, *pretty* boy?"

The "pretty boy" line was not in the script, and its effect on Reynolds was electric: "Old Burt Reynolds acted like I'd scalded him, you know." More than that, Rickman had played out for real the sort of table-turning menace the whole movie was seeking to achieve.

Rickman also doubled as Glass's voice coach. Boorman asked him to teach Glass "to talk like you Rabun County hillbillies." Rickman tried but with no success. So Boorman went ahead and shot Glass's scenes and later dubbed in Rickman's voice in the finished film.

The crowning irony is that it was Frank Rickman, location scout and technical adviser extraordinaire, who suggested to James Dickey that Ned Beatty should be made to squeal like a pig during the rape. How paradoxical. While Rickman was allowed to bubble creatively with better ideas about how to make Bobby the insurance salesman suffer, the fictional hillbilly characters were coached into a depiction of awfulness that would be used against Rickman and his kin forever.

## Andy Griffith as Masculine Monster

I'm gonna be a free man in the morning!
—Lonesome Rhodes, in *A Face in the Crowd*

The hillbilly male monster comes from the same threshold territory that produces the hillbilly as fool—the threshold of suddenly ambiguous potential. *A Face in the Crowd* (Warner Brothers, 1957) was Andy Griffith's first movie, and it's a good one for studying our deep nervousness about the blurring of the hillbilly fool into the hillbilly male monster, our fear that maybe the rural clown is not so harmless and laughable after all. Maybe he is really the old devil Male Singularity, another visitation from Satan.

"Women are bonkers for bad boys," said Rita Kempley. And that ambiguous fact is what *A Face in the Crowd* is really all about, even though critics at the time insisted it was about the sinister power of television. The film's main character, Marsha Jeffries (played by Patricia Neal), falls for the personification of country Vice, is bedded, and then is bereft of him. Director Elia Kazan explained it all in his amazingly frank autobiography:

[*A Face in the Crowd*] is the story of women as conscience. The film can be told this way: A bright and idealistic young woman who comes down from Sarah Lawrence College [to "the depths of Arkansas"— Bosley Crowther] to build a career for herself in radio discovers someone she considers a "find." He is a country boy with country horse sense and a gift for storytelling. . . . As she guides him on and up, she falls in love with him, as much for his potential as for his person. He becomes her voice. Then she notices that he's going bad and tries to restore him to the self she loves. But things have gone too far; she sees that success has corrupted his honesty. Since he is her creation, what he has become, a corrupting influence, is her responsibility. And, figuratively, she kills him.

Kazan follows this explanation with an even more suggestive one: "This story, as you can see, has little to do with American politics or even with life behind the scenes of the television industry. It is both more fundamental and more intimate. . . . [Scriptwriter Budd Schulberg] drew on what he had to draw on: his own life. This other story applies equally to me. There is a two-way autobiographical note here."

What Kazan is working around to saying is that the Andy Griffith character in the movie is a mirror projection of the way he and Budd Schulberg felt about themselves: Kazan the Greek-immigrant outsider and Schulberg the urban-Jewish outsider both found a mirror in the Arkansas hillbilly monster that satirized their male impulsive behavior (Kazan especially was an Olympic-class seducer) and flattered their roguishness—which Kazan, in his autobiography, obviously still prides himself on having in abundance. By engineering the story so that the seduced woman is the one who destroys the male monster, Kazan, like Boorman in *Deliverance*, can have it both ways.

The transformation of a sweet Carolina country clown (see Chapter 2) into Kazanian monster was almost too much for Andy Griffith. He wanted to play the part and thought he could do it well, but he was truly and blissfully ignorant both of Kazan's method and of "the Method," which were the same thing. Kazan set out to turn his unsuspecting actor into the movie's angry, dangerous hillbilly predator, to find the mean core in the vulnerable Griffith and expose that to the larger world, all of which caused great damage to Griffith's marriage and, coincidentally, to his view of himself as a human being.

Kazan did give Griffith fair warning: "I may have to use extraordinary means to make you do this. I may have to get out of line. I don't know any other way of getting an extraordinary performance out of an actor." Kazan's "extraordinary means" began with intimate, probing conversations with the actor; by revealing his own poor immigrant past to Griffith, he got Griffith to reveal his poor hillbilly past in Mt. Airy, North

Carolina. Kazan learned that as a boy the actor had been labeled "white trash" because of where he lived and who his people were. Bingo! Kazan had his key vulnerability and a core of hurt rage that, by viciously cornering, he could draw out into a great performance.

Kazan began to use the term "white trash" as a club on Griffith; sometimes, according to Gilbert Millstein, Kazan could merely whisper "white trash" at Griffith between clenched teeth before turning on the cameras, and the fury of the outsider would rise in the actor like Lucifer in starlight. Kazan also carefully engineered Griffith's isolation from the rest of the cast and crew, so that he would feel even more the hillbilly oddball. But Griffith was also the star of the movie, the person without whom there could be no commercial success, and Kazan pumped up that image, too, so that Griffith seesawed between deep humiliation and the illusion of powerful invulnerability. Once during the filming, at a cast and crew party at Patricia Neal's home, Griffith—who, now constantly in character as Lonesome Rhodes, seemed to some observers to feel he had to be the center of attention—showed his ignorance about art and literature in front of the very sophisticates from whom the real Andy Griffith sought approval, and his subsequent embarrassment made him withdraw sullenly from the party to brood. The next day on the set, Kazan suggested that members of the company line up and publicly mock Griffith for his dumb-hick ignorance of the night before. As a result, Griffith did "a fine psychotic day's work," Millstein reported.

In fact, Griffith the man was growing as dangerous as Lonesome Rhodes the character. Griffith made the tabloids during the filming as something of a wife abuser. He was said to "get out of hand." There was one item about his flying into "an ungovernable fury" at his wife, Barbara, and smashing multiple closet doors in their apartment. Griffith told Millstein at the time of the movie's release: "I did a lot of things to Barbara, mostly with silence. . . . I'll tell you the truth. You play an egomaniac and paranoid all day and it's hard to turn it off by bedtime. We went through a nightmare—a real, genuine nightmare, both of us."

In the movie, Lonesome Rhodes is all the more lethal as a bad seed because he is also country-appealing. We first see him in jail in northeastern Arkansas, joking and playing the fool, but with a clear subtext of cunning meanness (Fig. 6.3). He cons the pretty lady from the radio station: Marsha, the Patricia Neal character. For her, the attraction is partly that he's a "cultural find" she's naively proud to have stumbled on. But she has also gotten a whiff of some powerful animal magnetism. The camera captures Marsha's literal shivers as Lonesome howls his anthem, "I'm gonna be a free man in the morning!"

The movie contrives to set this force of nature free to prey on the world—to the end of his after all finite tether. Shortly after the jailhouse scene, when Marsha catches up to our apparent hillbilly naïf, who is hitchhiking out of town, and offers him the job that will begin his rags-to-riches upward spiral, he leans in the car window toward her in an overpowering way, eyeing her like the wolf eyes the rabbit, and she self-consciously covers her open throat with her hand, a telling gesture in the face of something both desired and dreaded. Though Marsha's uncle, who is driving the car, tells Lonesome to get in the back seat, he impudently climbs into the front seat instead, next to Marsha.

Randy Crutchfield has pointed out that clearly Lonesome doesn't want a job: "sounds too much like *work*!" But he takes the offer for a day—for a week maybe—on speculation, all the while eyeing Patricia Neal, the "'cold-fish girl' he means to fry." As Crutchfield puts it, "Natural men are not wage slaves, and Lonesome is a realbilly."

Marsha takes Lonesome to a hotel and discovers he's carrying souvenir female lingerie in his pitiful luggage. When she says something about the bras and panties, he becomes straightforwardly lustful: "How would you like to come over here and get acquainted early in the morning?" His mother was a prostitute, he later tells Marsha, and the unspoken implication is clear: aren't *all* women at heart? And don't they like a man who knows what he wants, whose purely animal power is uncomplicated by hesitation or doubt? "I put my whole self into everything I do," he tells Marsha, leering. When she catches him in his room with a hotel maid early in the movie, he admits frankly that he gets "extra hungry" in the morning, as though women were a double-order of fries, and when Marsha draws back, visibly winded by his virility, he contemptuously confronts her fears: "You cold-fish respectable girls! Inside, you crave the same thing as the rest of 'em." When he finally has his way with her, his version of foreplay is to be sardonic with her name: "Marsha . . . short for 'marshmallow.'" And he gobbles her up. Temporarily.

Lonesome Rhodes's male faithlessness is a foregone conclusion. On a triumphant return visit to Arkansas after he's found television fame, he

Figure 6.3. Andy Griffith and Patricia Neal in *A Face in the Crowd*.
(Courtesy of Wisconsin Center for Film and Theater Research)

encounters the very fetching high school baton twirler, Betty Lou Flee-
gal (played by Lee Remick in one of her earliest appearances on the
screen), marries her suddenly and impulsively, and parades her in public as his child bride. Earlier, the still trusting Marsha has met the first
Mrs. Lonesome Rhodes—technically the *only*, as there was never a legal
divorce. Mrs. Rhodes laconically observes, "Larry thinks he has to take
a bite out of every broad he comes across." Ironically, as she tells Marsha
this, the TV set is tuned to the newly popular *Lonesome Rhodes Show*, on
which the star, her worthless absconded husband, is spouting pious
phony-baloney about the evils of divorce while chorus girls sing "Just an
old-fashioned marriage is my kind of marriage."

The ending of *A Face in the Crowd* is bitter indeed. The ruined Lonesome isn't even allowed the dignity of death. That would be letting him
off too easily. As his former fans and friends desert him, he tries to hang
on to an illusion of power by demanding subservience from a group of
African American waiters he's hired for the big political rally that never
happens. They represent America's other outsider group, but they give
Lonesome nothing but passive resistance. At the end of the movie he is

standing alone in his penthouse screaming Marsha's name (the nascent monster revealed at last as just a big baby boy), an ending that reminds Wes Saylors of Brando's Stanley Kowalski—in Kazan's version of *A Streetcar Named Desire*—screaming pathetically for Stella.

The thrill of setting this rogue male loose, followed by the more ambiguous thrill of bringing him down, seems to have been missed in *A Face in the Crowd*'s first broad cultural reception. Reviewers at the time of the film's release read it as just a couple of city boys' worst nightmare of what might slouch into power by way of mass commercial popularity. Coincidental to that emphasis was the satirization of the American public as eagerly gullible for whatever product TV packagers wanted to dish up. Is it any wonder the movie was never popular, that it never found an audience willing to see itself in Andy Griffith's best, most unforgettable, most coruscating performance?

I'm just

a naive

hillbilly.

—Helen

Gurley

Brown

# The Mama's Boys

At first blush, the handful of extremely influential mountain mama's boys in the movies might appear to be rejecting the Roosevelt-Man posturing of their counterparts. After all, the movies discussed below starred cuddly boy-men, eternal little shepherds of kingdom come. But every one of these stories ends with a living affirmation of the necessity to be very, very dangerous. Consider the standard plot elements:

1. *Tol'able David* (Inspiration Pictures/First National, 1921). A Shenandoah Valley boy must rise like young David in the Old Testament and kill an evil trio of invading hillbillies, symbolic Goliaths. He must do

this in defense of his mother (and of hearth and home, for which she stands) and of his sweetheart (the future of the race). All the adult males in David's world are effectively neutered, and David, as an incipient true American male, perforce must rise. He must. And rising necessarily means having the courage to kill—which, it turns out, he has. Once young David has slain the giants and survived his wounds, he is declared a man by his mother.

2. *Stark Love* (Paramount, 1927). A sensitive and weak young mountain boy must let the mountain nature beast rise in himself in order to defend the memory of his mother, as well as the person of his own sweetheart, again against an evil giant who also happens to be his own father. In the mama's-boy movies, when the father isn't neutered outright, as above, he frequently becomes the necessary Goliath himself—another species of neutering and another invitation to ambiguity.

3. *Sergeant York* (Warner Brothers, 1941). A fatherless and immature mountain man must find his manhood by defending mother and motherland (and sweetheart, too). He goes off to war in France, there learning that he is indeed quite competent at what he has long thought himself incapable of: righteous killing (albeit of furriners). In *Sergeant York*, Germany is America's collective evil giant.

4. *At Close Range* (Hemdale Film Corp./Orion, 1986). An innocent but rough Pennsylvania hill boy is lured by the magnetism of his own father and initiated into robbery, the fencing of stolen goods, and attempted murder. But the love of his sweetheart and his mother and even his mother's mother saves the boy, who discovers almost too late that he has the courage to turn and oppose the power of his father. At the end, badly wounded, the son points a loaded gun at the father's head, and we think he is certain to pull the trigger. "No, I am *not* you," he mutters and puts down the gun. He will make it to American manhood *without* becoming his father.

Frederick J. Hoffman, in his important intellectual history of this country during the 1920s, pointed to the publication of *Civilization in the United States* in 1922 as a bellwether of attitude. A sophisticated symposium written by a group of this country's most disaffected citizens, *Civilization in the United States* was an assault on the intellectually bankrupt power structure of the fathers, "the old gang," which was responsible for all sorts of absurdities such as World War I itself, over which the new gang of younger American males had been brooding since 1919. World War I had been a monstrosity in their view, and it was all the fault of the fathers. Harold Stearns, one of the "literary vagabonds" of the 1920s and editor of *Civilization in the United States*, wrote in his contribution to the volume that "our cultural interests and activities have been turned over to the almost exclusive custody of women, and the only hopeful sign in 'The Intellectual Life' is the disrespect the younger people have for their elders" (paraphrased by Hoffman). Things are bad indeed when hope takes the form of disrespect. And note Stearns's jab at the cultural influence of mere women, too. As an example to his readers, Stearns abandoned his country and sailed for France as soon as he had finished the preface to this very pessimistic volume. But what might look like father hatred at a distance turns into "father hunger" when seen up close.

In his book *Iron John: A Book about Men*, Robert Bly grappled with the problem of American father hunger in the later twentieth century. Bly took as his text an ancient tale which taught that male virtue equals the willingness and ability to take action—that is, be violent for good cause. Obviously, we cannot say that all masculine violence is evil. Violence is good when it is defensive, when it saves and preserves. But Bly believes that mainstream modern American men, by selling themselves as wage slaves to corporations, bureaus, and institutions (a bitter complaint in the 1920s, too), have individually lost their capacity for virtuous action, for fighting when a fight would be right. Bly thinks that too many men around him have sunk passively into bureaucratic structures that do all their acting for them; as a result, individual male passivity has become the seemingly natural but actually unnatural state in which war and other violent actions are removed to a safe corporate distance. It is this perverted corporate masculinity that most actively oppresses both women and men. Caught in such structures, ordinary men "feel their opinions do not matter," writes Bly, and they "become secret underground people, and sometimes drown themselves in alcohol while living in a burrow under the earth." Or they cope by becoming superagreeable "soft males," husks who have been drained of all natural fierceness (and who are drawn to the fantasies of violence that the movies provide).

This sorry state of affairs has come about, according to Bly, because of the severing of the bond between fathers and sons (caused, says Hoffman, by World War I). In Bly's view, earlier Americans thrived because their fathers were mentors who initiated their sons into work, into sweat, into pain, into all that was male virtue. But the growing dominance of a perverse economic system has diminished the influence of fathers. Sons learn that the only things their fathers make anymore are *connections*. Salaried men serve a massive machine of a scale and scope not only beyond control but also beyond the ends of vision. What men do to get money is mysteriously office-obscured, hidden from the eyes of boys. Ergo, Bly suggests, these same boys see wage work as contemptible and weak. For a couple of generations now, at least, the most common father figure on TV has been either a businessman or the (un)willing worker for a businessman, and therefore, according to Bly, a joke: "a fit field for suspicion" or "a bad-tempered fool" or "a weak puddle of indecision." Think of the father of the hour in the early 1990s—TV's Homer Simpson. Very simply, the nation is suffering from what Bly calls "father hunger," which makes adolescent males and young adults, collectively, both vulnerable and very, very dangerous.

Is it any wonder that a powerful and recurring theme in much of our folklore and pop culture is that of the boy who must father himself into manhood either without or in spite of his biological sire? For example, in the *Star Wars* trilogy, the boy Luke Skywalker must bring himself into brilliant and virtuous manhood by overcoming the evil giant Darth Vader (who is—surprise—also his father). In one indelible sequence set on Yoda's soggy planet, Luke is sent into a cave to find his true but hidden nature. There he encounters a phantom Darth Vader and cuts off its head. Yoda has told Luke that he will find in the cave "only what you take in with you." So when the helmet on Vader's severed head is removed, Luke sees his own face, a mirror image of his own native potential. Americans, especially, seem obliged to fight that ambiguous potential hand to hand and to validate their ferociousness as commendably defensive. In other words, "father hunger" and the "mama's-boy syndrome" in American pop culture are, I take it, two expressions of the same quest.

Hillbillies in the movies can represent our American Darth Vaders— dark figures in touch with the Force (nature)—and, simultaneously, idealized versions of fetching boyishness who can, if necessary, cut off their own heads. In purely functional terms, the mountain boy ought to frighten us more than the mountain man. Sergeant York, after all, is far more lethal than all the bad hillbillies in *Deliverance*.

## Tol'able David

*Tol'able David* premiered in December 1921 and created an instant sensation, remaining a box-office leader throughout 1922. For mass appeal, broad popularity, and the staying power of its story, *Tol'able David* remains to this day one of the most influential of hillbilly pictures. It was the first of a handful of movies—*Sergeant York, Thunder Road, Deliverance, Coal Miner's Daughter*—that were seen by millions, movies, in short, that dictated for a time the meaning of the southern mountains.

Exhibitors from all over the country raved about *Tol'able David's* power to draw a paying audience and the believability of star Richard Barthelmess in the title role:

A great picture and one that appeals to all. The more we get of these, the better our business will be.
—Elk Point, S.D.

One of the best this year. . . . Holds them to the finish.
—Quincey, Ill.

In my opinion Barthelmess is a genius. . . . A few more like this one from Dick and I will have my bacon in for next winter.
—Rome, N.Y.

A sure winner for me; some few saw it the second time.
—Northfork, W.Va.

It's human!
—Greenville, Ohio

The best dramatic picture ever produced.
—Madisonville, Ky.

Just as good as they can make them. Book it and raise your price.
—Russellville, Ky.

The best mountain drama we ever had. Kind of a picture you are proud to face your patrons after the show.
—Bellaire, Ohio

Patrons perfectly satisfied at increased admission. If there is anyone who could not hate the villains, love the mother, and admire the hero, such a person should not be classed as human. Such pictures make friends.
—Grand Gorge, N.Y.

I cannot praise this picture too highly. Patrons talked about it; said it was a beautiful picture.
—Baltimore, Md.

This last comment was published in *Moving Picture World* a full calendar year after the film's initial release, a testament to its staying power. *Tol'able David* was voted the best picture of 1922 by the readers of *Photoplay Magazine*, and it was still mentioned three years later as a perennial box-office moneymaker, at a time when a new film typically played for one week tops, or even, more typically, for three quick days before sinking into the oblivion of obsolescence.

*Tol'able David* made Richard Barthelmess one of the aristocrats of Hollywood. By 1923 he was declared the "reigning favorite" of moviegoers—girls especially—in a survey of high school students conducted by the Committee for Better Films, the Russell Sage Foundation, and First National Pictures. The "survey" was really a publicity stunt. The last-named sponsor, First National Pictures, also happened to be the distribution combine that had signed Barthelmess to a three-year, twelve-feature deal, of which *Tol'able David* was the first product. After that film's huge success, First National hilariously promoted Barthelmess as "Our Dick," an apt boast in the big-money male culture of 1920s Hollywood and absurdly appropriate for the bottom-line gender politics of *Tol'able David*.

*Tol'able David*'s hillbilly setting and hillbilly formula—the feud melodrama—might seem anomalous in light of the film's popularity. Indeed, the movie environment of the time makes *Tol'able David*'s sudden success downright unlikely, because feuding hillbillies were definitely not selling by 1921. The feud melodrama, along with the moonshiner melodrama, had been movie clichés since 1908. From their beginnings in the nickelodeons in 1904 and 1905, pioneered by Biograph with *The Moonshiner* and *A Kentucky Feud*, violent southern "actioners" featuring moonshiners or feudists had hit a remarkable peak of popularity in 1914. For that year alone, I've counted some seventy-one new titles—on average more than one new hillbilly movie a week—portraying all kinds of desperate southern mountaineers: vicious outlaws, sadistic fathers, jealous and hotheaded rivals, all usually struggling over moonshiners' daughters or "daughters of the feud," some of whom are virginal and sexless and therefore, by the working of Victorian logic, highly desirable, and some of whom are untamed and willful and also, therefore, doubly desirable by the same logic. All of them, mountain nymphs and hellcats alike, are tamed and tasted, usually by superior "gentlemen" from the lowlands but sometimes by noble mountain brutes. These movies, which bore such titles as *The Moonshiner's Daughter* (Kalem, 1908), *A Mountaineer's Honor* (Biograph, 1909, directed by D. W. Griffith), *The Law of the Mountains* (Kalem, 1909), *Primitive Man* (Kalem, 1913), *Breed o' the Mountains* (Nestor, 1914), *Mountain Blood* (Big U/ Universal, 1916), *Brute Force* (Bison/Universal, 1917), and *The Power and the Glory* (World Pictures, 1918), all provided dependable violence, life-threatening dilemmas, and "virile action," but also obvious stories, heavy-handed morals, hackneyed themes, and standard character types. But by 1918 and the end of World War I, most of these hillbilly narratives had been replaced by big-city stories, and consequently *Tol'able David* looked like the umpty-umpteenth retooling of a plot now stigmatized as old-fashioned: the rural revenge drama wherein the "child of the feud" must face the ultimate sacrifice. Who would want such stuff in 1921, when heavy city sex had become the soup *du jour*?

Yet along came Richard Barthelmess, who transformed himself into a prince of the trade by playing a prince of the mountains. Barthelmess had been in pictures only since 1916, taking mostly juvenile parts, mainly under the dictatorial thumb of the crashingly Victorian D. W. Griffith. In 1919 Griffith had featured Barthelmess as the tragic young "Chink" (as he was identified in the titles) Cheng Huan opposite Lillian Gish in *Broken Blossoms*: "In [London's] slummy Limehouse, a young Chinaman loves the daughter of a brute, who kills her; the Chinaman then kills him and commits suicide." Barthelmess was electrifying.

Everyone recognized his million-dollar potential, not least Barthelmess himself. In 1921 he broke away from Griffith and went independent, forming his own company and contracting with giant distributor First National for a whole string of starring features, the first of which would be *Tol'able David*. The script was adapted from a short story by Joseph Hergesheimer that Griffith had owned for years but never got around to making. (Despite the remarkable box-office fortune he had reaped in 1915 with *Birth of a Nation*, by 1918 Griffith provoked cringes among critics and yawns at the theaters. He was known by then for making "old-fashioned rural melodrama" like *Way Down East*, which was released a few months before *Tol'able David*, and which was parodied unmercifully in a Universal one-reel comedy called *Way Down North*.) Griffith's affinity for sentimental rural weepies had led him to Hergesheimer's story in the first place. This precedent did not seem to bode well for Barthelmess, but the actor bought the story from Griffith anyway and hired Virginia-born Henry King to direct it on location in the very Virginia mountains where the story was originally set.

This scenario was not only a retooling of old-fashioned material but a replication of earlier Hollywood career moves. By taking his shot at fame with a mountain feud story, Barthelmess was following an already musty Hollywood tradition. Many other young stars had ridden to the top at the box office on a mountain nag, "Little Mary" Pickford first among them but also her little brother Jack Pickford, Mary Miles Minter, and Mabel Normand among others. Mary Pickford had played backwoods virgin/hellcat types since at least *The Mountaineer's Honor* (Biograph) in 1909, but it was *The Eagle's Mate* (Famous Players, 1914), an epic tale of wild mountain blood and male competition for breeding rights, that sealed her popularity and hence her wild profitability. Her younger brother Jack played several tol'able mountain boys himself (discussed at the end of this section). Minter made notable splashes in *Melissa of the Hills* (American/Mutual Star, 1917), *Her Country's Call* (American/Mutual Star, 1917), and *A Cumberland Romance* (Realart Pictures, 1920), and Normand, the formerly anonymous Keystone comedienne, made herself a name as the backwoods gal in *Mickey* (Mack Sennett/Mabel Normand Feature Film Co., 1917) and again in *Sis Hopkins* (Goldwyn Pictures, 1919).

Those crude mountain desperadoes who had largely populated the nickelodeon "Easterns"—the southern mountain melodramas—became in *Tol'able David* the subsidiary characters the Hatburns, symbolic monsters only, the Goliaths that young rural prince David would justifiably and ritually kill. Perhaps, after the Great War, the symbol of Good slaying Evil was a restorative for the greater number of Americans who did not read *Civilization in the United States* and who did not expatriate themselves to France and who wanted to feel all right again about an idealized American past. In a sense, *Tol'able David* flattered the old gang by presenting a mirror image of its own largely imagined and conveniently lost rural innocence: beautiful pictures that turned justifiably violent at just the right time to defend a good rural people against an awful invading evil. The majority of mama's-boy movies that I've identified were made soon after America's acutely felt experience in Europe in World War I, and they were a comforting parable of American patriotic virtue, a reaffirmation of the vision of the ideal American male as at-home boy, backward but virtuous (Fig. 7.1), an innocent bystander passing into manhood in a dangerous world where he can kill when he must. Are not the invading, degenerate Hatburns in *Tol'able David* projections of the Kaiser's troops? Is not young David a stand-in for wholesome doughboys rallying to defend our plowed ground from the dark rapacious powers in Europe?

And consider, too, the obvious connection this movie makes between the fictional Hatburns and the notorious real-life Hatfields of West Virginia's Tug River Valley, who were, as every literate American knew, symbolic enemies of American progress in the mythic Hatfield-McCoy feud. One of the title cards in *Tol'able David* even has Iska Hatburn saying that he and his sons are running from trouble "over Tug Valley way."

The single essential element in what I am dubbing the "mama's-boy" formula is that the boy must kill his giant or giants both because of and also, ironically, *in spite of* a strong mother figure—in fact, the Idea of Mother and therefore Motherland (and maybe, by extension, some encoded racial integrity). The various scenarios accomplish the transition of boyhood into manhood by way of violence inspired by a corporate-sponsored female with a conceptual halo around her head. By killing virtuously, dumb American innocence paradoxically redeclares itself through force rather than boulevard sophistication or coolly detached irony; it is not, in other words, associated with the new American char-

Figure 7.1. "The ideal American male as at-home boy": Richard Barthelmess in *Tol'able David* with his (doomed) dog Rocket. (Courtesy of Wisconsin Center for Film and Theater Research)

acteristics presented in the jazz-and-sin movies that replaced hillbilly melodramas as popular movie fare after World War I.

By 1918 audiences had traded in mountain landscapes for a largely interior urban world peopled by predatory "clubmen" and female "vampires" who engaged in European-style upper-class shenanigans; rich and idle playboys cavorted with Nasimova, Pola Negri, Louise Glaum, and a veritable host of feline others in "stories of sexual intrigue and exotica" that exhibited an exhilarating but ultimately unnerving flippancy about things that older Americans always did and still do find sincerely shocking: infidelity in marriage, open drunkenness, and naked bodies. The frankly and straightforwardly named *Sex*, the big hit of 1920 with Louise Glaum as the cheerfully amoral femme, did not warn people away from city sin with its spectacle of ruined marriages and foolish suitors. It lured. So, in a different way, did the thrillingly warped *Cabinet of Dr. Caligari* (Decla-Bioscop, 1921), another big hit.

The ordinary itself was bending strange, to general applause from a crowd ostentatiously weary of traditional reality. The rural just no longer fit the urban sophistication of flaming youth. American culture was no longer John Fox Jr. but had turned into Hemingway almost overnight. And yet there was in the city a reservoir of unresolved guilty nostalgia for America's rural past, just waiting to be focused and released by *Tol'able David*'s fond agricultural romanticism. Barthelmess made a vast American urban audience of both sexes feel good again about home and whitebread.

Also working to Barthelmess's advantage in making the mountain feud formula successful again was that he was popularly typed as the embodiment of adolescent male innocence ("the celestial idealist," as Griffith dubbed him in *Broken Blossoms*), the opposite, in other words, of the typical mountain men in the old nickelodeons—the cold-blooded killers, the potential rapists, the dark others. Barthelmess seemed to be light itself, male innocence, and his boyishness appealed greatly to an important economic segment of the moviegoing public. In 1919 Ben Grimm of *Moving Picture World* warned movie exhibitors: "It is *the woman* who holds the purse strings; who controls the dimes and quarters that pay admissions for the family; who is the head of the house always when it comes to the question as to what movies her family is going to." An exhibitor in Southington, Connecticut, complained about the Jack Pickford vehicle *The Hill Billy*, released in 1924: "Not a woman's picture and the women are the backbone of our business."

In *Tol'able David* Barthelmess gave audiences a woman's picture that was ironically a brutal man's picture, too, a story about a boy every mother would want to adopt as teenaged pet, in whom sexual acquisitiveness has not yet dawned, but in whom nevertheless the tidy need to kill in hand-to-hand self-defense could be sanctioned. Some moviegoers complained about the prolonged and painful violence at the end of *Tol'able David*, but most accepted it because the farm boy's heart is pure, his cause is just, and he is devoted to his mother. That sounds as improbable as hell for the biggest hit of 1922, but amazingly, it worked.

Star Barthelmess and director King made their improbable magic by taking the cast and crew on location to one of the most underpopulated areas in Virginia: Highland County, on the western uphill rise that flanks the northwestern Shenandoah and adjacent to the state of (darkest) West Virginia. In and around the county seat of Monterey, King made sure his camera recorded only what conformed to his notion of an idealized nineteenth century, with nothing of the twentieth (though a power line is plainly visible in one scene shot on a Highland County dirt road). This movie might be in a sense King's homage to the idea of his own (lost) past in the nearby Shenandoah, on a farm near Christiansburg where he grew up and worked and from which he escaped as a teenager to join a traveling show, the proverbial circus. King made many movies as both actor and director before *Tol'able David*, which is now generally regarded as his masterpiece. (He afterward directed over a hundred movies in his long career, including *Lloyds of London, Jesse James, Song of Bernadette, Twelve O'Clock High, The Gunfighter, The Sun Also Rises*, and *Tender Is the Night*, all for Twentieth Century–Fox.) Highland County appealed very much to King's eye for authentic farm detail and to his "common touch," as opposed to D. W. Griffith's thundering aristocratic condescension and sentimentality.

The story focuses on farm boy David Kinemon, an impetuous and clumsy specimen. But since this is a David of the David-and-Goliath mold, appearances are deceptive. The biblical allusion is, in fact, explicit. At the beginning, the titles pokily but reverentially introduce the Kinemon family hierarchically one by one, starting with the father/ patriarch; when young David is finally shown lying on his stomach on the bare floor of a simple cabin, his feet kicking idly in the air behind him, he seems almost more a ten-year-old than a sixteen-year-old. (Barthelmess was actually twenty-six at the time.) David is studying an illustration in the large family Bible. The camera closes in on a lithograph of wee David confronting a massive, armored Goliath. The contest has not yet begun, and nobody is betting on David.

The Goliath of this film is Ernest Torrence as bad Luke Hatburn, the biggest and meanest of the Hatburn boys from deepest West Virginia. This was Torrence's first movie, and his résumé didn't look particularly promising for him to play one of the worst screen villains in American cinema: he was a Scottish opera singer. But his strikingly long face and his tall body would so memorably express the very epitome of Arnold Toynbee's Celtic-fringe degeneracy that Torrence typed himself forever after as a screen heavy (although he played parsons, too, and also big lunky comic sidekicks as in James Cruze's *The Covered Wagon* [Paramount/Famous Players–Lasky, 1923]).

The three Hatburns, father Iska with his sons "Buzzard" and the more dominant Luke, are on the run from the law in West Virginia, and they come down to the idyllic valley of Greenstream like wolves on the fold, moving in forcibly on their hapless Hatburn cousin, an elderly valley farmer who acts as guardian to his peach of a granddaughter, Esther (a character who is not in Hergesheimer's short story but who proves fairly useful in the movie, adding lust to Luke's menace and another biblical name to this parable of duty). The invading Hatburns quickly establish their brute cruelty. They represent an undiscriminating voraciousness. When they first stalk onto their cousin's thrifty little farm, Luke and the dim-witted Buzzard wade destructively into the precise and pretty kitchen garden patch, uprooting adolescent vegetables and cramming them greedily into their mouths. It's a scene of surprising horror that perhaps only a farm boy like director Henry King could have visualized. (James Still included a similar scene in his classic 1940 mountain novel *River of Earth*, in which hungry relatives strip a growing garden while its starving owners look on in despair.) With his mouth full of onion, Luke literally drops his jaw when he first sees Esther, another and more tasty morsel. Luke's eyes glitter with erotic threat, and his mouth is juicy. He approaches and towers over her. His glitter-eye stalks her through the picture until passion and opportunity erupt in near rape (the threat of which is the key subtext to most hillbilly masculinity in the movies, though not to the mama's boys).

If young David is his mother's true son, if his very presence in the story depends on his status of being "mothered," then surely the Hatburns assume even greater symbolic evil because they epitomize the *un*mothered. Luke Hatburn is the mamaless boy. That's why "a peculiar humor" has developed in him "to destroy whatever he encountered" (as his opening title card announces), especially weak and innocent things. David Reynolds has suggested a comparison between Luke Hatburn and Leonard Smalls in *Raising Arizona* (see Chapter 2). Smalls's tattoo, in fact, rationalizes the evil of the unmothered: "MAMA DIDN'T LOVE ME."

The Hatburns are pure symbolic mountain, "natural" in the negative, while the Kinemons are pure symbolic valley, good corporate rural. Bill

Lightfoot has pointed out that although Kinemon obviously means "cattleman" (*kine* being the archaic word for cattle), the name also suggests "kind man," one who, in *Tol'able David* at least, is ideally *settled* on a farm, bothering no other man's settlement—achieving, in other words, a symbolic gentle relatedness to the landscape, a kindness/kinship. The movie's plot arranges a test for this native kindness, a test it is bound to pass, in which David's family with its more progressive ideal of neighborliness receives a visitation from what America ideally isn't: the three antitheses to American progress, the Hatburns from West Virginia. The American who roams the uneven uplands is criminal by definition, in essence *un*-American.

But the despoiled garden and the terrorized cousins are nothing compared to what's coming when the giant Luke kills David's dog and cripples his elder brother Allen. The universally admired Allen drives the mail hack twenty miles into West Virginia and back, a daily employment that baby brother David idealizes as the one true proof of manhood. One fateful day, as Allen passes the Hatburn cabin in the mail hack with David's dog Rocket on the buckboard beside him, Rocket jumps down and chases a cat into the Hatburns' yard. Luke, feeling his "peculiar humor" teased, grabs a large stick and kills the dog. The conventionally resolute Allen then comes into the yard and tells all the Hatburns in no uncertain terms that, although he cannot delay the mail to deal out justice now, he'll be back. For this effrontery Luke blindsides Allen with a rock, knocks him down a bank, and literally stomps his head under his boot. Allen is carried home a hopeless cripple for life.

Now the feud motif kicks in. In rapid succession we see Allen's tragic arrival home, David's frantic emotion, their father's grim and growing resolution. Presently the father lays hands on his rifle. His wife, David's mother, looks on resignedly; she knows what must happen next. The man of the family must kill the evil. He *must*. David's mother embraces her husband, takes his hand, and then turns away her face, still holding on to his hand until he pulls gently free. It's an important moment, the full articulation of the female as saint of hearth and home. Conveniently, she is signaling both her acquiescence in what male culture demands and her sure fatalistic belief that what she stands for will go on because her husband must die.

Meanwhile the agitated David is grabbing his old muzzle-loader, his ramrod, and his powderhorn, preparing to accompany his father on his quest for vengeance. But the father, who repeatedly has reaffirmed David's lower status as mere boy—excluding him from the male ritual of brandy and cigars to toast the birth of the family's first grandchild, for example, and saying it's "because you're not a man yet"—now further emphasizes David's lack of manhood: he orders the boy to stay home with his mother while he himself goes out to face certain death (as any *man* would and must do, the movie preaches). David, forestalled again from what he knows he must do eventually, is emotionally devastated.

But then a higher fate intervenes (this is a melodrama, after all). David's father suddenly drops dead of a heart attack before he has even reached the door, and young David, still hot with the need to act, grabs up his own gun again and marches out to revenge his family on the Hatburns.

Thus commences the central thematic sequence in this mama's-boy movie. David's mother, down on her knees trying to revive her dead husband, realizes where David is going and hurries after him, crying. She is a large woman, but she overtakes him, grapples with him, clutches his clothing, gets a hold on his arm and then loses it, grabs his waist with both hands, slips down in the barnyard muck while she hangs on to his legs and feet, and finally stops him in his hell-bent forward progress. *Not you too, not my baby!* As David stops, listens, considers, gives in, his face is a mask of pain and humiliation. Brought to the brink of desperate manhood, he is held back by the number-one woman in his life. Her symbolic nature as Mother dictates reticent acceptance of the desperate acts that men must perform, but she'll hinder the passage of her son into that arena for as long as she can. He has to go against her wishes, or at least behind her back. And once he makes the passage, the idea of Mother presides like a blessed saint over the carnage. The ending tableau in *Tol'able David*: Mother cradles her wounded but triumphant son in her arms and pronounces him at last a man.

The acting out of David's manly courage brings all symbols together in a thrilling climax. He first succeeds in driving the mail hack into West Virginia and back. But he inadvertently loses the mail to the Hatburns and must restore the property of the United States of America, and in the process he saves the peach of a granddaughter from rape and kills all three Hatburn men. All in one day. The climactic hand-to-hand struggle with Luke Hatburn, especially, features realistic brutality that, according to some complaints at the time, went much too far. "Not for the squeamish," said one exhibitor. But of course, part of what made this movie a certifiable hit was its frankly visceral message.

Several of my students have noticed the neat congruence of David's ascent to full participation in the American male fraternity while he is carrying the government *mail*. Nancy Collins sees a trinity of applications: David announces himself to the bad Hatburns, saying, "Don't hinder me, I'm the government's agent," and then he adds, "and David Kinemon, too"; he is carrying the mail, wearing the mail (in chivalric defense of sacred womanhood); and finally, he *is* the male. Such symbolism reinforces the interpretation of this film as an encoded piece of patriotic propaganda that was bound to resonate well among viewers who vividly remembered our experience in World War I.

Barthelmess did not invent the mountain mama's-boy type. Jack Pickford had played it earlier in at least two mountain plots: the excellent *Bill Apperson's Boy* (First National, 1919), which survives in the collection of the Library of Congress, and Pickford's version of John Fox Jr.'s *The Little Shepherd of Kingdom Come* (Goldwyn Pictures, 1920). (Barthelmess also did a version of *The Little Shepherd of Kingdom Come* called *Kentucky Courage*, released by First National in 1928.) Pickford's movie specialty, too, was pettable albeit lethal waifs found in strictly rural settings, usually mountains. After Barthelmess made it big in *Tol'able David*, Pickford returned as the same type in *The Hill Billy* (Jack Pickford Productions, 1924), another John Fox Jr. story about an innocent mountain boy initiated into ideal manhood through desperate acts against his necessary giant, in this case a hillbilly murderer named "Groundhog" Spence. Goldwyn Pictures had promoted Pickford in *Little Shepherd* as "the living symbol of youth," and *Moving Picture World* described him in *The Hill Billy* as "a very likeable sort of chap, especially in the emotional scenes where he is struggling against almost insurmountable odds." As in *Tol'able David*, the point in the Pickford films is that the mama's boy must kill and yet remain "wistfully appealing," which is how Quinn Martin, film critic for the *New York World*, described Pickford in *The Hill Billy*.

David Kinemon was obviously imitated two years later by Charles Emmett Mack, who played a similar character in *Driven* (Charles Brabin/Universal, 1923), summarized thus by the *New York Times*: "The story . . . is that of a mountaineer mother. She is the wife of a beast and three of her sons are beasts. Moonshining is their business and brutality their recreation. But the woman has a fourth son, a slender, youthful dreamer, a weakling, if you will, but tender, too, and all the love in the mother's life is centred in him." According to formula, the idealized mountain mama's boy rises eruptively to defend Mother. But whereas in *Tol'able David* the evil is an invader, an outsider, in *Driven* the evil comes from within, from the putative men of the family. Like *Tol'able David*, *Driven* could brag that it was made on location in the southern mountains. But it was an imitation without wit, and it stumbled. One very irritated exhibitor in Saranac Lake, New York, wrote to *Moving Picture World*: "The picture was advertised to the limit here in the East, principally for exhibitors to pay a good rental. It ran merely for exploitation purposes in New York City. I think the picture very, very ordinary. . . . A poor imitation of *Tol'able David* . . . a program concoction." "Program concoction" was the kiss of death.

The 1925 movie version of Lula Vollmer's Broadway play *Sun-Up* (Metro-Goldwyn-Mayer) showcased the same mountain male character type again. In *Sun-Up*, a fierce old mountain matriarch must give up her only son to World War I. Her burning desire for him has been that he fight for Mother, but in the family feud, not in Europe. Now he must go abroad for her, in a sense, but he also goes against her will. She neither understands nor appreciates that she is part of something larger than family. The son's wartime experience abroad ironically "civilizes," or at the very least spiritualizes, him. (He learns to carry the government mail/male.) He returns home to Ma to lead her, too, out of the Old Testament of mountain backwardness and vengeance into the New Testament of peace and coexistence with her feud enemies. The mama's boy becomes a kind of cultural Moses, arising out of bullrushes and swaddling clouts and into a soldier's garb. The mama's boy as military recruit looks backward to World War I and ahead to World War II—the connection that *Sergeant York* exploited so well, as we will see later.

## Stark Love

*Stark Love* is one of the little-known masterpieces of American film. Whereas *Tol'able David* is available to modern viewers on VHS videotape, *Stark Love* all but vanished after its initial brief run, and even now it can be viewed only through the benevolence of the Museum of Modern Art or the cooperation of the Library of Congress, both of which obtained their 16mm prints through the beneficence of the Czechoslovakian government, which allowed the 16mm duplication of their single surviving 35mm print of the film. Part of the reason *Stark Love* almost disappeared for good was that, at the time of its release early in 1927, it was considered even more "a freak" (*Variety*) than *Tol'able David* might have been, and for similar reasons: the "old-fashioned" stigma that had settled on mountaineers. In addition, it had no star power. It used a wholly "native" cast of "real hillbillies." Talk about toxicity at the box office!

*Stark Love* was going to fail, and its parent studio, Paramount, knew it. The prevailing opinion there was that the movie should be shelved indefinitely, but its young creator, Karl Brown, forced his bosses' hand by successfully premiering it himself at the Broadway Cameo in New York City out of his own pocket, to some rave reviews, especially among what *Variety* called the "high-brows in the neighborhood." But a broad popular appeal never materialized for Brown's arty re-visioning of the southern mountains, even though the studio squeamishly released it. Witness Paramount's lukewarm pitch in *Moving Picture World*: "It is different from the usual run of plays, and can be sold as a novelty with *reasonable* assurance that the picture will please" (emphasis added). The advent of movie sound experiments in 1927 hadn't helped much either; all silent movies suddenly seemed dated and silly, especially an innovative one using a cast of real mountain people. After a perfunctory nationwide run, *Stark Love* was withdrawn. It reappeared briefly (at Broadway's Cameo again) during July 1928, but showings after that were a novelty indeed. The movie disappeared, almost for good.

Why, then, did sophisticated Paramount, which supposedly purveyed to advanced tastes, give Karl Brown, a lowly former studio cameraman on his first directorial assignment, $50,000 to write and direct an old-fashioned rural melodrama featuring woman abuse and a hand-to-hand fight to the finish between a hillbilly father and his son?

One reason was that Brown's track record had been steady and impressive. The son of show people and musicians, Brown practically grew up in Hollywood and worked in films from the time he was a teenager, first as a technician at Kinemacolor, then as Billy Bitzer's assistant cameraman on D. W. Griffith's *Birth of a Nation* and *Intolerance*. He knew movie people, he knew the movie business, he knew how to work a movie angle. He made a name for himself as an innovator, a tinkerer, an inventor of moviemaking hardware. Eventually he moved to the Lasky studios (Famous Players), the forerunner of Paramount, and he became famous among cameramen for his photography on *The Covered Wagon* (1923), the sweeping epic that mythologized the conquest of the American West. *The Covered Wagon* was a notable hit, the first really big Western, and Brown's photographic ("documentary") realism was often singled out for praise. Paramount executive Jesse Lasky solemnly presented a copy of the movie to the Smithsonian Institution as a valuable "record" of America's past, although reputable historians were less enthusiastic: "Almost never in all the history of western migration did an Indian war party descend upon a circle of covered wagons"; "bull-trains never swam rivers with neck-yokes on. . . . [W]agon trains never camped for the night in box-canyons. . . . Jim Bridger was not that kind of man [a drunkard with two Indian wives]. . . . [F]our hundred wagons never travelled across the plains in a single caravan, for where would the oxen pasture?" But despite all that scholarly caviling, at Paramount the cameraman who shot *The Covered Wagon* was suddenly worth money.

But Brown still had to bulldoze his way into studio bigwig Jesse Lasky's office by telling Lasky's secretary that he must see the boss immediately "on the matter of the utmost importance, a completely new and unique story idea about the pioneers." *Pioneers* was the key, but misleading, word to describe what Brown actually had in mind—a story about southern hillbillies—but as Brown himself wryly noted, "After the enormous success of *The Covered Wagon*, anything having to do with *pioneers* was like money in the bank."

Another reason Paramount green-lighted *Stark Love* was the recent success of Robert Flaherty's electrifying *Nanook of the North* (Revillon

Frères, 1922), followed in 1925 by Ernest Schoedsack's *Grass* (Famous Players–Lasky)—the latter, incidentally, backed by Jesse Lasky. These freaky, arty "documentaries" using nonactors in fictional situations that approximated their real lives became big hits. But when Brown made a pitch for his hillbilly docufiction, Lasky hedged and made Brown write his ideas down on paper for circulation among the top Paramount management. "There are quite a large number of people who must be sold on the idea before we can make any commitment," Lasky told him. Brown dutifully wrote the idea down, turned it in, and then waited. And waited some more. Finally a studio middle-management flunky summoned him. Brown recalled the kiss-off scene this way: "He tossed [a mimeographed copy of my story idea] onto his desk and said, 'We've all read this—this *thing*—and we are all agreed that it would make an exceedingly bad motion picture. That will be all.'"

But even with that door seemingly slammed in his face, Brown got the go-ahead anyway by exploiting a logistical oddity in the corporate structure at Paramount: the top brass were split between the East and West Coasts, with the real head office in New York City commanded by Adolph Zukor and the almost equally powerful production office in Los Angeles nominally headed by Lasky. Brown knew how to work a trick with night letters sent by wire, and before anyone knew it, he had created his own in-company hype and gotten his movie funded by Adolph Zukor himself.

The plot of *Stark Love*, as it evolved, was calculated to twist irony out of the mama's-boy formula: a lordly old brutal mountain man, the boy's father and his necessary giant, has made a virtual slave and involuntary breeder out of the boy's Ma. The boy pines to help her but he is passive; he can't rouse himself yet to challenge his father. This weak, idealistic son—he's been tetched with "chivalry," ideas he's gotten from picture books he can barely read—has slept all his life alongside the very bed where his father has repeatedly mated with his mother, so close beside it on the floor that he can reach out and touch the bedcovers (which the camera shows him doing). Devoted to his mother as an ideal of Woman (there is also his sweetheart, the neighbor girl), the boy sells his horse and goes off to Berea College to become his own version of the cultural Moses, bent on delivering the women from slavery. But while he's away on this chivalric quest, his overworked and over-bred mother dies, and his father "marries" (essentially buys for use) the fine and headstrong neighbor girl.

The log cabin itself, in which the boy and his father and his mother and all his siblings live, forces the inevitable conflict because of the very closeness of quarters. In fact, writer/director Brown had wanted to call his movie *The Log Cabin*, but Paramount overruled him, insisting that *love* had to be in the title if the movie were to have any chance on the market at all.

In Brown's imagination, the empty textbook symbol of the pioneer log cabin had been suddenly filled with what he took to be a vision of reality. Late one night in 1923, while reading an installment in the *Atlantic* of missionary Lucy Furman's serialized novel about Kentucky hillbillies, *The Quare Women*, and after working all day on the set of *The Covered Wagon*, he came to his sensational insights about the awful steamy closeness of living and procreating in such crude quarters. Think of it, Brown said, just *think* of adolescent children sleeping and dressing in the same room with active adult carnality. *That* was frontier reality.

At the end of *Stark Love*, within the confines of that log cabin, all the energies, suppressed hatred, and aroused lust dormant in the mama's-boy formula congregate and explode. Here is Brown's own synopsis of what happens:

It's beginning to grow dark and a howling wind presages a violent storm. There'll be no going out that night because the river that washes almost to the cabin door will be in full spate and everybody will be house bound until the waters subside.

Which is all right with the old man [the boy's father]. He's itching to try his new woman anyway. So he orders everyone to bed. The older kids scramble up a makeshift ladder to the loft. The baby and smaller children are bedded down in their corner.

The old man closes the slab door and fits the wooden latch into place, pulling the latch-string inside. He begins to unbutton, getting ready for bed.

The girl looks wistfully, almost apologetically at the boy as she begins to unbutton the top of her bodice. He can do nothing but stand and stare, paralyzed by the thought of what is to be happening in his very presence.

The girl hesitates, shrinking back against the wall. The old man is enraged. When he gives an order he expects instant obedience. He reaches for her. She shies away. He becomes enraged because of her attitude. [And Helen Mundy, the teenager hired in Knoxville to play the girl, had "attitude" to burn.] He grabs her and flings her onto the bed, down below the bottom frame-line of the camera. We can see nothing of the actual action, but from the old man's motions we know that he is tearing her clothes off, ready to take her right then and there. [This last sequence was later censored by Paramount, though the studio left in an earlier view of Helen Mundy's nude backside.]

The boy, horrified, is goaded into action. He flings himself at the old man. He might as well have flung himself at the rock of Gibraltar. After a split second of surprise, the old man flicks the boy aside with a careless backhanded swipe that sends the boy sprawling, after which he devotes his attention to the business in hand, which is to start the girl on her way to motherhood.

By now the boy is literally mad, insane, utterly reckless. He recovers his footing and again hurls himself against the old man's body.

But Brown's mama's boy isn't strong enough for his giant. As David Reynolds has parsed the experience: "*Stark Love* confirms the dreaded suspicion in the back of most men's minds: 'When backed into a corner, I may need some help.'" The boy's help comes from the girl, who saves him from his father's wrath and herself from the rape by threatening the old man with an ax (Fig. 7.2). Seeing her eyes glint in the firelight as she raises the blade, the old man knows she'll do it, and we know she'll do it, too—we've seen her chopping wood. The ferociousness we respect in men obviously ain't exclusive to that gender (see Chapter 8).

The fight sequence took Brown's crew two full days of hard shooting. He insisted on doing it as a sequence of close shots, "covering the action bit by bit in very short scenes"—fifty-one in all. These he edited into a believable and alarming struggle that allowed audiences to vent their accumulated hatred for the father and all he stood for. Most audiences, in fact, still show that their desire to see the old man chopped up by Helen Mundy's ax is roughly proportional to how intensely they have felt the boy's desperation, and that is palpable indeed.

What makes *Stark Love* a surprise in the mama's-boy tradition is its dif-

Figure 7.2. Frame enlargement of Helen Mundy wielding the ax in the climax of *Stark Love.*

ferent tone. Most other mama's-boy movies sentimentalized the land-scape and romanticized its settlers. But Brown had no intention of flat-tering a rural nostalgia that he clearly despised. In being "pastoral," the earlier mama's-boy films had offered—implicitly by comparison—a cri-tique of what urban life lacked, at least in the minds of their creators. Brown recognized no such urban lack, and *Stark Love* is shockingly anti-pastoral. He believed in American progress, he loved American cities, and he was not fool enough to think that pioneer conditions were in any way an improvement over contemporary city living, especially in Los Angeles and New York. Brown wanted to show how bad life had been in the American rural past, not how potentially ideal. The log cabin in our collective heart, as far as Karl Brown was concerned, had made us mean.

To turn the mama's-boy movie on its ear, Brown needed his own real location. And perhaps he thought he had found it in the highest peaks of North Carolina's Great Smoky Mountains. Clearly, what he thought *should* have been there—some highly colorized vision of pioneer America—was no longer effectively real, if it had ever in fact existed as Brown imagined it. Brown knew nothing of mountain people or of mountain living except what he had gleaned through the media (namely, Lucy Furman's fiction and a zillion other similar presentations, including, probably, many of those old nickelodeon movies).

In addition to the Secret of the Log Cabin, Karl Brown's mental landscape was possessed by another hoary hypothesis that could account for all other supposed facts: hillbillies represented the complete isolation of a strange "culture." When Brown was interviewed in 1927 by the *New York Times*, he said he remembered most vividly this key point in Furman's novel: mountaineers "have lived in their high fastnesses for 200 years *untouched by civilization*" (emphasis added). Describing his trek to find the location for *Stark Love*, Brown told the *Times* how, "after climbing lofty trails, breaking thick ice so that he could ford streams, he eventually reached the home of the mountaineers," as though he were acting out some of the wackier plot developments in *The Lost Continent*. Much, much later, when film historian Kevin Brownlow finally tracked Brown down in the late 1960s, the director told Brownlow (evidently in all seriousness) that there "were only 5,000 mountaineers left and it proved hard to locate them." The very first title in *Stark Love* repeats this myth as fact: "Deep in the North Carolina hills, far from civilization, lives an isolated and primitive people."

That ridiculous notion, prevalent in the early 1920s, had been a stubborn and prolific mind virus since the 1880s. Irene Hudson's "The Schoolma'am of Sandy Ridge"—which appeared in the January 1921 issue of the *Atlantic,* two years before Brown read the fateful installment from Lucy Furman's novel—was a wholly representative "real" account of life in the contemporary Virginia mountains. Hudson's *Atlantic* piece took the form of a series of letters home to Minnesota from her missionary post in bleakest Russell County in the Virginia Blue Ridge during the summer and fall of 1918 and the winter of 1919. Hudson was doing in Virginia what Furman had been doing over on the Kentucky side, the same thing that many well-educated, heavenly intentioned, and "progressive" middle-class women and men were doing during the first two decades of the twentieth century: they went into the isolation chambers of the poorest mountain regions they could find to minister good deeds as penance for real or imagined sins. Hudson served her turn as a teacher-missionary in the most isolated and incommodious spot she could personally locate, but one that was not, as a matter of fact, very far uphill from Dante, Virginia, the bustling, railroading seat of Russell County. Hudson's letters contained terse and effective descriptions, and she made a stab at trying to suspend her middle-class conditioning. But what she emphasized from the beginning was the extreme *isolation* of the place, "being as remote and isolated from the rest of the world *as if they were on a desert island*" (emphasis added).

We perceive the isolation of a desert island as absolute; and the abstract concept of such seclusion comfortably allows the city beholder to completely dissociate him- or herself from the "island inhabitants": "That is not me. That is something wholly other, which explains my permissible curiosity and my forgivable need to collect these people as specimens."

But immediately following Hudson's reference to desert islands came some purely incidental information that indicted her own imagery. She mentioned in passing "every house along the *road*" but failed to make a plain connection: this *road* led from this *community* of houses through a series of other communities and coal camps, with jobs and wages and sellouts—very much the "modern world," of which the residents of Sandy Ridge had plenty. But no, to Hudson this place was an island, and she believed in her ideal against all physical evidence to the contrary. Historical geographer David C. Hsiung has recently reminded fervid urban imaginations that the remotest log cabin in darkest Tennessee was *always*, from the earliest times, tied to the national economy by trails, tracks, roads, or rivers, rough and "impassable" as they might have seemed to those urbanite visitors who passed over them and survived to write articles for the *Atlantic*. Isolation is in the eye of the beholder; it is seldom in the actual landscape.

But Karl Brown's conception of mountain isolation, and hence of isolated mountaineers, didn't reckon with a central problem: to find the splendid isolation he imagined, he would have to go where there were literally no mountain people. He finally found his spot in Graham

County, North Carolina, in some of the higher coves of the Smokies on Big Santeetlah Creek, in a former small neighborhood that had been recently and utterly cleared of human habitation to make way for the federally funded Santeetlah Dam (completed soon after Brown finished his movie).

Brown's search for his "tribe" of mountaineers—considering his fund of knowledge—is hilariously detailed in his manuscript *The Paramount Adventure*. To find hillbillies, he incongruously went first to New Orleans, the most interior southern city he could think of, and there he asked a journalist friend if he knew where there were any benighted mountain people. His friend had vaguely heard of a Berea College in Kentucky that was supposedly civilizing such types. And presto, Brown just happened to stumble on "a young man leaning on a push broom" who also just happened to be a proud graduate of Berea College and who incidentally got so mad at Brown that he blurted out what the Hollywood denizen wanted to hear all along: "[Y]ou get right down to cases on what goes on in them cabins after the dark comes down and they're all locked in together and—well, you show that around for people to laugh at, and brother, you better look out, that's all. You look out real good or you're liable to wake up some morning deader'n a nit. And don't say I didn't never warn you, neither."

So Brown took the hint and got himself by train to Berea—everyone went everywhere by train then, including deep into the southern mountains to make movies—where he got the none-too-surprising official cold shoulder from college people eager *not* to be associated with any such "truth." Next Brown bounced to Nashville, where he asked hotel desk clerks if they knew where any real isolated mountaineers lived. They didn't, but they pointed him in the direction of Knoxville, Tennessee, where someone else told him that those kinds of hillbillies were all over the line in North Carolina. Naturally, he went to the biggest city he could find, Asheville, and there, very near the end of his urbanbound rope, he happened to limp into a bookstore, where he found a copy of Horace Kephart's *Our Southern Highlanders*, an exceptionally well written and therefore believable account of the "isolated" inhabitants of the Great Smokies circa 1907. It was Brown's great luck, he thought, to then discover that Kephart himself was living not too far away, on a rail spur in Bryson City—deeper into the heart of our history, as Brown wanted to imagine it.

Kephart's influence on Brown is both an interesting accident and hard to overestimate. Brown himself reported several times (in his book manuscript and in published interviews in 1926) that Kephart had been at times a daily fixture on the movie set, an adviser and consultant on many matters from the meaning of "mountain primitive" to the art of camping out in the open in December and not freezing to death.

Kephart left no evidence (that anyone knows of) that he ever met Brown or helped him make an on-location movie that would libel mountain manhood. And Kephart might not have known how his writing played into Brown's hands. Kephart had, after all, recorded with a librarian's cool frankness the harsh truths about mountain people that he believed he saw all around. Kephart liked harsh truth; he thought it was the avenue that would return him from overeducated sophistication to the Kephart family's "frontier traditions" (in the Allegheny Mountains of central Pennsylvania), described by George Ellison as "a strenuous, do-without, log-rolling, shooting-and-fishing, camp-meeting, wagoneering, lumber-rafting type of existence" supposedly lived with gusto by the mythic Kephart fathers on the 1800s frontier. The Kephart son who came to the Carolina mountains in 1903 was a highly educated, alcoholic denizen of research libraries, a world-traveled linguist and scholar who took an intense interest in touching his own personal truth through what he believed to be the pioneer savagery of the Great Smoky Mountains. When he came to those mountains, abandoning his wife and four children in St. Louis, he kept a small bound notebook that he labeled "The Joys of Barbarism."

There was another paradox in the nonfiction book Kephart eventually published in 1913 as *Our Southern Highlanders*: for a scholar who would become one of the major research sources for documentary evidence on turn-of-the-century mountaineers, Kephart lived a rather odd (and highly suspicious) "theory of the value of personal isolation." That is, one might think that an anthropological study of such lasting impact would require more actual interaction with living people. But Kephart was notoriously antisocial. One of his former employees back in the St. Louis library said of him, "Kephart lived almost exclusively in a world of his own." No wonder the "highlanders" seemed "so picturesque" to him. In the idea of them he found what was lacking in himself, the living possibility of "the past in the present," "a Back of Beyond" that justified, ironically, his own "capacity for being alone"—the savage in him, the drink perhaps, that made him unfit for company. Real isolation, having no obligations to another living soul, was Kephart's chief intoxicant, and it was a myth shared by the visiting moviemaker: Karl Brown was drawn to Kephart as to a magnet.

According to Brown's account, Kephart treated him cordially and was immensely helpful in explaining North Carolina mountain character and the nature of life there. From Bryson City, Kephart sent Brown further into the mountains to Robbinsville, the county seat of Graham County, and got him a local "guide" to lead him ever higher into the Snowbird Mountains. On the drive up to Robbinsville, Brown took some movie footage of the Nantahala Gorge, which became the opening image in his finished movie; it shows some of the wildest and most rugged landscape in North Carolina, hardly representative of where actual mountain people lived.

Brown never found his tribe of isolated hillbillies, though he bumped into one or two hunters, who were friendly and helpful, and he found a large, flat meadow above Rattler's Ford on Big Santeetlah Creek for his on-location camp and plenty of abandoned log structures for his set (Fig. 7.3). His meadow was bounded by Long Hungry Creek, which could be temporarily dammed to produce the ending flood sequence. (There were no obstacles to his doing so, since the whole area would soon be under water anyway, as it still is).

It was December 1925 when Brown staked his location. He came back to Robbinsville in the summer of 1926 with $50,000 and went to work on his movie, the first task being to acquire a "native" cast. But Brown had a major problem. He wanted to hire local people for parts in a movie that was guaranteed to insult them. He got around much of that problem by keeping the storyline to himself and by shooting out of sequence. The Graham County extras would be none the wiser as to the story's ultimate message: the degradation of women by a cultural system that makes men monstrous. After all, Brown was a man from California with money to spend. For his movie set he leased old log cabins and tub mills and spinning wheels and coverlets, and for tactical support he

Figure 7.3. Readying a shot for *Stark Love* on Big Santeetlah Creek. Karl Brown is in the white shirt, with Helen Mundy second from left. (Photograph courtesy of Nancy Love, Andrews, N.C.)

paid for some of Robbinsville's modern accoutrements, like the taxi and lodging and food. He hired many people to pantomime disconnected actions that told no narrative they could rightly follow. This is how the *New York Times* later reported Brown's cruel estimation of the Graham Countians:

Because of the ignorance of the native cast Mr. Brown said it was possible to secure remarkable natural acting. The men and women of the mountains went through their pantomime without the realization of its context to the plot. They were like children, Mr. Brown declared, in their implicit obedience. While families occupy cabins with a single room, women do all the hard work. The men are lazy, drunken, good-for-nothings, he said, who hunt, fish, fight and get drunk.

If Brown actually uttered such opinions in New York City, he was careful to keep them to himself in Graham County. But he couldn't ultimately conceal the central plot from his four principal players because the men who took the parts of the two fathers would have to know what sort of men they were supposed to be—lazy and lordly old tyrants—and that one of them would attempt rape. And, of course, the girl who played the boy's sweetheart would have to know what was in store for her. So Brown eventually had to look outside Graham County for these four characters. He found the girl and the boy in Knoxville and the two fathers "on the norther [*sic*] side of Cumberland Gap," possibly in Middlesboro, Kentucky. And while filming the touchiest scenes between these four principals he maintained a strictly closed set. "They wouldn't let anyone close to where they was filming," remembered one county resident.

Not that Brown didn't try at first to hire local talent for the main parts. But he met with a ferocious Puritanism that held movies and "movie people" in contempt. Apparently Brown had several unpleasant experiences trying to cast the part of the girl. Ollie Mae Holland (later Ollie Mae Stone) was in her late teens in 1926 and was attending school at Western Carolina Teachers College in Cullowhee. She had come home on the bus from Topton, and she had just stepped out on the main street of Robbinsville that day when she saw a man with a movie camera taking shots of various people. The man saw Ollie Mae and made a beeline for her: "He stood there and looked at me awhile, and then asked me if he could make some pictures of me. And I said I guessed it was all right. So he had me pose this way and that and had me walk up the street and back." Ollie Mae was, by her own testimony, very young and quite interested in this man with the camera. He asked her for her name:

But a friend of my father's—Walt Wiggins—saw what was going on, and he came over right then, and because I was a teenager, he said that I would have to talk to my father about this—and at that time I didn't even know what it was all about, that they wanted to make a movie. And the man with the camera said, "I would like to go with you to talk to your father." But Mr. Wiggins sent me on home.

By the time I got there, the man with the camera drove up with Mr.

Wiggins, and there ensued a heated argument which I was not permitted to take part in. I heard my father say, "My child will have nothing to do with that!" And then he said to me, "Young lady, you cannot have any part in it." . . . My father was a nice-looking, well-educated man, but he didn't want his daughter anywhere near the movies.

Apparently Walt Wiggins was working for Brown as a local troubleshooter. It was Wiggins who got Bob Roberts his job as company chauffeur. Roberts, who was hired for four months to drive the cast and crew around in his Model T ("wherever they wanted to go, no questions asked"), remembered another local girl, Dorothy Stiles, who was also seriously sought for the lead role of Barbara Allen, but whose stern parents would not budge either. "She was an awful pretty girl," Roberts remembered.

Brown himself wrote a much more romanticized version of the Ollie Mae Holland encounter: high in the Snowbird Mountains one day, rather than downtown in Robbinsville, he supposedly met a raven-haired mountain beauty, already tragically condemned to a life of thankless servitude by her dark and bearded and sinister father, who sternly prohibited her from taking part in Brown's movie, even after the director tested her with the camera and found her a natural for the part of Barbara Allen. Ollie Mae Stone told me that indeed her hair was jet black but that her father never had a beard, nor did she ever go wandering in the higher Snowbirds. Perhaps Brown's account was not intentionally fictional; perhaps his memory merely gilded the lily.

For the two fathers, Brown eventually cast two perfect Kentucky men, Reb Grogan and Silas Miracle, who were placated into acting as mountain monsters by being told that they were impersonating *North Carolina* monsters, not Kentuckians. Brown found his boy (and his girl too, eventually) in Knoxville. The boy, Forrest James, was out for the evening with three of his football teammates, celebrating a victory, and Brown spotted him in a restaurant. No country boy, James was later portrayed by the *New York Times* as some pure mountain throwback: "never seen a railroad train, automobile, electric lights or a telephone," the *Times* lied. It was even suggested that James "went off into the woods with his gun" after the movie wrapped, but this Knoxville football player would have felt more at home on a streetcar. Much later Karl Brown told Kevin

Brownlow the truth about the boy: "He was very silent. He would sulk in his tent like Achilles. He had very little to say to anybody. But he got through with his part and as soon as he got through it he was gone [back to town]. Nobody ever heard of him again."

And though Forrest James was technically the star in this mama's-boy fable, there was never anyone to compete with the girl they finally found to play Barbara Allen: Helen Mundy, the Knoxville high school flapper with a head on her shoulders and a fire in her furnace (Fig. 7.4). Mundy took the movie by storm, so naturally good at what she did that Paramount afterward signed her as a contract player and even gave her a role in another movie. But she was difficult and headstrong enough to be fired promptly after she went to New York, or else she simply quit. Anyway, she disappeared permanently from public view after one of the most memorable film debuts in that or any other year.

Helen Mundy took Robbinsville by storm, too. Brown sent Bob Roberts in his Model T to pick her up in Knoxville, and the two rode back to Robbinsville (by way of Murphy in those days) in silence: "She didn't have anything to say to me, and I didn't have anything to say to her," Roberts remembered. But Brown in his memoir says he was absolutely panic-stricken to see Helen step out of that car in Robbinsville alone. He had assumed she would be accompanied by her mother or by an older sister. An unchaperoned girl was trouble even when she wasn't a Helen Mundy. This particular girl's penchant for setting emotional brush fires could invoke the wrath of the Mann Act on Brown's Hollywood head in this unsympathetic place. So Brown gave the local sheriff money to hire extra deputies just to keep an eye on the unpredictable Helen.

When Brown got around to writing about the local cast members in the late 1960s, he could remember virtually no names, only part of one, "a Mrs. Queen" (Adeline Queen), who played the central icon of the boy's silently suffering Ma. But local memory in Graham County identifies many others: Roy, Ray, and Quince Ghormley, who played three of Helen Mundy's brothers; Wylie Underwood, as the miller; Sim Hooper, as the visiting preacher who takes the boy to Berea; George Rogers, as "the widower from Black Creek"; Nathaniel ("Nathan") Burchfield, as the old hunter who welcomes the visiting preacher; "Uncle" Grant Stewart and Dave Stewart, as mountain musicians; Earl Wall and Kelly

Figure 7.4. Forrest James and Helen Mundy in *Stark Love*. (Courtesy of Wisconsin Center for Film and Theater Research)

Wall, aged seven and five, as two of Forrest James' siblings; and Frank Forsyth, Ben Grant, Robert Elmer Rogers, Jim Carver, Della Davis, Jake Davis, Fay Davis, Carrie Davis, George and Mary Roberts, Posey Stewart, Martha Walters, Alice Patterson, Henry Stewart, Ollie Collins Crisp, Forrest Denton, Alma Stewart Buchanan, Alice Williams, Rena Blevins, and Nate Blevins in various extra parts.

The *New York Times* obligingly trumpeted *Stark Love* while it was still being edited: "The most unique motion picture ever made" (29 August 1926). And Brown gave the big-city reporters exactly what they wanted to hear: "These [people] are proud and secretive and resent invasions of their privacy, but they are interesting. Their lives duplicate the lives of the original American settlers." *Moving Picture World* called the film "the true picture of Southern mountaineer conditions." But although crowds were said to be flocking to the Cameo Theatre to see *Stark Love* during its short run, it never did better than mediocre business in its national release. It died just the way Paramount figured it would, and the studio melted the prints. Apparently no copy of *Stark Love* survived in the United States. In the late 1960s Kevin Brownlow discovered one surviving 35mm print in Czechoslovakia, with Czechoslovakian subtitles, and this was copied in 16mm for the Museum of Modern Art and the Library of Congress in the early 1970s, with the subtitles retranslated into English.

I borrowed the Museum of Modern Art's copy of *Stark Love* and held a public showing on the campus of Appalachian State University in April 1990, and in July of that year it was shown twice again in Cherokee County, very near the Graham County locale where it was shot. Several hundred Graham County residents saw the movie at these three showings, several of them more than once, and many of them could name people they saw on the screen—their parents, grandparents, and neighbors. Although one man said conditions like that might have been common in the 1800s, they were not common in 1926, and although one woman said that women never did all the work, that survival was a partnership, public reaction from the Graham County audience was overwhelmingly positive. They simply chose to overlook any negative intent on the part of the filmmakers. One very elderly woman even confided to me later that the old men in the mountains "back in those days really were *like* that," and other local women especially seemed to approve of the essentially feminist perspective that Brown more or less stumbled into because of Helen Mundy's fierce power as the bought bride. The bottom line for most Graham Countians was that *Stark Love* was a very good movie that presented *them* to the rest of the world. Their lack of defensiveness is instructive. A student in my "Hollywood Appalachia" class, John O. Haynes, observed this about the showing of the movie in Boone:

> It seemed that the audience from Graham County all had a link to someone who had participated in the making of the film or were very familiar with it. I think that now, 64 years after *Stark Love* was made, the people there are still dazzled by the Hollywood producers who immortalized their county on film. Of course, the irony is that in 1926 the makers of *Stark Love* saw fit to portray the resident mountaineers as primitive and lazy. The audience witnessed a man ask another man for his daughter and then practically rape her, and they

took it completely in stride. They seemed detached from the symbolic meaning but submerged in the glamour of being on the screen. This shows the *endearing* impact the medium of film has on people.

## Tol'able Alvin: *Sergeant York*

He was fighting in a sanctified cause and so his soul is at peace.
—George Pattullo, describing Alvin York in the *Saturday Evening Post*

Moses with a blue tick.
—Randy Crutchfield

Before, throughout, and beyond World War I, the American mass public was swept by exaggerated fears of foreigners—as demonstrated by the great Red Scare of 1919, for example, along with mass arrests of people with funny names and weird philosophies. In the face of these largely imagined threats, the mama's-boy movie heroes, especially the overtly mountain ones, served partly as comforting projections of Anglo-Saxon strength and solidarity (*Stark Love* being the decided exception). Since the 1880s, the mass-circulation middle-class American magazines had promoted endlessly the firm belief that southern mountain people were genetically *pure* Anglo-Saxon stock. In other words, southern mountaineers were perfect and already well-formed symbols ready to march in the mass-media parade against degenerate Huns (*Kaiser Wilhelm—The Beast of Berlin* was a popular movie serial during World War I).

It's an interesting coincidence that at the very time American urban mass culture was being introduced to mountain mama's boys by way of Barthelmess and company, a *real* Tennessee mountain boy, Alvin York, had indeed become America's greatest war hero. York, who performed "the most remarkable individual feat of fighting" in World War I, was as improbable a case of cornered adolescence as David Kinemon. Eventually, the movie about his life would produce an even greater patriotic glow.

On 8 October 1918, a month before the end of World War I, Corp. Alvin York and seven privates were advancing on a German position in the Argonne. Suddenly they found themselves facing—and pinned down by—an entire machine gun battalion. (The machine gun was one of the more baleful technological "improvements" of World War I, along with tanks and planes; machine guns were capable of spewing 450 rounds per minute.) Against such fire from three sides, York nevertheless managed by sharpshooting to kill 20 Germans, put 35 machine guns out of action, and take 132 German prisoners, earning for himself the Congressional Medal of Honor, America's highest military decoration. By the time the American people heard his name, he had been promoted and would be forever remembered as Sergeant York.

Outside the American Expeditionary Force (AEF), in whose ranks York's geometrical feats of warfare were not, as a matter of fact, all that uncommon, his performance in the Argonne remained totally unknown to most Americans for months. York spent the winter after the armistice (1918–19) performing "Christian service" for the army and showing up in French towns to receive decorations from various mayors. He was particularly devoted to the Christian service. For six weeks he and the division chaplain conducted prayer meetings with small groups of soldiers that actually sparked a boomlet revival through the 328th Infantry. York became choir leader at the swelling services. But on Christmas Day, 1918, York was detailed to Paris, where President Woodrow Wilson was in residence for the peace talks. York was to be "received" by the president, but this disastrous day hurt his feelings. York was primarily a husky and gregarious redheaded country blurter. He was ushered in to meet Wilson, who was for his part a very cold fish, a pained university intellectual, the epitome of American refinement at the time. And, as it turned out, a cruel host. According to historian David Lee, "Wilson cared little for soldiers of any rank or achievement, so York was politely dismissed after a few moments of bland conversation. . . . At no time during the day did Wilson or anyone else offer [York] a bite of Christmas dinner."

After *Saturday Evening Post* reporter George Pattullo finally stumbled on the York story in the early months of 1919 and realized what a scoop he had for American readers, he staked the *Post*'s exclusive claim to the story. He approached Gen. John J. Pershing's chief of intelligence, Gen. Dennis E. Nolan, for help in tightening army censorship about York's feat to prevent the story's leaking out to other American publications. By 1919 the *Post* had a circulation in excess of two million, the largest in the world, and "was probably the nation's most influential periodical," according to Lee. It was already famous for peddling Norman Rockwell's sentimentalized, soft-focus portraits of Americana. But Pattullo faced a potential problem with General Pershing. Although Pershing was not adverse to publicity for his army, he did not want to see York singled out. Alvin had been a reluctant soldier, after all, a conscientious objector. York's own commanding officer, Capt. E. C. B. Danforth Jr., had previously passed York over for promotion to sergeant because of it: "The Captain could not see his way to promoting a man with his ideas," Pattullo reported. And Pershing himself preferred that the publicity go to an army professional, a career man like Sgt. Samuel Woodfill, who had singlehandedly silenced five machine gun nests just four days after York's feat.

But General Nolan helped Pattullo keep a lid on the York story behind Pershing's back. The *Saturday Evening Post* got its scoop on 26 April 1919, under the title "The Second Elder Gives Battle." It created a sensation across the nation. In many ways, just like *Tol'able David* two years later, the story offered a vision of America as a cornered adolescent that was every bit the match for the meanest bullies on the block.

The "second elder" of Pattullo's title referred to York's status in the Church of Christ and Christian Union back in Pall Mall, Fentress County, Tennessee. And religion, incidentally, gave Pattullo his chief improbability in the story of Tol'able Alvin: York's Christian piety had made a virtue of turning the other cheek. But there was no cause for worry; religion may have been a drag on Alvin York (like David Kinemon's mama clinging to him in the barnyard), but York was still at heart and truly to the marrow of his bones an all-American boy: he had the gonads to fight like a man. According to Pattullo: "[Before he got religion] he frankly . . . went blithely along the road so many red-blooded youngsters have traveled. He had many a bout with John Barleycorn, settled many an argument after the fashion of mountain men—and he was no slouch at stud poker, either." Basic *cojones*, uninitiated as yet in the new arena of the high calling of war. But this roisterer got religion, and his religion said it is wrong to fight and kill. Christian humility proscribes it. However, practical reality, the harsh Facts of Existence, the Law of Nature that sets up a less-than-ideal democracy, demands it sometimes. War was the will of a stern God who luckily thought the same way as, say, Theodore Roosevelt did. Captain Danforth finally convinced York of the necessity of wartime killing by reading to him from the thirty-third chapter of Ezekiel:

> Son of man, speak to the children of my people, and say unto them, When I bring the sword upon a land, if the people of the land take a man of their coasts, and set him for their watchman; If when he seeth the sword come upon the land, he blow the trumpet, and warn the people; Then whosoever heareth the sound of the trumpet, and taketh not warning; if the sword come, and take him away, his blood shall be upon his own head. . . . But if the watchman see the sword come, and blow not the trumpet, and the people be not warned; if the sword come, and take any person from among them, he is taken away in his iniquity; but his blood will I require at the watchman's hand.

The stand-up, knock-down, but redeemed and sanctified former stud poker player of the Kentucky-border blind tigers discovered that his whole natural life had been essential training for the work of the watchman. The older Yahweh of the chariot was calling him. Pattullo wrote: "Once his conscience was at ease the second elder went in for fighting in earnest—and he surely did one fine job."

By the time his return boat docked in Hoboken on 22 May 1919, every American knew Alvin York's name, and most worshiped the idea of him, the paradoxical improbability of it all. He was given a ticker-tape parade through New York City, put up at the Waldorf-Astoria, feted first by New York and then by Washington society (but characteristically, he was invited to the White House while Wilson wasn't at home), displayed before Congress, and featured in June in a Kinogram newsreel that proclaimed him "the greatest hero of any war in the annals of history. The Tennessean mountaineer, who not until his captain and the major of his battalion established to his understanding by the reading of the Scripture that he was justified in trying to kill the enemy did he go into battle as a business. Pictures are shown of his mountain home in Tennessee."

Justified killing was the business of the certified mountain mama's boy, and it might have made York's fortune as it made Barthelmess's. Monetary offers poured in, including a bid of $50,000 from Hollywood producer Jesse Lasky for the right to make the movie version of York's life. (It would take another twenty-one years for Lasky to talk York into that movie.) According to David Lee, York rejected almost all the blandishments, such as the *New York Herald*'s offer of $10,000 for a single article on his experiences in France. A theatrical company offered him $52,000 for a year's worth of vaudeville appearances, and another newspaper offered him $1,500 a week to write a personal column for 104 weeks. Similar propositions tumbled in at the rate of fifty to seventy-five a week, eventually totaling between a quarter- and a half-million dollars of unrealized revenue.

The theatrical schemes and the movie offer from Lasky were too strange even to contemplate: "I'd look silly in tights," was York's joking remark, which "covered a real fear of being exploited or made ridiculous," according to Lee. Too, York really did believe that making money on his wartime actions would be like Judas taking his thirty pieces of silver. He had, after all, grown up in Fentress County "valuing land or guns or character above money. To York, money was simply another tool, like a rifle or a hoe, that was used for a purpose but not sought for its own sake. Never rich, he had always gotten by, and the prospect of substantial wealth meant little to him." But because he also had his dreams and ambitions—in particular, he wanted to start a school for boys in Fentress County—he found that it made sense to take to the lecture circuit, and he did promote some brand names if they were products he had actually used.

Sometimes his endorsements were amusingly backhanded. For example, in 1920 he authorized the publication of the following statement: "My mother has used in our family for years, Thedford's Black Draught for torpid liver, stomach trouble, headache and other troubles . . . and we, when children, dared not complain unless we wanted to be dosed with [it]." The funny honesty of that testimonial, with its prominent mention of "my mother" as a banner and a benchmark, is significant for the way it fits the formula of the mama's boy. And the makers of Thedford's Black Draught visualized that very concept in their newspaper ads: there was Alvin York framed by soldierly and patriotic bric-a-brac, like a sainted icon, with his wife as an attendant cameo on the left and, even more important, his mama on the right (Fig. 7.5).

York's devotion to his mama was already legendary. He had attempted to reach her by telephone when he first got home to the States and

Figure 7.5. Ad for Thedford's Black Draught showing Alvin York as iconic hero, flanked by his female saints. (Courtesy of Tennessee State Library)

expressed his frustration at failing. (The movie *Sergeant York* makes this telephone call successful, and it provides one of the big emotional payoff scenes in the movie.) On the last leg of his trip from France to Pall Mall, at a stopover in Knoxville, he had told a large crowd of well-wishers, "I want to go home and see my mother first of all." Though Mother York had only a brief mention in Pattullo's article, it was clear nevertheless that she occupied a special saintlike position in Alvin's heart. She was religious authority, history, philosophy—the symbol of home and goodness that Alvin finally realized he was divinely sanctioned to fight for. It was due to her influence that his soul was saved both in the first place and in the last place.

Also at work in the York legend, and keeping him symbolically adolescent in the public mind, was his connection to a southern mountain "culture" that could be viewed as essentially and psychologically immature. Though Pattullo went somewhat out of his way to say that hillbilly was *not* the right definition for York, he nevertheless could not quite prevent himself from seeing the Tennessee mountaineer as an unspoiled child of nature. "He seems to do everything correctly by intuition," Pattullo wrote. As a matter of fact, York often resented his treatment by others, both in France and later back home while he was on display as a kind of overgrown babe of the backwoods, "a child of the mountains" who miraculously did the right thing when no one expected he could.

In reality, of course, he was no child. He was thirty-one when he picked off those twenty German gobblers. And he was, in point of fact, a mountain "modernizer," a follower and advocate of "progress" in the contemporary world, as Lee explains: "Far from working to preserve an agrarian Appalachia, York struggled to bring industrialization and modernization to the mountains, but the irony of this escaped his biographers." Those biographers—Samuel K. Cowan and Thomas Skeyhill—were, like Pattullo, intent on feeding the established expectations that York fit the mold of an American throwback, the unsophisticated yet instinctual child of nature, the good American boy whose initiation into manhood assumed patriotic dimensions. In fact, this idea was too important a rallying symbol to be spoiled by dragging a lot of controverting fact into view. Instead, Cowan said York had in his veins the blood of the "purest Anglo-Saxons to be found today," and Skeyhill subtitled his children's version of York's story *Last of the Long Hunters*, giving York a totemic crown of coonskin (which the movie version also did, making three explicit references to Daniel Boone).

All that remained to cement Alvin York forever in American mythology as the improbable boy-initiate was a movie deal. The catalyst that finally got York's signature on Lasky's Hollywood contract in 1940 was the behavior of Germany and Japan in the late 1930s. Many people saw World War II coming. It didn't take special insight. Japan invaded China in 1937, and Germany invaded Poland in 1939. Yet there was a strong isolationist movement in this country—"America First!"—that loudly remembered World War I as a waste and a mistake. Led by the likes of that other boy-hero, Charles Lindbergh, the America-Firsters said the United States had been duped by unscrupulous Europeans into joining the fray in World War I, and they were by God determined it wasn't going to happen again. Asked what he thought of Lindbergh's views, York the reformed pacifist warned, "[A]fter [Japan] conquers [China] it is going to come over here. I'd just as soon we got into it now as later," and then he added, "I believe if we want to stop Hitler we must knock him off the block."

So York was already primed for image seduction when movie-producer-now-down-on-his-luck Jesse Lasky approached him once more about a movie deal in 1940. Lasky told York he wanted to discuss "a historical document of vital importance to the country in these troubled times." York knew very well that the "document" was to be a film biography, but with world events tending as they were, York could now think of a movie script as Godly writ in service to his country. He agreed to meet with Lasky in Crossville, Tennessee, in early March 1940.

York's decision was prompted in part by the York Agricultural Institute, the school he had founded, which was struggling right then, and he also had a new dream of a nondenominational Bible school. Lasky's renewed interest in a Sergeant York movie came at an opportune time; after listening to Lasky's proposal, York would not commit at once but first took Lasky on a tour of Fentress County, softening him up by showing him his Agricultural Institute and the site for the proposed new Bible school. York saw Lasky off the next day, only saying to reporters, "All I know about this movie job is that Mr. Lasky visited me . . . and left after making me an attractive offer which will not require a great deal of my time away from home."

However nominally "attractive" the offer was, the money wasn't quite right yet. Four days later Lasky was back. He invited York to a Nashville hotel, and York (like the untutored child of the mountains he was) brought his attorney with him. According to David Lee, Lasky initially offered $25,000, half of what he had estimated the worth of York's story at back in 1919. Apparently York did not agree that his value had depreciated so precipitously in the intervening years. But Lasky was not so flush as he had been earlier. He had been ousted from Paramount, the famous studio he had helped make rich, after producing a string of unsuccessful pictures; these were followed by an even more dreadful congregation of flops he made as an independent. Lately he had been reduced to producing radio programs. He needed a surefire comeback project, and he instinctively felt that the York story was it.

But York was amazingly stubborn, a mule-headed mountaineer when it came to money. For hours Lasky pleaded his poverty, and periodically, as the jawboning got intense, York would get up and leave Lasky's hotel room, vanishing off down the hallway. When Lasky's curiosity got the better of him and he followed, he found the sergeant kneeling in prayer. Exasperated, Lasky broke off negotiations and returned to Hollywood to brood about the deal that now appeared to have the Protestant Jehovah as a third party. Outnumbered and outgunned, he returned to Tennessee a week later to accept York's terms: $50,000 up front and 2 percent of the gross, a figure that Lasky estimated to mean roughly $100,000. More amazing, York also had ironclad script and cast approval, conditions unheard of in standard Hollywood contracts of the day.

As proof of good faith, Lasky gave York a downpayment of $25,000 with a postdated check, then rushed to borrow against his life insurance to cover it, meanwhile scrambling around Hollywood trying to find a studio to back him. The balance on the initial $50,000 was due to York in sixty days. Warner Brothers showed some interest in the film and said they'd consider it if Lasky lined up the star and a suitable director. Lasky invited Howard Hawks to direct. When Hawks, famous already for *His Girl Friday, Only Angels Have Wings, Bringing Up Baby, Road to Glory, Barbary Coast,* and *Twentieth Century,* signed a contract, Warner Brothers accepted the project readily, and Lasky was finally rolling in the dough.

From the beginning, Lasky had imagined Gary Cooper in the title role. As soon as he had York's signature on that contract, he had composed and sent the following telegram to Cooper from Crossville, signing York's name to its contents—perhaps with York's consent: "I have just agreed to let the motion picture producer Jesse L. Lasky film the story of my life, subject to my approval of the star. I have great admiration for you as an actor and as a man, and I would be honored, sir, to see you on the screen as myself." Though Cooper evidently believed that it had been York's idea, Lasky's ruse almost backfired. The more Cooper weighed the sincere expectations of the legendary man-child of Tennessee, still inconveniently alive and very much concerned about the accuracy of the finished film, the colder his feet got. He came to think that York "was too big for me, he covered too much territory. . . . Here was a pious, sincere man, a conscientious objector to war, who, when called, became a heroic fighter for his country," Cooper later wrote. He concluded reluctantly that "I couldn't handle it."

But Lasky had additional leverage. He had given Cooper his first break in the movies and now needed the favor returned. Lasky and

Hawks both cajoled until Cooper gave in. The last hurdle was getting Cooper released from his exclusive contract with MGM. Studio head Samuel Goldwyn, himself no slouch at negotiation, agreed to loan Cooper to Warner Brothers in exchange for the use of Warners' contract star Bette Davis in *The Little Foxes*. The deal was put in writing and signed by all parties in September 1940.

Though Cooper was obviously the right choice to play Alvin York, not all of Lasky's casting ideas were as inspired. He wanted Jane Russell for the part of York's sweetheart Gracie Williams (who would become his wife at the end of the film), but York and the real Gracie wanted no sultry painted Hollywood hussies playing that part. The Yorks insisted that the actress selected to play Gracie neither smoke nor drink nor wear ungodly makeup, a potentially tall order in Hollywood. But Warner Brothers promoted one of its own contract players, sixteen-year-old ingenue Joan Leslie, about whom there were no salacious rumors, and the Yorks were mollified. Cooper and Leslie would be joined in the cast by Walter Brennan as Pastor Pile and by the great Margaret Wycherly as the pivotal Mother York. These major players were backed by a veritable platoon of Hollywood's best character actors, including George Tobias, Ward Bond, Noah Beery Jr., June Lockhart, and little Dickie Moore (formerly of *The Little Rascals*) as Alvin's brother George, among a host of other speaking parts.

York demanded accuracy, and that's what Warner Brothers, following its own lights, attempted to deliver. The studio was determined to portray and name real York family members, friends, and fellow soldiers in the 328th Infantry, an aim that involved tracking them all down to sign releases and to accept token payment. Warners convinced ten members of York's former squad to accept $250 apiece. Family and neighbors in Fentress County were tougher negotiators in some cases, one of them wrangling as much as $1,500 for his cooperation. But there was one notable hold-out—Gracie Williams's father—who was subsequently deleted from the script.

Lasky, along with a cameraman and two writers, made a weeklong trip to Pall Mall and its neighborhoods for background and research. They interviewed two hundred people, took pictures, witnessed a sharpshooters' match. Then they went back to Hollywood and constructed an elaborate series of 123 studio sets (a record number, to go with the

Figure 7.6. Gary Cooper meeting with Alvin York before the filming of *Sergeant York*. (Courtesy of *Now and Then*, Center for Appalachian Studies and Services, East Tennessee State University)

near record number of speaking parts), including a forty-foot mountain on a turntable that could show sixteen different faces of rock and soil and 121 live trees. So although Sergeant York may have gotten a form of accuracy, the movie audiences certainly didn't get reality. These Tennessee mountains were abstractions of the art director's romantic imaginings of where the adolescent soul of America ought to be living in 1918—let alone 1941.

The film premiered in New York City on 2 July 1941, a scant five months before Pearl Harbor, with Alvin York and party in attendance. The enthusiastic audience gave him a fifteen-minute ovation after the show. Asked to say a few words, York replied modestly that he hoped the film would contribute to "national unity in this hour of danger," when "millions of Americans, like myself, must be facing the same questions, the same uncertainties, which we faced and I believe resolved for the right some twenty-four years ago."

At the film's Washington premier several weeks later, York, Lasky, and

Gary Cooper were all received at the White House by President Franklin Roosevelt, and a very different reception it was from the last time York had been hauled in to meet his commander-in-chief. Roosevelt told York he had been "really thrilled" by the movie. "The picture comes at a good time," Roosevelt continued, and then added piously: "I didn't like that part of it showing so much killing. I guess you felt that way too." It was a cynical and calculating presidential film review. Roosevelt's foreign policy had been openly pro-British and anti-German in dealing with the war already building in Europe, and his bellicosity had earned him enemies in the America First movement and in the U.S. Congress. *Sergeant York* was the best propaganda he could ask for, delivering the punchy message of visceral initiation into blameless American manhood.

Roosevelt's leading congressional enemy, North Dakota senator Gerald P. Nye, put his finger on the irony of the president's enthusiasm for *Sergeant York*. Speaking to an America First rally in St. Louis, Nye said, "The movies have ceased to be an instrument of entertainment [and instead are now] operating as war propaganda machines almost as if they were directed from a single central bureau." Nye was darkly alluding to the president himself as a kind of thought-control dictator. Referring to Roosevelt's oft-quoted comment to York about not liking "so much killing," Nye said it was curious that a man so squeamish about death in a Hollywood film nevertheless seemed delighted to have the American people roused emotionally to scream for war with Germany.

A good portion of the movie's emotional impact came from music director Max Steiner's cunning blend of patriotic airs and Baptist hymns. The music that plays as the credits roll is sufficient by itself to make us weak-kneed: Steiner's rich symphonic syrup of "America the Beautiful" blending into "Give Me That Old-Time Religion," "Beulah Land" leading directly into "My Country, 'Tis of Thee." The music conveyed the subliminal doctrine that the religion of America is and shall be patriotism.

Also contributing to *Sergeant York*'s impact was the comfortable believability of the actors, primarily Gary Cooper in the title role and Margaret Wycherly as his mother. Wycherly was a British-born actress well known on the American stage but not in movies. She had been in *The Thirteenth Chair* back in 1929 and didn't appear on the screen again until *Sergeant York*. Though the sets were fake, Cooper and Wycherly and what they represented seemed as actual and as palpable as dawn, and as common and unremarkable too—in other words, wholly representative (which is the key to our surprise and pleasure when this mama's boy rises to action in a wholly unrepresentative crisis). Mother York is a rock, yet her stolid gaze in the scene where she has to part with her big-boned baby boy so he can go off to war has been known to choke tears out of automobile repossessors.

Though tiny in stature, she is as strong a mother as Tol'able David's. Early in the film, she sends brother George to bring Alvin home, drunk and at gunpoint, from saloons on the Kaintuck border. Alvin and his friends have been drinking toasts to never getting sober again. When his little brother George enters the saloon and pronounces laconically, "Alvin, Ma wants you," a loudmouthed drunk bellows in derision, "His *ma-a-a-a* wants 'im!" and it is important for Alvin York's inclusion in the mama's-boy syndrome that this blaspheming of his mother gets his dukes up. A satisfying chair-flinging, window-smashing, table-collapsing fight ensues, with player piano going madly along. After Alvin wins the fight and is banging the abuser of ma-hood's head against the Tennessee side of the blind tiger's floor, little brother George repeats his message with the same neutral intonation, "Alvin, Ma wants you."

Alvin, who has evidently been forced home in this condition before, stands outside the York cabin trying to sober up, while his ma watches him with those big, frank, enigmatically sad eyes of hers. "Fetch me a pail of water, George," she says with resignation, and Alvin takes off his hat quickly and pulls up his collar for the dousing he knows is coming and knows he deserves. Mother York dumps a bucketful on him because he's still her boy, and he needs correction; he takes the punishment because he accepts his status as boy. Against her he does not rebel, and she loves him dearly. After the dousing, she immediately serves him breakfast, proudly offers him salt for his pone (she'd been "plumb out of salt" but traded eggs for it), and smiles at him with nurturing warmth. How could we not cherish the idea of Alvin York's ma?

She sews the seat of his pants while he bends over obediently in front of her, a big gawky boy. Ironically, he wants his pants stitched because he's going to call on Gracie Williams. He asks his ma for the family history, against which he must now measure himself:

*He*: Ma, when you and Pa got hitched, what did Pa have to set up with?

*She*: Well, he had this here farm and a mule and five—no, six—dogs.

*He*: What did Grandpa have?

*She*: Your grandpa had this here farm, pair of horses—the mare was in foal.

If anything, the men of the York family have come down in the world, a fact that soon begins to eat at Alvin York. He tells his ma he's aiming to get married to Gracie. A dark cloud crosses her face, and Alvin notices: "What's the matter?" She replies, "I ain't said nothing," but her eyes have said a great deal, and we soon learn that it's the relative poverty of the York family compared to the relative wealth of the Williamses that worries her for Alvin's sake. There is such a thing as class differences in these mountains.

Alvin goes calling at Gracie Williams's house and has a run-in with rival suitor Zeb Andrews (played by Robert Porterfield, founder of the Barter Theater in Abingdon, Virginia). Zeb's family owns good bottom-land, and Zeb, at least, thinks of himself as being of a clearly superior social class. He says he figures to get sixty bushels of corn an acre, compared to Alvin's twenty bushels from the York's poor scrub. Zeb mocks all of Alvin's opinions, but Alvin won't take this. Behind Miss Gracie's back and off-camera, Alvin gives Zeb a walloping and sends him hobbling back home. Any audience is pleased by the demonstration of York bravado. But Gracie Williams is outraged (like most women in these fictional worlds, she is set up as a governor over the "natural" in men). She considers fisticuffs *boy* stuff, and she stamps her foot at Alvin's behavior: "You ain't fitten to come visit a girl! . . . I wouldn't have you on a Christmas tree, Alvin York! . . . A fine husband you'd make!" She doesn't mean any of it, but Alvin thinks she does. He argues with her: "Zeb Andrews has a piece of bottomland. *That's* it, ain't it?" This only exasperates her more, for she already loves the big dumb lug and doesn't care at all about bottomland and who has it and who doesn't.

On his way home from Gracie's, Alvin picks up a fistful of good creek-side soil and stares at it, then takes it home. At the cabin his mother is sitting up late, sewing. Alvin puts the fistful of dirt in a plate and studies it. Mother York looks at it, too (Fig. 7.7). Her instinct has been right:

Figure 7.7. "That there's bottomland soil, ain't it?": Gary Cooper and Margaret Wycherly in *Sergeant York*. (Courtesy of Wisconsin Center for Film and Theater Research)

"That there's bottomland soil, ain't it?" When he nods that it is, she goes on: "Queer how folks that lives on the bottom looks down on the folks on the top. Were always that way. Ain't no changing it." Bearer of history, philosophy, and now political science, Ma York explains the workings of class and land ownership. But something new rises in Alvin, a manly resolve to do something about it:

> *He*: Well, I'm a-goin' to change it. I'm going to get us a piece of bottomland.
>
> *She*: Your pa set out to get hisself a piece of bottomland once. Nary a man ever tried harder. Liked to kill hisself a-tryin. It was a long time before he give up, but he had to in the end.
>
> *He*: I know where there's a piece of bottomland, and I'm a-goin' to get it!

She looks at him, her face lightening, the cloud lifting, and she smiles. "Maybe you will," she answers. She admires and loves his spirit, but like David Kinemon's ma, she will not—cannot—actively help it bust loose.

Figure 7.8. Gary Cooper, as Alvin York, gets right with God after being struck by lightning. (Courtesy of Wisconsin Center for Film and Theater Research)

And of course he doesn't get his bottomland, though he works like a slave to raise the money. He falls into bed every night exhausted. One evening Mother York gets up and covers him and then pauses to pray: "Lord . . . Lord, if You can, help him to be a-gettin' his land. Amen." But the Lord works in mysterious ways. First, Alvin must be cheated out of his bottomland because old Nate Tompkins, who promised to sell it to him, doesn't keep his word. The land is sold instead to archrival Zeb Andrews. York, in despair, goes on a bender to the Kaintuck border, and in his cups he determines that he must kill Nate Tompkins to satisfy his honor. He sets out on his mule in a thunderstorm to do what he knows any man would do: avenge a grievous, soul-stabbing wrong. But like Saul going to Damascus, he's struck down on the road by a lightning bolt, his rifle split and bent symbolically. God does not want him wasting his initiation into manhood on old Nate Tompkins when there's a whole continent of Germans that'll be needing some trim, although Alvin doesn't know about that yet. God leads him, stumbling, out of the storm and into church. He walks in with his hat in his hand, dripping wet, and to

Figure 7.9. "Moses with a blue tick": Alvin York goes to the (fake) mountain-top to unify his obligations to God/country. (Courtesy of Wisconsin Center for Film and Theater Research)

the congregation's enthusiastic singing of "Give Me That Old-Time Religion," he converts, reforms, turns around, is born again (Fig. 7.8).

He self-consciously sets out to ask forgiveness of those he feels he has wronged, Old Nate and young Zeb Andrews, and he is settling down to teach Sunday School ("Blessed air the peacemakers," he tells the children), when the message comes galloping in from "Jim-Town" (Jamestown, the county seat) that the president has declared war on Germany and its allies. Men are to be drafted for the cause. Most of the boys down at Pastor Pile's store are shown volunteering, not waiting to be drafted. But it is Alvin's destiny always to go down hard: "The Book's agin killin'," and I follow the Book," he says.

He refuses to register for the draft, and a struggle commences. First Alvin applies for and is denied exemption for conscientious objector status. Then, in basic training at Camp Gordon in Georgia, he is singled out for hazing by his sergeant (to whom "conscientious objector" means goldbricker) and preached at by his captain and his major. He's proved himself a model soldier, a master sharpshooter on the firing range, and a natural leader of men, and the major wants to promote him to corporal, but York says he'd rather not be promoted because he just isn't comfortable with what the army ultimately wants him to do. The captain quotes scripture (though, in the movie, it is never Ezekiel as in the *Saturday Evening Post* account), but Alvin quotes it right back at him and tops him every time. Then the major tries a different tack. He hands Alvin a history of the United States of America—the other and mightier Bible in this piece of propaganda—and grants him a furlough to go back home, to read the book and to try to get his head straight.

In filming York's climactic visit home to the everlasting hills, the Warner people made full use of that forty-foot studio mountain with its sixteen faces and 121 live trees. The anointed one (York) goes to the mountaintop and listens for the still, small voice of the Lord (Fig. 7.9). Instead, he hears Max Steiner's swelling symphonic religio-patriotism ("Beulah Land" flowing seamlessly into "My Country, 'Tis of Thee") and the conflicting voice-over layering of Pastor Pile on the one hand ("Them that live by the sword will be perishing by the sword") and Major Buxton on the other ("Defend your country!"). The voices speak faster and faster, with Pastor Pile's "God" being jostled by Major Buxton's "country"—"your God . . . your country . . . your God . . . your country"—until they actually mesh, becoming in effect one and the same ("Godcountry . . . Godcountry . . . Godcountry") and penetrating Alvin's doctrinal armor. A soft breeze then blows open the pages of Alvin's Bible to a passage that Gary Cooper thoughtfully reads aloud as only Gary Cooper could do it: "Render therefore unto Caesar the things that *air* Caesar's and unto God the things that *air* God's." York has his sign, the divine dispensation to go and kill without blame for his Godcountry.

The mama's boy kills and returns innocent to his ma's embrace. As York checks into the Waldorf-Astoria at the end of the movie, he discovers that his fancy city hosts have put a picture of his ma in the hotel room and that, lo and behold, they've gotten Fentress County on the telephone line, too. He talks first to his ma and then to Gracie Williams, the female attendant saints who always frame the mountain mama's boy in his initiation.

Percentage change,

since 1991, in the cir-

culation of *Women and

Guns Magazine*: +50

— *Harper's* Index,

April 1993, p. 11

 **Hillbilly Gals**

If a hillbilly is a democrat, then hillbillyland grants extraordinary equality to women. At times. A few mountain women in the earliest silent movies were known to pick up a gun and shoot it, too, and some would cross-dress and go about successfully as men, at least temporarily. Strong backwoods women with weapons have regularly appeared in movies ever since, fighting back against whatever threatened them—with guns especially. Never mind for the moment how such women typically ended up in those movies. Most important for now is that in at least a scene or two, or in a series of scenes, or oc-casionally through a whole scenario, *they fought back*, sometimes to good effect. I think of these appearances as a glimpse of the same democracy of violence that men have always assumed for themselves: equal freedom possessed at physical hazard.

But the democracy of violence is not the only democracy open to hillbilly women in the movies. An implied equality of fellow-feeling, however ironic, also resides in the democracy of victimization. Especially following LBJ's War on Poverty in the 1960s, Appalachian (or "mountain" or "hillbilly") women have often been depicted as sympathetic victims of unjust power, no matter who or what these movies ultimately blame for the inequality and no matter what absurd and hurtful ends our sympathy drives us to.

And finally, the democracy of sexuality found its hillbilly fulfillment in Blaze Starr, the stripper from West Virginia who made a fool out of the governor of Louisiana. Dolly Parton, interestingly, continues in a different way that tradition of the boundary-crossing hillbilly female. Her sexual authority is twinned with an irrepressible backwoods uppitiness, the willful assumption of equal status. And what's a democrat, if she don't backtalk with a backwoods twang?

## The *Thunder Road* of Feminism

Only lately have we witnessed the arrival of Thelma and Louise, who should have been there in movies all along, as they were there in life. *Thelma and Louise* (Percy Main Productions/MGM-Pathé, 1991) roused the spirits of both sexes—but especially of women—in the best democratic tradition of making Americans root for the underdog. The movie packs an emotional wallop, along with enough hillbilly gal defiance that the Donald Wildmons of this world felt inspired to condemn it as Satan's own plot against goodness and radio windbag ego-artist Rush Limbaugh denounced it as "femi-Nazi" propaganda. The fear of female freedom victimizes men and women. But countering this powerful backlash are the improbable Thelma and Louise, who can't, as a matter of fact, win, but who look so good in trying. The pair's concluding gesture of sailing out into space in Louise's mint-green 1966 Thunderbird convertible transcends their actual defeat in the manner of all great tragedy. Death represents freedom from a power that cannot be outrun, whether it be the gods or fate or the entire state police of

Arkansas, Oklahoma, and New Mexico. "You get what you settle for," Louise says, and these two women ultimately won't settle for anything less than taking a flying leap. They want it all, or nothing.

Louise is played by weary veteran Susan Sarandon, who should have won the Best Actress Oscar in that year and in every year. She plays an unmarried waitress in Arkansas, tough and resilient (both Louise and the locale). Her buddy Thelma is played by Geena Davis, a willow to Louise's oak, a young married woman who has bent more easily to the economic winds of middle-class suburban Arkansas housewifery, putting up with traditional domination by a frustrated (because he's self-centered) petty tyrant of a husband named Darryl. But this willow is surprisingly resilient, too. In fact, the story is set in motion by her defiance. Thelma doesn't ask Darryl if she can go away for the weekend with Louise; she just leaves, taping a note for him to the microwave.

Thelma and Louise take off for "the mountains," an updated psychic hillbillyland traveled by Jesse James and Luke Doolin in earlier years—a behavioral periphery of drink, rebellion, and outlawry, but also the last surviving bastion of the small-*d* democrat, the place of equal freedom. The very first image on the screen is that of a beautiful but vaguely disturbing rural landscape, seen first in black and white and then gradually in color. A country road leads straight ahead from the foreground into unforested, clean-shaven hills, above which float white, puffy clouds. Clearly a symbolic place, this "West." Wesley Saylors saw the transformation from black and white to color in this opening shot as signifying a blossoming or a magical beginning—an interpretation that fits well with what happens to the Geena Davis character—but undercutting any positive sign in this scenic shot is Hans Zimmer's soundtrack, low and darksome Dobro and bass subverting any sunny pleasure we might feel in this apparently decorative image of Americana. The unnatural black and white, the innocent-looking road disappearing behind the deceptively pleasant saddle of hills, the deep shadows on the road: all convey the ambiguity of this freedom. Near the end of the movie, this same landscape reappears, only now the trapped and cornered Thelma and Louise are speeding down the pleasant road toward their final destiny in those mountains. In such a place, on psychological hilly ground and under the spell and threat of equal freedom, Thelma will grow, Thelma will blossom, Thelma will take charge. The hopelessly trapped housewife and gullible prey of men will become a gun-wielding sibyl imparting useful secrets to the dominant sex.

The first recipient of Thelma's new-found assertiveness is the trig highway patrolman who stops them in New Mexico for speeding, a cocky strutter whom Louise immediately identifies as "a Nazi." While he's writing up Louise for going 110 mph, and just as he's about to radio in to headquarters, Thelma, *Thelma*, puts her gun to his head and sweetly requests that he drop the radio and put his hands on the steering wheel, then that he get out of the car and into the trunk. To help him comply, Louise shoots out two radios, and Thelma thoughtfully plugs the turtle for air vents. With guns going off around him, the patrolman's demeanor crumbles. He blubbers: "Please don't shoot me. I have a wife and kids." Thelma, as armed equalizer, replies: "Well, you be sweet to them, especially your wife. My husband wasn't sweet to me. Look how I turned out."

Later the two of them teach a sleazebag trucker the lesson of his life. This road hog with nudies-in-chrome on his mudflaps has harassed them several times in a game of cross-country tag, wiggling his tongue at them and pointing at his crotch. It's Thelma's idea to put a stop to it. She decoys him off the road, and Louise, after lecturing him about his repulsive behavior, demands an apology. He declares he's not apologizing to *anybody* and calls her bitch (which is a disrespectful thing to say). Louise shoots out his tires, but Thelma one-ups her by hitting the gas tank and blowing the shiny long phallic truck all to hell and gone. Thelma will never be the victim again.

But she has been the victim before, and very recently. She and Louise aren't an hour out of town on their fishing vacation when she talks Louise into stopping for a drink. It's the fateful turn in this tragedy of free will. Inside the Silver Bullet saloon, Harlan the honky-tonk stud immediately zeroes in on Thelma as fair prey; he buys her drinks and dances her around the floor, his Rambo arm not merely encircling her but holding her in a virtual headlock. She's having a good time, but she's getting drunk. Harlan twirls her around and around to the Western swing until she gets sick. Saying, "You need some fresh air, little lady," he takes her to the parking lot, where he immediately starts pawing her, pushing up her skirt, claiming that he just wants to kiss her, that he won't hurt her. She tells him no, to stop it, and she tries first to push him away, then to walk away herself. He stops her with that arm of his, and she fights back with a slap. This sends him into a violent rage. He hits her several times hard across the mouth, which stuns her. He has her bent over a parked car, his pants open, and clearly he means to rape her, but into the frame comes a gun, its barrel pushed against his neck, and we hear Louise's voice telling him to let Thelma go or his brains will be splattered "all over this nice car"; as the camera moves back, we see that she has the know-how to do that very thing. Thelma gets away. With some effort, Louise controls her anger and tells Harlan, "In the future, when a woman's crying like that, she isn't having any *fun*." She turns to leave, both women walking away free of him, when Harlan, by now a badly humiliated and frustrated two-stepper, shouts, "Bitch! I should have gone ahead and fucked her!" Louise stops and turns around: "What did you say?" He replies, "I said *suck my cock!*" And she shoots him. Then she tells his corpse to watch its mouth in the future. Most audiences cheer, because her action feels like justice at a time when justice is subversive (and no wonder Limbaugh puffed up like a horny toad).

It's important to note that, immediately after the killing, Louise is not yet *running*. She's all poise and confidence with the gun. She saunters away from Harlan's body. But when she gets into the mint-green Thunderbird with Thelma, she is beginning to realize that the law will call what she's done cold-blooded murder, and then she drives like hell, and drives and drives.

Louise has been here before, when she did not have the equalizer in her hands. Something—we never know exactly what, but something bad, a rape probably—once happened to her in Texas, so she drives the long way around that state from Arkansas to get to Mexico. "Look, you shoot off a guy's head with his pants down—believe me, Texas is *not* a place you want to get caught," she tells Thelma. "Just *trust me.*" With the power and gumption finally to fight the Harlans of the world, she takes a stand and becomes not only Thelma's custodian but also Thelma's role model, for soon it will be Louise who crumbles, who loses that poise and that confidence, and Thelma who rises and takes Louise's place in the vanguard.

In shooting Harlan, Louise refuses victimhood—for herself in retrospect, for Thelma in the present, for all women from now on. Shortly before the end of the movie, but before they know they've been cornered, Thelma says, "Something's crossed over in me, and I can't go back." A little later, when they are indeed cornered at the rim of what appears to be the Grand Canyon, Thelma, with tears of joy in her eyes, suggests they just "keep going" over the rim, making the only gesture of refusal still open to them, defying power even in death. Something crosses over in both of them. And through any audience there sweeps a wave of exhilarating identification. Many cry. Many applaud.

On the hillbilly highway, rough masculinity is the norm. But rough masculinity extends to more than just potential rapists in every honky-tonk, because this landscape is also the setting for the first real sexual fulfillment Thelma has ever experienced. This hillbillyland—as in the hillbillyland of the good old boys—is the only place left to get properly laid. At least that's the case for Thelma. And the message is that it's a good thing she's hightailed it onto this uneven ground, this hillbilly possibility, "Deep Shit, Arkansas." For Thelma, this life is better than life with Darryl (and all the talk-radio swagger and ultimate infidelity he stands for). Hillbillyland may be an uncomfortable place in many respects, but philosophically the only road to freedom leads through it.

But like all nature, hillbillyland is also ambiguously terrifying, still the free range of the Harlans of this world. In several highway scenes, director Ridley Scott and cinematographer Adrian Biddle photographed Thelma and Louise in the Thunderbird in dark, road-warrioresque landscapes dominated by black, bull-shouldered eighteen-wheelers, ominously pumping oil wells looming huge and black all around them —the machines, the systems, the apparently unconquerable power of man(un)kind. This is a tragedy, after all, the theatrical enactment of human vulnerability meant to make us *soar* (and also *sore*) in spirit.

A puzzling tic in this movie is a series of cryptic scenes inserted into the action: brief images of old rural faces that seem to watch enigmatically at various moments. The first of these takes place soon after the attack on Thelma and the killing of Harlan, while Thelma is still sniffling and wiping her bruised face. Cut to an old man's face with red, ruined eyes, an apparition of eerie waste. A little later, after the hitchhiking cowboy J. D. (Brad Pitt) has made good love to Thelma, given her a useful line for polite armed robbery, and then absconded with Louise's precious nest egg, Thelma, who is driving now while Louise grieves for her lost money, stops the car at a country store and enterprisingly robs it, using the technique she's learned from J. D. Meanwhile, Louise sits dejected and defeated in the Thunderbird. Two older women's faces suddenly appear on screen, framed in the window of a roadside house, seeming to watch Louise as she waits for Thelma. Louise looks up, sees she's being stared at. One of the two women staring is ambiguously in deep shadow, the other in very bright but equally ambiguous light, as though they are peering at Louise out of a different reality (potential reality?). Louise is self-conscious under their gaze; she fumbles with her lipstick as though these other eyes somehow judge her looks and know her secrets and condemn her. The camera moves dramatically in on the woman in light, framing a close-up of her fiercely expressionless, still face. One of her lips twitches, maybe with disdain. But as Louise looks at herself in the rearview mirror and puts the lipstick to her lips, she suddenly changes her mind and throws the lipstick away. She's crossed over.

The third inserted scene begins like the first two but develops into a complex scene in its own right. In the desert Southwest, where Thelma and Louise have stopped for water, an ancient man with a straw hat and a white goatee stares at Louise with kind and watery eyes, and she looks back at him, searching his face for signs. She goes over to him, stands before him, and says "Hi"; then she sits beside him and, without explanation, removes her rings (including the long-awaited but poorly timed diamond from Jimmy), her watch, and her earrings, and holds them out to the old man in her palm. This is alien junk now, another system's imposed schedule (the watch) and feminine role (the jewelry). The old man continues to stare kindly but uncomprehendingly, as though he might speak if he could. Cut to moments later: Thelma and Louise are driving off together. Louise has the old man's hat (an obvious gender marker to signify her achievement, a kind of coonskin-cap trophy). We know she's traded her watch and jewelry for it. But when Thelma asks her where she got it, and although we know very well that she bought it at great cost, Louise replies, "I stole it." And by her own sense of transformation she did.

These inserted elderly faces are more than mute and mysterious witnesses to the tragic passing of Thelma and Louise through the landscape. The two old women who watch Louise fumble with her lipstick are framed distinctly by a window in a home, under glass, where women are "supposed to be," passive, in reach, put to use—where Thelma's husband, the feckless Darryl, wants her all the time. The women become a mirror image of every woman's married possibility, the obedient and flightless trap. Ironically, this potential is what Louise has long been struggling to attain before her showdown with Harlan. In the very first images of her in the movie, she is serving food, wiping counters, as much a female servant as Thelma except she gets a salary plus tips. And much later we learn, in her scenes with Jimmy, that she has wanted in fact to marry him, that her motive in going off for the weekend with Thelma is to teach Jimmy a lesson.

The old women framed in the window are a mirror, and so are the old men, haunting visions of the male gender's ultimate human potentiality, decrepitude and rheumy eyes. The old man whose hat Louise acquires looks as though he has something to say, something to impart— a great wisdom perhaps, or a great apology.

In the history of hillbilly gals in the movies, *Thelma and Louise* is unique because in it, for the first time, the women are allowed the full implications of their egalitarian potential without being repossessed in every way by the close of the story. By sailing out into space and being held there in a freeze-frame, they effectively forestall any necessity of ever hitting the ground.

## Uppity Women: Seen but Not Heard

Although the earliest movie industry, the nickelodeon trade, liked to flirt with dangerous hillbilly women in film stories, the earliest silents never dared what *Thelma and Louise* proposes: a female duo who help and reinforce one another's bid for uncompromised freedom.

Isolated opportunities for what I think of as the democracy of violence were fairly plentiful for individual women. For example, in the final scene of the earliest known hillbilly movie and pioneer in the field, *The Moonshiner* (Biograph, 1904), the moonshiner's wife seizes a gun and shoots the lawman in the back, a display of wicked but invigorating potentiality that made early urban nickelodeon patrons cheer and call for more. And in *A Mountain Wife* (G. Melies, 1910), a hillbilly woman "does something that requires pluck and determination—she makes [a revenue officer] mount a horse and straddling another, she compels him at pistol point to ride." *The Little Moonshiner* (Nestor, 1912) featured a hillbilly daughter who quite competently takes over the family moonshining business when her father dies; In *The Power and the Glory* (World Pictures, 1918), "Jonnie" Consadine, "a daughter of a shiftless mountain stock," becomes forewoman at a local mill. Mavis Dawn of the poor backwoods in *Heart o' the Hills* (First National, 1919), played by Mary Pickford, "runs wild," goes "target shooting on horseback and fishing with a boy chum," and joins an otherwise all-male gang of nightriders to prevent the theft of coal lands by outsider industrialists. The title character in *Bonnie of the Hills* (Champion, 1911) uses a gun to turn the tables on a couple of highwaymen. In *Twilight* (Deluxe Pictures, 1919), the hillbilly gal shoots a man in the leg when he attacks her. The title character in *Judith of the Cumberlands* (Signal, 1916) forces her distant cousin (who lusts after her) to do the right thing at gunpoint, then shoots the horse out from under him when he backslides. In *Her Country's Call* (American, 1917), Jess Slocum, played by Mary Miles Minter, the brilliant and tragic Mary Pickford wannabe, shoots a dastardly, un-American troublemaker for tearing down an American flag. In other words, these hillbilly gals were allowed symbolic moments of equal power through violence. They could ride as well as men and sometimes shoot as well, but none of the above plots ultimately afforded the women anything approaching permanent equality. All these momentarily forceful women were, in one way or another, reconciled by the final scene to the tradition of masculine rule, so that their previous violent actions were rendered obsolete.

The qualifying description "shiftless mountain stock," which appears, for example, in the synopsis for *The Power and the Glory*, in fact frequently anchored a silent movie's narrative strategy for dismissing or explaining these unusual outbursts of female freedom. Action leading to violence, in a hillbilly gal, was often attributed to bad mountain genes or, by extension, to bad mountain neighborhoods. "The girl" in *The Revenue Man and the Girl* (Biograph, 1911; directed by D. W. Griffith) is described as "rough *in nature*"; seeing her father killed by revenue men "sets [her] fierce *mountain* spirit ablaze" (emphasis added). But by the end she's trooping off "for a new life in the city beautiful" and marriage to—wouldn't you know it?—a revenue man. Likewise, the moonshiner's daughter in *The Stranger at Hickory Nut Gap* (Imp, 1914), though she works her father's still and handles a gun like an experienced pro against the advances of an unwelcome suitor, by the end of the story she has burned her father's still in repentance and married the revenue man. In *Bawbs o' Blue Ridge* (Ince, 1916), Bawbs turns out to be (gasp!) the long-lost daughter of these, um, really rich dead parents and goes off—married—to Philadelphia at the end. As a final example (but see the Sources): in *Her Man* (Advanced Motion Picture Corp., 1918), Juanita Holland is "born to wealth and refinement," she thinks, but her ancestors were "the people of the Cumberland Mountains," where she presently goes, of course, and where "the old spirit rouses in the girl. . . . She stands off the feudists." But she ends up married to Anse of the rival family anyway, "and a new condition arises in the valley"—in other words, a happy ending that precludes the necessity of Juanita's ever putting her fingers on a firearm again. Marriage plus town is the preferred antidote for too much female freedom. (Ironic, isn't it, seeing that the urban landscape has more often represented equal freedom for women in the movies, while the *rural* one often connotes emotional and physical prison.)

Insidiously, women were allowed their moments of gumption in theatrical fiction primarily as a way of controlling such moments of gumption in real life. Nearly all the nickelodeon films mentioned above, as well as others of the same type, embedded outbreaks of hillbilly gal violence in stories ultimately aimed at reestablishing patriarchal control. To a man, a gun is "the great equalizer," remember, a symbol of democratic leveling, but democracy has not yet been fully extended to women, so at the end of all the movies mentioned above, any guns in play are safely back in the hands of "the proper authorities"—the sheriffs, the feds, the husbands. The world is left perfectly ordered and controlled through the efforts of the strong, dashing, purposeful, granite-jawed leading men, who undertake the care and feeding of *wives*.

The vast majority of hillbilly gal silents—not to mention literally hundreds of other moonshining and feuding melodramas and assorted southern mountain romances in which women had prominent roles—ended in traditional matri*money*, with the former gals becoming "ladies" because they accepted the weaker role and financial dependency. Former hillbilly gals often wound up trussed into ballgowns, stuck in some urban drawing room far away from wild mountain possibilities, and the audience was supposed to buy that outcome as a good one. None of the nickelodeon hillbilly gals ever said with Thelma, "Let's keep going," because it never occurred to the moviemakers of that culture to let them.

## Cross-Dressers: Who's Wearing the Pants?

Uppity, democracy-embracing hillbilly gals were often cross-dressers in the earliest movies. Several silents featured a scene or a sequence in which the hillbilly gal actively disguises herself as a man and temporarily gets away with it, usually not for laughs but for serious plot advancement. For example, in *Battle in the Virginia Hills* (Kalem, 1912), Nancy Tucker dresses as her brother to avenge his shooting by a rival clan; Clara in *Nature's Touch* (American, 1914) dresses in the clothes of the eldest son of her employer, who has subjected her to "extremely revolting abuse" (we can only imagine what this means, as the movie does not appear to have survived), and hops a freight train to momentary freedom; the *Daughter of Devil Dan* (Buffalo Motion Picture Co., 1921) disguises herself as a newsboy and puts up her dukes on the street to defend her territory; Alexander McGivens in *The Mountain Woman* (Fox, 1921), played by *Perils of Pauline* star Pearl White, "wears the name and personal attire of a man" and roughnecks successfully with a gang of lumberjacks; Norris Gradley sports both a boy's name and a boy's ways, playing fiddle at rough country dances in *Cinderella of the Hills* (Fox, 1921); in *Red Margaret, Moonshiner* (Gold Seal, 1913), Margaret is possessed of enough "sagacity and commanding personality" (*cojones?*) that, dressed as a man, she leads a notorious all-male gang of moonshiners that the lawman can't catch—at least not at first.

These open cross-dressers end up very much like all the other nickelodeon hillbilly gals: married off in a conventional happy ending or otherwise reverting to conventionally dressed female roles. Their cross-dressing therefore becomes a scenic novelty and ultimately a negative example that has to be corrected before the audience is allowed to go home. But even while the cross-dressing clearly was signaling that women should "KEEP AWAY from trying to be like men," it nevertheless—and paradoxically—suggested the thrill of that very possibility.

A string of big Hollywood musicals, made much later than these early silent films, painted cross-dressing as a kind of fraudulent joke: *Annie Get Your Gun* (MGM, 1950), *Calamity Jane* (Warner Brothers, 1953), and *The Unsinkable Molly Brown* (MGM, 1964). In these musical extravaganzas, the hillbilly gal is always scapegoat and clown. In her cross-dressing she parodies masculine power politics, openly satirizing the structure of domination, but ultimately she succumbs to the masculine hierarchy by doffing her pants and donning a dress. All formerly free country gals eventually give up their male display (and their symbolic as well as their real independence) to become standardized wives of the most traditionally eligible male characters available. And they always give up willingly, for love.

In other words, insofar as these movies hint at a female challenge to male expectations, they are elaborate frauds and retrograde to boot. The three movie musicals I discuss here do not pit female against male, or even rural against urban devilment, so much as they expound corporate Creation myths. The prototypical First Male is a kind of successful arbitrager, and his real love object in all three movies is not a woman at all, but the acquisition of land and/or capital. The only functional lust is the lust for gold, for empire. (Watch Debbie Reynolds making love to $300,000 in cash on her wedding night in *The Unsinkable Molly Brown*.) These are Western-themed musicals, after all. Western expansion of the young nation provides the most apt metaphor for ideal American masculinity: manly patriotic virtue, which happens to encompass a lot of necessary roughness including invasion (market share) and domination (monopoly). And on the way to achieving his expansionist goals, the First Male will, coincidentally, kill the Indians, settle and consolidate, build and grow, write the history, and generally overcome—with violence, if necessary—all rivals to power.

There in the midst of all this normative reactionary male doctrine stands the hillbilly gal, who might have posed an instructive challenge to the habits of capital acquisition, not to mention male exclusivity, but whose real function turns out to be actively helping in the acquisition of empire and revalidating restrictive male/female gender roles. For example, though Annie Oakley can outshoot Frank Butler in *Annie Get Your Gun*, she learns that she is better off as a woman if she lets him win. And she turns out to be a talented capitalist, too, raising more cash than all the men put together. For Frank Butler's part, his overbearing arrogance supposedly learns a more domestic gentleness. Love melts his heart, or rather bloats it, because now he can be sentimental about his dominance: he becomes gracious in letting the now gender-stable little lady have her way occasionally.

The sheer necessity of surviving in an all-male world has made the unsinkable Molly Brown, at the start of her movie, boyish in dress and boyish in scrappiness in the rough male democracy of her Colorado mountains. She won't give in to the bullying of the locals: "Nobody wants me *down* like I want me *up!*" she yells, as three husky lads hold her face in the dirt and demand that she say uncle (Fig. 8.1). She'll never say uncle. Later, when she makes it into Leadville, she's green as gooseberries, but a saloonkeeper has "a job for a man," and ironically she fits the description. That mannishness is her essential core of democratic freedom, which most women aren't supposed to have, let alone exercise.

But she who said she'd never give in when her mouth was full of side-yard dirt and three big boys were sitting in the small of her back gives in almost immediately when she meets Johnny Brown, the phenomenally lucky dominant male played by the seriously strapping baritone Harve Presnell. Molly's father (Ed Begley) warned her when she lit out for town, "Be careful of the love of money," and it is interesting to see how *Molly Brown* turns the formulaic plot of the hillbilly gal rags-to-riches story into a darker consideration of just exactly what Molly has given in *to*. In some ways Molly Brown bears a striking resemblance to Burt Lancaster's Big Eli in *The Kentuckian* (discussed in Chapter 3), the coon-skin-capping "natural man" from the mountains who loses his juice in town. The message in both movies is that money and city ways are deadly to freedom, male or female, and that the fighting spirit belongs to both sexes naturally.

In town, Molly's marriage to Johnny Brown does not go well, but the acquisition of wealth goes very well indeed, and soon Debbie Reynolds is trussed up, like many another hillbilly gal, in extravagant gowns, swathed in jewels and flamboyant headgear (Fig. 8.2). And money does indeed prove to be the trap that Daddy had prophesied, for upper-crust Denver society rejects the newcomer wholesale. She flees to Europe and finds her friends among the titled aristocrats there, grand duchesses and dukes and barons who ironically practice the democracy lacking

Figure 8.1. "Nobody wants me *down* like I want me *up!*": Debbie Reynolds as Molly Brown, with her mouth full of sideyard dirt, in *The Unsinkable Molly Brown*. (Courtesy of Wisconsin Center for Film and Theater Research)

in Denver; they recognize in Molly's backwoods roughness a true equal. With its frank depiction of the buying and selling of human freedoms, the movie teeters on the verge of breaching early 1960s matrimonial fantasies. But it pulls back at the last moment and saves the marriage of Molly and Johnny Brown with romantic love and the soaring strains of Meredith Wilson's music.

The most interesting of the three hillbilly gal musicals is *Calamity Jane*, mostly due to the potency of what it suggested on its way to the closing nuptials. As the cross-dressed frontier scout named Calamity, Doris Day brags like a man. In fact, early in the movie Calamity boasts about herself in Henry Miller's Golden Garter saloon in the style of a man no other man would take seriously. "Why, I must've shot thirty In-juns," Calamity declares. (Annie Oakley indulges in a similar parody of male braggadocio in the song "Anything You Can Do, I Can Do Better.") Meanwhile Rattlesnake, a toothless dumpling of a stagecoach driver

Figure 8.2. Debbie Reynolds ends up like many another hillbilly gal, trussed up in extravagant gowns and flamboyant headgear, symbols of her loss of freedom, in *The Unsinkable Molly Brown*. (Courtesy of Wisconsin Center for Film and Theater Research)

who witnessed the true incident, is holding up two fingers behind her back, making all the men laugh at her. When Calamity discovers she's being mocked, she imitates a *dangerous* man. She is, after all, potentially lethal; she wears guns (Fig. 8.3). But on this occasion she grabs a bullwhip and lashes the defenseless Rattlesnake around his face, his *face*. "How many of them Injuns do you reckon I shot?" she demands. Rattlesnake answers like a subordinate: "I guess it was thirty." Calamity releases him contemptuously—"You toothless old buffalo!"

What's remarkable about the scene is how palpable Doris Day makes Calamity's meanness despite the context of comedy: in a closeup, her features visibly and literally darken, as though an emotional thunderhead had just moved across all that blondness. What has been ordained an exclusively masculine right to power has been usurped by a woman; the same dark cloud crossed over Louise's face right before she blew Harlan away. The only time the men of Deadwood pay any attention to

Figure 8.3. Doris Day as the armed Calamity in a publicity still from *Calamity Jane*. (Courtesy of Wisconsin Center for Film and Theater Research)

Calamity—except when she's singing—is when she uses physical violence. She punches and shoves, elbows and slaps, and pulls and fires her gun in a crowd no fewer than five times before the movie is over. It all seems like a parody of male impotence.

But if this exaggerated distortion of woman can be taught manners, then all preexisting structures will be saved. Calamity must give up her guns and become feminine in order for American masculinity to go on thinking well of itself.

In *Calamity Jane*, the conventional feminine ideal against which Calamity is judged is embodied in the famous actress Adelaid Adams, the highly decorative current adornment of the New York stage, a lady who has great power over men and therefore unusual freedom, so long as she holds the stage or appears to men as an image on the back of cigarette cards. Howard Keel, playing the normative male hero Wild Bill Hickok, preaches the text of the ideal woman while gazing at a painting of Adelaid: "She's everything that a woman ought to be. . . . She's a hope, a dream, a vision. You see her carved on the prow of an ancient ship."

But his words are propaganda aimed at Calamity more than they are something actively believed by men.

Next to Adelaid Adams—actually next to her image—Calamity is a monstrosity with "a face nobody would paint." Wild Bill urges her to notice other women when she gets to Chicago: "how they act, what they wear. Get yourself some female clothes and fixin's—you know, dresses, ribbons, perfume, things like that." It is interesting, in these hillbilly gal musicals, that the female stars are made to go on a pilgrimage to the city to learn about "normal" femininity; it is the same for the Heidis (see below). Compare with this the city *men* who make the opposite trek in serious films like *The Winter People* or in comedies like Danny Boyd's *Invasion of the Space Preachers*; they are husbands, usually, who have to go to the mountains to recover their masculinity, like *Deliverance*'s Ed and Lewis and Bobby and Drew on the banks of the Cahulawassee. Calamity Jane, in a sense, has already been to that psychic frontier, so she is driven in the opposite direction. In fact, the happy ending to come depends on whether that psychic backcountry in her can be removed or at least contained. Whichever direction a movie plot is headed—the gals' progression toward an inevitable loss of freedom in town or the guys' march toward freedom's terrifyingly full potential in the mountains—the hills represent a decidedly ambiguous state of equality.

In Chicago, Calamity is first mistaken for a man on the street and is winked at by another woman. She is dumbfounded, hasn't an inkling what flirting means or how it involves her. Later she walks into Adelaid Adams's dressing room and finds another woman, Adams's maid Katie Brown, in her bustier. Calamity thinks Katie is Adelaid, and Katie at first genuinely believes that Calamity is a man. In fact, Calamity *plays* the man. She bursts into an obviously sincere adolescent male rhapsody at the sight of Katie's body: "Gawd Almighty! You're the prettiest thang I've ever seen! Never knew a woman could look like that!" From that point forward, almost to the end of the film, Calamity courts Katie, even seems to marry her at one point in a very strange honeymooning interlude.

There is no warning lead-in for the Calamity-Katie marriage. From comic high jinks, the movie suddenly cuts to Katie and Calamity climbing into a buckboard together. Wild Bill Hickok approaches. Obviously enamored of Katie himself, he asks Calamity where the two are going.

She replies that Katie is moving in with *her*, and her manner is strangely defensive, even angry. Wild Bill laughs mockingly (or is it lasciviously?). Katie's doe-eyes coyly glance from Wild Bill to Calamity, as though she is stringing along two suitors (Fig. 8.4). She says to Wild Bill: "There aren't very many women in town [in fact, *none*, until the closing sequences], and Calamity had the idea that we should live together, sort of *chaperone* one another." Wild Bill is astonished: "*You* chaperone Calam, and *she* . . . " He doesn't finish the thought, but his derision is clear. Then he adds, "Oh, *this* ought to be interesting!"

And indeed it is. At her dilapidated cabin, Calamity plays the virgin husband to Katie's virgin bride. Calamity's a bundle of first-night nerves. Alternately bubbling with suggestive imagery ("We two will batch it here snug as two bugs in a blanket!") and full of despair that her shack is no fit place for this ideal female, she plays the parody of a nervous groom on his wedding night. She wants so much to please Katie, and Katie accepts the overture: "We can fix it up. All it needs is a woman's touch. . . . Never underestimate a woman's touch." And she paints the front door with "Calam & Katie" inscribed in a kind of lover's knot of flowers.

But at this most dangerous moment in the logic of her cross-dressing, Calamity is wedded to the idea of Katie Brown and not her body. This is a fairy tale, after all, and Katie Brown turns out to be the fairy godmother instead of the fairy princess, while Calamity is not the Frog Prince but actually Sleeping Beauty. She awakens from her trance of inappropriate masculinity. Calamity and Katie burst into a duet, during which a montage shows us a cabin- and Calamity-transformation. Before the song is over, we see Doris Day first in clean men's clothes and then in lacy, full ballgowns that'll take two trips to get through a door. Calamity becomes feminized before our eyes and in her own eyes, too, and from this point on she abruptly stops courting Katie, indeed falls out of love with her, and begins her ineluctable track toward subordination as wife to Wild Bill Hickok. She has rid herself of the ambiguous and forbidden freedom of acting like an equal.

## Mannish Misfits

Sometimes the usurpation of masculine equality is accomplished by strong hillbilly gals without cross-dressing. Such a strong gal is

Figure 8.4. Katie Brown (Allyn McLerie, center) strings along her two
suitors, the frowning Calamity (Doris Day) and the mocking Wild Bill Hickok
(Howard Keel), in *Calamity Jane*. (Courtesy of Wisconsin Center for Film
and Theater Research)

Mammy Yokum in the 1959 musical *Li'l Abner* (discussed in Chapter 2).
She presides at the beginning of the movie as "Society's queen . . . and
head of the local machine," according to the perpetually overruled
though nominal head of the Yokum dynasty, Pappy. So Dogpatch is,
from the git-go, a world in which proper patriarchy has become a joke.
The very landscape is dominated by a statue of the supposedly hallowed
patriarch Jubilation T. Cornpone, who has become a fool of wonderful
proportions in the song all the Dogpatchers sing about him. The men
in this society are presented as mere comic pawns in a ruthless female
power play that makes men into mere breeders and legally hunted
game on Sadie Hawkins Day.

Mammy Yokum's eventual comeuppance and the return of Dogpatch
to masculine dominance are starkly political themes. The whole happy
outcome of the plot hinges on the scene near the end when Pappy

Yokum finally reasserts the divine right of masculine rule. All through the movie, Mammy has been the decision maker and bossy little tyrant ("How is your sweet, gentle, and relentless little self?" Marrying Sam greets her). She loves to end arguments by stating, "I has *spoken!*" with her stiff little digit pointing heavenward. But late in the movie, Pappy overpowers Mammy with an uncommon and unexpected "*You* hesh up!" He sends her home. "*I* has spoken!" he says, in exactly the same way Mammy has always done it. She promptly capitulates, violating her own character as written, and is little heard from again in a musical comedy she has fairly dominated heretofore. But there is no suggestion that she prefers things this way, unlike Goldie Hawn's character in *Overboard*.

This mannish potentiality in Mammy, Al Capp's perversion of the customary mother's role of nurturer, turns out to be actually hurtful to the future of the species. Mammy still forcibly doses her grown son Abner on Yokumberry tonic, which, as we learn from no less an authority than the federal government, is a direct cause of impotence in men. Although Mammy's Yokumberry tonic miraculously transforms the scrawny men of Dogpatch into bodybuilding hunks, they're of no use "romantically" to the wives who bagged them during the most recent Sadie Hawkins Day. The women complain about this in the best musical number in the show, singing, "Put 'em back the way they was!" Masculinity is sunk until Pappy reasserts patriarchal rule. Men in the audience applaud.

In *Spitfire* (RKO, 1934), Katharine Hepburn plays the mannishly usurping misfit in one of her earliest screen roles, which wasn't exactly a hit. As Trigger Hicks, the fiercely independent though poor hillbilly gal, she changes moods and tempos rapidly and seamlessly, but Hepburn can't wrap her stiff aristocratic palate around the dialect, which is insistently metaphorical and odd. Physically, though, she is just right for the part, all square and flat and hard as a griddle, big-shouldered and full of rangy sinew. Though she never dons a man's clothes, she's a mannish challenge to the neighborhood; not surprisingly, at the end of the movie this community takes the form of a mob of men to drive her out of her homeplace.

That core plot is pretty engaging, especially Hepburn's showdown with the mob, when she stands unarmed and unafraid before her detractors, exposed to their hatred and their fury, and she won't give an inch and won't fight back either, forcing their hand of cruelty. She's hit in the head with a thrown rock, which floors her, but falling down saves her from further, worse violence. The outsider engineer who has grown to love her thinks she's near death, but she rouses when the mob is gone: "I ain't above playing possum a little myself," she confesses. Mere men and rocks can't keep her down.

But playacting is what Trigger is all about in the politics of this story, and that includes her mannish command of every situation. This is an ugly-duckling fable, after all, in which the unprepossessing little hillbilly wart is really a swan waiting to be hatched and mated. When she kisses her true man at the end, all preexisting power relations are reaffirmed: every woman needs a man; any woman can get one.

Mannish behavior by a hillbilly woman is taken to comic exaggeration in Edwina ("Ed"), the character played by Holly Hunter in *Raising Arizona* (see discussion in Chapter 2). Ed is the more powerful McDunnough, the boss of Hi. She "wears the pants" symbolically and literally too, for she is gainfully employed for a while as a cop and chief breadwinner for the McDunnough "starter family." Interestingly, her usurpation of masculine power is coupled with her female "barrenness," which is actually the central comic proposition that motivates this foolshow.

A searing portrait of a mannish hillbilly woman was painted recently by Vanessa Redgrave in the movie made from Edward Albee's theatrical version of Carson McCullers's novella *The Ballad of the Sad Cafe*. As Miss Amelia, Redgrave appears in a boy's haircut and overalls, playing a tough landlord-overseer of the men working her cotton patch; in addition, she is a kind of granny woman–witch who mixes secret salves and ointments and doctors her people both physically and psychologically. When one poor woman says her man "whacked" her upside the head, Redgrave tells her to whack him back. A potent gender-bender, this character. She also makes the best moonshine in her hiding place in the swamp and sells it to the local men, who are passively but resentfully under her power. The indelible image of Redgrave wading waist-deep in swamp water, her shoulders square and massive, her head a lion's of power and command, makes us wish she could have played Gertie Nevels in *The Dollmaker*, instead of Jane Fonda.

Love for one man and the hatred of another conspire to bring this strong woman down. The love is highly improbable, and even grotesque. A misshapen dwarf ("the broke-back," the mean and ignorant townspeople call him) comes hobbling into Miss Amelia's life one night. Cousin Lymon (played by Cork Hubbert), a distant relation by marriage, is hungry and houseless and pitiable, not to mention four feet tall, but he stirs in the super-tall Redgrave first a maternal instinct and later a more erotic femininity. With Lymon in the house, she puts on a dress for the first time, in fact a shockingly red and revealing dress that had been her mama's, and in one wild sequence she bears cousin Lymon on her back to her secret swampy still, where they get drunk and she dances before him with abandon in the rain and rolls in muck and kisses him impetuously. Perhaps they mirror one another, misshapen misfits, and her love is the fatal affection of Narcissus for her own reflection.

But the dwarf is evil. Amelia's love seems to trigger in him a psychotic need: as half-man, he can think only of how to bring down the half-man in Miss Amelia. He forms a wicked covenant with her long-banished husband, Marvin Macy, played like a snake by Keith Carradine. We learn in a tiresome flashback that Macy, like leading men in other hillbilly gal movies, had at first swept the independent woman off her feet and into matrimony. On his wedding day, he was practically smacking his lips over the prospects of Miss Amelia's body. But she physically threw him out of the house, rejecting his masculine right of bedroom liberty on its very first outing. She owns everything in sight, after all. But with that fateful decision to defy her husband, this hillbilly gal headed for her own kind of tragedy.

Eventually she has to stand up to Marvin Macy in a literal barefisted fight to the finish. She and Marvin pound the bloody bejesus out of one another while all the townspeople—along with the evil dwarf, who like Iago has engineered the whole conflict—look on. The dwarf chortles. When Amelia finally pins Marvin Macy fair and square, and we think she's won the fight, the gremlin dwarf leaps on her back, which allows Marvin Macy to knock her down for the count. She cries, sobs, at this defeat. But it is not enough for the dwarf and the frustrated husband. Unable to end completely her intolerable female freedom any other way, Cousin Lymon and Marvin Macy come back that night and torch Miss Amelia's sad, sad café. It's a brutal moment for any audience, which must share the blame in this conspiracy against her independence.

Our last image of Redgrave shows us her ruined face many years later: a survivor, yes, but a bitter and gaunt old crone who stares us down from behind torn curtains, an outcast who scares children, the witch now, indeed, that the town always said she was. This is Thelma and Louise's window-woman potential lived to fulfillment. There is no transcendence in this tragedy.

## Heidi and the Poverty Mamas: Fooling with Economics

An idyllic rural family plods into the frame with bent backs, indicating hard labor and the dignity of oppression.
—Andrea Frye, describing the opening scenes of *Where the Lilies Bloom*

Quite often of late, mountain women have been portrayed on film as poverty goddesses, making *hillbilly* synonymous with *poor* when poor is meant to be noble. Since these films were made by the nonpoor and for the nonpoor, the flattery is both insidious and misleading.

*Heidi*, the 1937 Shirley Temple vehicle, is the perfect example of such a film, though not the earliest (see the Sources). It is the story of a poor and virtuous mountain girl who is "uncivilized" but who teaches goodness to the urban rich anyway. In Heidi's world, it is "civilization" that's theoretically sick, and the adorable little poor backwards mountain girl brings psychic health wherever she goes and forms natural bonds with the oppressed and outcast: an embittered old hermit, a henpecked butler, a crippled rich child, an organ grinder's monkey. Every one of these, she helps to health or to happiness. Meanwhile, a witch of a governess, herself ironically a servant and underling, plots to sell Heidi into slavery. The witch is thwarted, and Heidi returns willingly to her mountain environment, ascending again into the Austrian Alps like a transfigured saint. Meanwhile, the city is said to be better off because of her visit, and yet it is blessedly free of her, too, in the end. Make no mistake: those things the city stands for—money and power—still determine how the world rotates. Nothing structural has changed. Heidi is back in the never-never land of romanticized but relegated-to-the-fringe mountains, and the world is free to go on creating witches and burning them, too.

Another Heidi hillbilly was portrayed by Debbie Reynolds in *Tammy and the Bachelor* (1957). Debbie plays the dirt-encrusted granddaughter of disreputable old moonshiner Walter Brennan (of the Louisiana swamp league). She falls in love with a rich city man (the young Leslie Nielsen) who crash-lands his plane in her swamp. Naturally she goes with him to his mansion in town, where she becomes the object of scorn and amusement for her dumb-cluck mistakes but also the perfect little backwoods saint and healer. Hillbilly Tammy can read people's souls; she teaches wisdom to the urban sick. And despite her class-based per-secution by the social snobs, Tammy thrives. That is, she is rewarded for being poor and tractable: she marries the rich Mr. Right and lives on in his mansion in a conventional happy-ever-after ending.

Another variation on the hillbilly sainted for her economic denial was *Coal Miner's Daughter* (Universal, 1980), starring Sissy Spacek as Loretta Lynn, which drew a phenomenal audience particularly in rural areas. In *Coal Miner's Daughter*, a poor and ignorant hillbilly girl strug-gles against great odds; she goes to town and grows rich but never gets corrupted. The damned Big Time system doesn't change her, except to wear her out. She remains one of the good rural poor of Butcher Hol-low. Along the way, though, the getting of wealth seems mystically or-dained yet improbably distant, and any mud-in-your-eye hillbilly defi-ance is never given full voice.

Director Michael Apted took his production on location to the east-ern Kentucky coalfields, very near where Loretta Lynn grew up, and he created a compellingly believable rural world that engaged the deepest sympathies of even urban audiences. ("The box office—$38 million and counting—and the public response have exceeded expectations," *People* magazine reported a couple of months after the film's release. "Even city-slick *cinéastes* found themselves surprisingly moved.") Tom Rickman's script, a clear-headed and efficient screen adaptation of Lo-retta Lynn's own disjointed memoirs (published by Regnery in 1976), and Michael Apted's eye for country naturalness in his casting of east Kentuckian Phyllis Boyens as Loretta's mother and Arkansas homeboy Levon Helm as her father combined to create an energizing mirror that country people, especially, found elegantly flattering.

The movie did phenomenal business in the South generally, but especially in the upland rural South. In Boone, North Carolina, in

Figure 8.5. Sissy Spacek as the perfect little Heidi in *Coal Miner's Daughter*. (Courtesy of the University of California at Los Angeles Arts Library, Special Collections)

Kingsport, Tennessee, in Pikeville, Kentucky, in Elkins, West Virginia, and in many another small town in Appalachia as well as other places I've heard from all across the rural American landscape, *Coal Miner's Daughter* drew whole families into the theaters, which was not at all the norm for the movie industry by 1980. Mothers and fathers, some of whom hadn't been to a movie since John Wayne Westerns went out of style, came with kids in tow—and frequently grandparents who could have counted on the fingers of one hand all the movies they had seen since *Sergeant York*. One local woman I know took her elderly father to see *Coal Miner's Daughter* a second time, because he asked to go again.

The movie flattered, like most rags-to-riches tales do. But rags to riches is a deceptive fantasy. The rags are romanticized as symbolizing a somehow ennobling but dull condition that can and will be cured (Fig. 8.5).

Sometimes that condition is simple dollar poverty, but often it is cultural "backwardness." In the rags-to-riches milieu, a wholly new system of values comes to dominate all propositions, one of which is—it should come as no surprise—an insistent idealization of Nature, under the cover of which false abstraction all kinds of schemes operate to dominate, subjugate, and subdivide nature on every hand. That's the irony of the rags-to-riches theme. The profit-driven philosophy is not just antithetical to rural democracy; it is, at heart, a betrayal of hillbilly freedom, though we aren't allowed to see or feel that in the Heidi movies or in the unique biopic *Coal Miner's Daughter.*

*Big Business* (Touchstone Pictures/Silver Screen Partners III, 1988) is a kind of twisted-sister version of *Heidi.* Bette Midler and Lily Tomlin both play their own doubles, so that there's a pair of city twins (Midler) and a pair of hillbilly twins (Tomlin), who get mixed on their birth day in the Jupiter Hollow, West Virginia, hospital. One hillbilly and one urban baby go back to town, while one urban and one hillbilly baby stay in the "slow-normal" hills. Forty years later, the country-trapped Midler twin is pining to run away to the charms of the big city, which somehow seem more natural to her than patchwork quilts and apple dolls. In the city, her urban twin has just naturally become the ruthless CEO of the Moramax conglomerate. The hillbilly Tomlin at home in West Virginia has become the feisty forewoman at the Hollowmade Furniture Company, a subsidiary of Moramax. This Tomlin has organized her fellow workers, in classic hillbilly gal style, to fight Moramax's plan to sell the Hollowmade Furniture Company to a strip-mining foreign conglomerate. In the meantime, her hillbilly twin, who is trapped in town but has no idea she's really mountain bred, just naturally has no head or stomach for business. Rather, she dreams of gingham dresses and country dinners on the ground and can't stop herself from obsessively worrying about stray animals.

On the surface, then, *Big Business* satirizes urbanity, especially corporate economics, and holds up hillbilly life as the better, more humane alternative, but the bottom line is just the opposite. The city actually provides the normative viewpoint here, particularly when the action shifts to Jupiter Hollow. Talk about Hollowmade Furniture! This movie's hillbillyland is pure cartoon, a silly city version of country life that thinks it's being generous and supportive in the classic liberal way.

In the end, the two proper sets of twins are reunited: the hillbillies return to hillbillyland, and the urbanites stay urban. Jupiter Hollow has been saved at the last minute by a simple vote of the Moramax board of directors, proving that the structure of power that allows dominant city wealth to routinely destroy people and their homes need never be undermined so long as there is hope that the bigwigs in control might take pity next time and not sell all us hillbillies down the river.

During the 1960 presidential election, when Democrats John F. Kennedy and Hubert Humphrey out-liberaled one another in the West Virginia primary, their political pity and piety were mythologized by enough TV and print media to transform "Appalachia" overnight from a previously antique folk culture, on the periphery and therefore vaguely threatening to urban America, into a liberal cause, a "social problem" just begging to be solved (and in fact *solvable*, given enough federal cash and volunteers in service). After Kennedy's election, he delivered on his campaign promise and in 1963 appointed the President's Appalachian Regional Commission, which eventually became a middling bureaucracy in its own right during the sudden administration of former Vice President Lyndon Johnson, who in the Kennedy spirit declared a great War on Poverty. In a dramatic display, Johnson flew to Appalachia and visited, among other places, the front porch of poor coal miner Tommy Fletcher in Inez, Kentucky, in April 1964. The media recorded the event. Tommy Fletcher and that tumbledown, starving, dirt-dumb spectacle became Appalachia forever after in the mass American mind.

Democratic Party liberalism came to dominate public imagery, but such imagery fed on symptoms and knew zilch about causes. The search for outrageous inequality in the American democracy, of which Appalachia was but one notorious example, was like the search of the blind men of the Orient for the elephant. The structure was much vaster than the searchers thought, and interconnected. Many well-meaning Americans ended up subtly blaming the victims of grinding economic systems for their own *overcomeable* misery and set out to minister unto them, to change them, to uplift them, to reconnect them even more firmly to the dominant economics, just so that, ironically, middle-class Americans could feel good again about the evolution of our political economy.

Those who saw economic domination as the enemy and used Appalachia to preach against the old pieties (that the United States of America is the guileless and favorite child of the Almighty Jehovah) were branded as dangerous, not to mention godless, Communists. Meanwhile, the American economic system that puts everything up for sale and creates two classes of owners and renters—the "free enterprise system" for which countless patriots have expended much energy and heavy breathing—was hauling Appalachia away. Mountain people have learned the hard way to beware the doer of good deeds bearing pity.

This string of events ushered in a late-twentieth-century low-art form of word and image on paper and on screen—the in-depth hillbilly feature story—and also spawned a string of hillbilly movies in which the sight of poor, struggling mountain people is supposed to trigger liberal guilt. Theatrical releases like *Medium Cool* (Paramount, 1969), *Where the Lilies Bloom* (United Artists, 1974), and *Norma Rae* (Twentieth Century–Fox, 1979) and made-for-TV movies like *Angel City* (1969), *The Incredible Journey of Dr. Meg Laurel* (1979), *The Pride of Jesse Hallam* (1981), and *The Dollmaker* (1984) often showed mountain people as the helpless victims of greed, but always in a context that never allowed the operative mechanism of greed to be understood.

Haskell Wexler's *Medium Cool,* set in and around the infamous 1968 Democratic Convention in Chicago, tells the story of a cold and intellectually disconnected TV news cameraman (played by Robert Forster) who begins to feel human again under the influence of an urban-migrant hillbilly woman from West Virginia and her bright but doomed little boy. Wexler makes the visual point that ghetto-poor African Americans and poor hillbilly Americans share the same economic victimization. In fact, Wexler tried valiantly to raise his audiences' consciences about unequal power in America, but his definitions of powerlessness, especially in the hillbillies' case, seem decidedly more cultural than economic (especially in a couple of brilliantly photographed memory sequences in which the boy learns the rules of manhood from his now missing-and-presumed-dead father). But *Medium Cool* does not cop out with a happy ending. It stops and chokes on bitter medicine, which partly explains why no one went to see it.

The most obvious hillbilly gal of this lot, Gertie Nevels in *The Dollmaker* (played, unfortunately, by Jane Fonda), is capable of mannish feats while she remains in her mountain setting but turns weak and indecisive when she moves to Detroit to become the martyr matriarch of

Merry Hill. The script labors mightily to demonize both the black factories that chug smoke literally over the migrants' heads and all the general inhuman meanness of everything in town. The intention is to assign clear blame for human misery to the unfortunate circumstance of Working for the Man in Town, but the inauthentic happy ending, which sends the migrated hillbillies back to safety in the hills, probes no more deeply into the question of who the Man is than did *Big Business*. Both movies end with the safe Heidi solution: the mountain women disappear into the hills, leaving the city system unaltered.

All these poverty films presume that good jobs, government help, and the ministrations of missionaries are what these poor hillbillies need. Either that, or they require immediate Heidi-like relocation back to the hills, which are ideal for *them* though not necessarily for the rest of us who are watching TV and buying tickets at the multiplex. The often unintended stinger in the tail-end of such romanticizing pity is that the hillbilly label becomes pure stigma, with all the potential freedom removed. The bottom line in the American college of hard knocks is this: if you fail economics, you deserve your *F* in social class and geography, too. And in the box for DEPORTMENT, we find the summation, "Needs improvement."

## Hillbilly Gals and Burly Cue

You can sit and talk with me for five minutes and
know that there's a little more to me than tits.
—Dolly Parton

The theatrical entertainment called burlesque was, at its heart, a display of female riotousness by way of imitation, a mocking mirror held up by women to reflect outrageously male values or male behavior. Burlesque women were unruly women in that they *took* masculine freedom shockingly onstage; in the earliest days of classic burlesque, they initially cross-dressed as men, appearing in pants and imitating dominant masculine swagger and talk. Burlesque was—and still is in its transmigrated soul (into Madonna, for example)—full of political possibility.

Robert C. Allen raises and pursues these topics in his excellent history of classic American burlesque, *Horrible Prettiness: Burlesque and Amer-*

*ican Culture.* The first two words of his title are an unwieldy oxymoron, but they signal a vexing yet potentially redeeming paradox about dominant American male culture: what men find "horrible," they also often desire out of need.

In the later history of American burlesque, when women began to disrobe more and more as women, they confronted their audiences with male fantasies made apparently and dangerously real. Strong women gave dominant men an hour's worth of altered perception, a sudden freedom to consider an impossible world wherein men are every bit as weak as women and women are every bit as powerful as men.

The spirit of burlesque—the willingness of women to display themselves devilishly before men and the willingness of men to see themselves reflected in that display as veritable fools—is a paradox of male reaction. Allen explains: "The burlesque performer represents a construction of . . . something [which has been named the "low-other"] that is reviled by and excluded from the dominant social order as debased, dirty, and unworthy, but that is simultaneously the object of desire and/or fascination." The burlesque performer, in other words, represents something very like a hillbilly.

Both the burlesque woman and the hillbilly are connected in some way to freedom. Allen quotes stripper Seph Weene as saying: "'The thrill I got from stripping was power. I was seen as powerful; more important, I *felt* powerful. . . . Ordinary restrictions on women's behavior did not apply on that stage.'" The problem, of course, is that the power an individual female performer might gain did not necessarily translate into any effective political empowerment of other women. Seph Weene again: "'There was [a] flaw; it was such relative power. If we were free in the real world, the stage freedom would not matter.'"

Any low-other is obviously a scapegoat for fears and frustrations but also represents a devil of a thought: up is down; everybody in power is a fool; freedom can be successfully learned. Dangerous thoughts. They fuel rebellions that can grow into full-scale revolutions. But when devil thoughts leak out onto a public stage, according to Allen's sources, the masters of the theory, the potential threat to dominant power dissipates once it has its hour, and any weird craving to play the fool ourselves against the "dominant social order" is controlled, regulated, because it is licensed to appear. When burlesque women proved too hot, too dangerous, and too free to be themselves, they were relegated to the back rooms, the back alleys, the backwoods of our culture.

This may be Allen's key observation: "The discourse [performance] of the 'low other' has the potential to challenge the ordering of officially sanctioned culture by pointing to the arbitrary nature of this ordering and the social interests that ordering conceals." A shocking mass experience at least has the potential to alter or liberate mass perception. In the case of burlesque, devil women unmask men. In the case of hillbillies, a rural devil jumps up and says "boo" to power.

The raucous fruition of the career of West Virginia stripper Blaze Starr, the underground hillbilly gal, provides a good example. Starr played a different kind of fool's role, one much more in the strict tradition of Allen's burlesque queens. Her real name was Fanny Belle Fleming, and she hailed from the West Virginia coalfields of Mingo County. When she got to the city, she unveiled a magnetic sex appeal, even as she scapegoated her hillbilly identity. Here is how David Lida describes her stage routine:

In time she developed a comedic talent. Exploiting her down-home West Virginia accent and idiom, the friendly Starr, carrying a long ebony cigarette holder, would saunter onto a stage decorated with a lamppost that read "Passion Street," narrow her eyes, and address her audience as "you li'l ol' evil tomcats." Patrons were invited onstage to help her divest herself of her clothes; after she had placed a rose between her unconscionably large bosoms, another would be asked to go "flower pickin' in the hills." He would be instructed to pluck the rose with his teeth, but not until he had pulled "the booby string," an imaginary rope above their heads that, when "jolted" by the fellow— now crimson-faced with embarrassment at the hoots of his cronies— would appear to make Starr's right breast jump. She never developed the muscle coordination to perform the same trick with her left breast. When asked to by the audience, she would adopt a pout and whimper, "She tired tonight."

Starr was famous for boasting, "Well, I'm a 38 double-D, and they all come to look at me." She boiled men like lobsters. According to the movie version of her life, she brought down the powerful Long family dynasty and reduced the all-male Louisiana legislature to a snarling, stymied mess.

The Blaze of the movie *Blaze Starr* (Touchstone/Silver Screen Partners IV, 1989), played by rookie Lolita Davidovich (Fig. 8.6), is at first an improbable torch for female freedom, being a woefully naive backwoods gal who sets out from rough poverty to find her fortune in the world. "Lookin for a man," is what she tells her mama, as though she could have no identity without one, and her mother replies, "You've got to sort it out for yourself," but wisely adds: "Never trust a man who says trust me." If Fanny Belle Fleming, taking off into the world from Mingo County, is pure democratic potential, the first man who says "trust me" is the pure antidemocrat. He'll take power by stealth and beggar freedom. The very first time she is cajoled into stripping onstage by a fast-talking operator played by veteran character actor Robert Wuhl, she does it in front of an audience of servicemen, good country-serving Americans, and as a result she feels both gratifyingly patriotic and invigorated by the boys' "warmth and love and . . ." ". . . *Respect*," the man who means to make her his property completes the sentence. But then this potential manager/boss says those ominous words, "trust me," and our fledgling democrat is promptly out the window, like that other bird of freedom played by Robert Mitchum in *Thunder Road*. The warmth and love and, yes, respect she felt onstage were real, a species of equality, the naked truth if you will— "a powerful presentation of basic human needs," which is how Louisiana governor Earl Long (Paul Newman) sees her.

"I must say, you look like a democrat to me," Old Earl later says to her in his mating dance, but he doesn't know the half of it. Blaze forces her full equality on him, won't settle for anything less. When the unmarried Long begins to take her with him surreptitiously in his white Cadillac limousine on his politics-and-junking sprees through the Louisiana backwoods, he doesn't invite her out of the car at their first stop. It's clear to her that he's ashamed. Before they reach their second stop, Blaze tells the governor calmly that she will not be left in the car again like disreputable baggage. And Old Earl immediately recognizes her doctrine as armored truth. So at their next stop, a state-owned hospital, he makes a show of introducing her, "Miss Blaze Starr," as she alights from the Cadillac like a princess from a coronation carriage. In grant-

Figure 8.6.
Lolita Davidovitch
as Blaze Starr
(a.k.a. Fanny Belle
Fleming of Mingo
County, W.Va.),
despoiler of gov-
ernors, in *Blaze*.
(Courtesy of
*Now and Then*,
Center for Appala-
chian Studies and
Services, East
Tennessee State
University)

ing her this symbolic equality, the governor becomes a better man, even as he becomes an easier target for his enemies: "They say I fell in love with a striptease dancer at the drive-in theater," he says to Blaze. "And they're right. I'm guilty." "Why, thank you, Honey," Blaze replies. Love can bestow equality quicker than any voting rights act. He finally presents her with a ring: "Maybe it's time for Old Earl to become domesticated. Might be a humbling experience." And indeed the social and psychological leveling that Blaze provides is the paradoxical province of that small-*d* democrat.

When Blaze Starr's story resurfaced in the cultural mainstream in the publicity surrounding the 1989 movie, she returned to the American consciousness not so much as an embodiment of low-other cultural challenge to urban standards, but as an unlikely aberration. John Ed

Bradley put it this way: "Back home in West Virginia . . . all told, there were 11 children in [her] family counting the boy who died at 2 months. And they all were smart-looking, especially when you stacked them next to what all else Appalachia had to offer." The hillbilly as an agent of rural devilment does not appear in Starr's movie. There is no hint of cultural championship in her public image.

So how different is she from Dolly Parton, our fullest embodiment of the hillbilly gal as cultural devil? Dolly Parton might have kicked John Ed Bradley's teeth down his throat. Parton's movies have been mainly forgettable, even regrettable, affairs, though her recent *Straight Talk* (Hollywood Pictures/Buena Vista, 1992) did better than most at giving her a handy vehicle in which her backwoods democratic backtalk could achieve its healing potential. But even if we exclude her movies from this discussion, Parton provides plenty to talk about.

Parton's big breasts are like Blaze Starr's, just part of a smart country girl's ample challenge to conventional taste, though Parton sees herself more as a celebration than as a revolt: "[About] my look, the way I dress, the image I have, with the clothes and the makeup and the hair. I've always said—and it's the truth—that it came from a serious place: a country girl's idea of what glamour is. I was impressed with what they called 'the trash' in my hometown. . . . They had blond hair and wore nail polish and tight clothes. I thought they were beautiful." The stories about "the trash"—the flamboyant and sometimes unmannerly tarts—have now transmigrated through Dolly Parton into the pop entertainment of an urban culture that commonly shuns flamboyance in the uppity poor, especially in uppity poor women (remember the outrage in some quarters over *Thelma and Louise*).

As the sweetly vengeful democrat, Parton the country low-brow dares to come knock-knock-knocking on heaven's door, and she expects to be admitted, too, and served some eats. Parton cheekily told Scott Haller in *People* about her migrated life in California: "I still like to pee off the porch every now and then. There's nothing like peeing on those snobs in Beverly Hills."

Parton is most powerful when she exploits her backwoodsiness, when she willingly makes herself the rural scapegoat of urban good taste. Just before the first broadcast of her ill-fated TV variety hour in 1987, she explained to the press: "The show will not be *mostly* country. It will definitely *be* country because I'll be on it." Country people take power from her power, and working people adore her. She's 9-to-5, just like them. She was one of *Ms.* magazine's thirteen Women of the Year in 1986, honored especially for "creating popular songs about real women" and "for bringing jobs and understanding to the mountain people of Tennessee." In 1988 an association of the world's chauffeurs, doormen, bellhops, and maids voted her one of the best-mannered rich people they knew.

And rich she certainly is. Early in 1985 the *Miami News* estimated Parton's net worth at $300 million. (In 1991 Kevin Sessums of *Vanity Fair* said the figure was probably closer to $100 million, but so what?) She owned, in 1985, a $9 million Hawaiian home, a twenty-three-room Nashville mansion, 410 wigs, 2,400 pairs of shoes, two production companies, five music-publishing companies, and of course Dollywood, her successful hillbilly theme park outside her home town of Pigeon Forge in Sevier County, Tennessee. She owns more now.

Parton began developing Dollywood in 1985. When she popped the question to the town fathers of Pigeon Forge, they jumped. They obligingly pledged several million dollars' worth of improvements to an existing but defunct amusement park, Silver Dollar City, which Parton then acquired and renamed after herself.

The city's investment immediately looked wise: by January 1986, several other projects were in development, all reportedly spawned by the publicity surrounding Dollywood (among them a dude ranch, a recording studio, and a "Dollywood University" for training tourism workers in public relations). Soon there were signs of more overt altruism. The Dollywood Foundation began giving grants to local education and health care institutions. In August 1990, Parton embraced environmentalism, announcing that Dollywood would build an "eagle complex," including a football-field-sized aviary, a breeding area, a 350-seat amphitheater, and a bird hospital for sick or wounded American eagles.

Current yearly revenues at Dollywood are estimated in the neighborhood of $30 million. The theme park itself employs up to 1,600 people at the height of its season and otherwise benefits hundreds of other local people, which Parton has said all along was one of her chief goals. Funneling the profits from her act into the pockets of her people, the rural scapegoat becomes a cultural savior.

But salvation based on stage freedom is often an illusion. While the success of Dollywood pumps cash into Sevier County, the locals act the fool for more damn tourists, only reassuring these "better others" that urban values are supreme and urban power is secure. Ultimately, country culture always appears dumb to urban culture, which is why it has so often been portrayed as a symbolic nightmare of the American frontier, sometimes merely dismissibly peripheral but sometimes posing a *Deliverance*-level threat.

Parton herself has acknowledged the resulting tension: "The Hollywood version of the country and mountain people has always bothered me. They usually make us a lot more stupid and dumb than we really are." The irony in this statement goes to the heart of her greater paradox: in rejecting only the degree ("*more* stupid and dumb"), she accepts the basic premise ("stupid and dumb"), just as her people accept the omnipotence of the bottom line in celebrating her financial success. That she has grown rich is good but ironic, because the acquisition of wealth reimposes the very structure that defines hillbillies in the first place.

The failure of Parton's 1987 attempt at a variety hour on network TV also reveals this irony. She negotiated a tough contract with ABC. She insisted on and got an initial order of forty-four guaranteed episodes for her own production company, Sandollar, unlike most new TV series, which usually receive an initial order for only six or thirteen or twenty-two episodes and then have to prove their commercial worth to earn renewal. When ABC signed its contract with Parton, it had no less than $44 million at risk up front. But even given that incentive to make the show work, the network first scheduled *Dolly* on Sunday nights, TV's number one prime-time spot, then shifted it to Saturday nights in a vain attempt to find a sufficiently remunerative audience, and finally canceled the show after just twenty-two episodes. Parton is said to have walked away from the wreckage with $11 million. And rural culture looked dumb again? Yes, because the upstart hillbilly gal had been put in her place critically even while she pocketed the money.

The point is that when urbanites and suburbanites enjoy hillbilly displays, as they do from time to time, they may be seeing someone else's heroic cultural gesture as nothing more than a clown show—the rural boobs let loose for an hour to provide the vicarious and therefore safe thrill of ignoring or offending the rules from a safe distance. Outrageous hillbilly transgressions committed in plain sight seem to dissipate any hidden desires in us to become unmannerly country tarts ourselves.

Another obstacle to Parton's potential power is her very sexual grotesqueness. In her, the great sex creature of male fantasy has taken itself all too literally, but the exaggeration smothers dread. And so she plays into the hands of Johnny Carson and other showbiz sophisticates, in whom she stirs no countercultural resonance and who therefore blow her up even more into just an anatomical curiosity. In this perception, it must be admitted, she has readily participated. In one concession to ABC's programming executives, she agreed to appear weekly in a bubble bath for the opening of her show. And she told Rita Kempley in 1989, "If people ask me if I get offended with the [big breast] jokes, I say, 'Absolutely not.' I mean if I was going to be offended, why don't I cover 'em up?" But she also added, "You can set and talk with me for five minutes and know that there's a little more to me than tits."

Still, most onlookers don't get to sit and talk with her, so in the discourse of popular culture, Parton is regularly assigned a seat next to hillbilly cartoons ("She's a Beverly Hillbilly, a Will Rogers stuffed in Daisy Mae's body"—Rita Kempley). She herself prefers the company of Mae West: "I'm little and overexaggerated [like Mae West], very outgoing and ballsy," she told William Stadiem. By claiming kinship with Mae West, Parton was both linking herself to a whole history of "transgressive" American burlesque women and also incidentally explaining the key obstruction that her sexual grotesqueness presents to what might otherwise be her more extensive power. When Mae West found herself increasingly censored, relegated, and marginalized in American popular entertainment, she increasingly became a parody of herself. Parton runs the same risk. Geoffrey Himes has made this point about Parton in comparing her to Elvis Presley: "Both singers grew up poor hillbillies with great voices and sure instincts. Both allowed themselves to be transformed into grotesque self-parodies; Dolly, the platinum-wigged, big-busted doll, and Elvis, the wooden B-movie actor."

So should we be glad we have a highly successful hillbilly scapegoat? Or should we be sad that her potential power is so easily marginalized and controlled? There is no one answer. The answer is both. And that's the pain.

# Sources

For the comprehensive filmography of over eight hundred titles on which this work is based, see J. W. Williamson, "Southern Mountaineers Filmography," available on Internet. Gopher to gopher.acs.appstate.edu. From the first menu, choose University Library. From the University Library menu, choose Appalachian Collection.

Sources are cited below in the order that they have been referred to in the text.

## Chapter 1

The Hunter S. Thompson quote is from his *Generation of Swine: Tales of Shame and Degradation in the Eighties* (New York: Summit Books, 1988), p. 10.

William Willeford, *The Fool and His Scepter: A Study in Clowns and Jesters and Their Audience* (Evanston, Ill.: Northwestern University Press, 1969), pp. 71–72.

A major collector of hillbilliana is Jean Haskell Speer, who has abetted me at times in my weird interests.

I am grateful to Nancy Collins for introducing me to the monsters of mountain tradition—the Whang Doodle, the Taily-Bone, and the Boojum.

The first *TV Guide* quote is from a description of *Lobo*, 19 Dec. 1983, p. A54. The second *TV Guide* quote is from an article on incest as depicted in the TV movie *Something about Amelia* (ABC), 7 Jan. 1984, p. 42.

John Higham, *Strangers in the Land: Patterns of American Nativism* (New Brunswick, N.J.: Rutgers University Press, 1955), p. 181.

The Herblock cartoon was printed in the *Washington Post*, 5 Nov. 1985.

Elmore Leonard, *The City Primeval: High Noon in Detroit* (New York: Arbor House, 1980), pp. 156–57.

Rod Davis, "I'm a Nazi until Death," *Texas Monthly*, Feb. 1989, p. 134.

Johnny Fullen, quoted in an AP story in *Troublesome Creek Times*, 20 Aug. 1986, p. 4.

Minnie Pearl, writing under her real name, Sarah Cannon, in the *Nashville Banner*, quoted by Fleur Paysour, *Charlotte Observer*, 11 Nov. 1986, p. 20C.

On Dwight Yoakam, see Geoffrey Himes in the *Washington Post*, 24 May 1987, p. G2, and Joe Sasfy in the *Washington Post*, 9 July 1987, p. C11. The Ken Tucker quote first appeared in the *Philadelphia Inquirer* and was reprinted in the *Charlotte Observer*, 31 Oct. 1986, p. 1C.

The Judds accepted their Horizon Award on the evening of 8 Oct. 1984.

On Marty Stuart, see Ed Bumgardner in the *Winston-Salem Journal*, 4 Oct. 1991, pp. 27, 32, and Joe Edwards (for the Associated Press) in the *Mountain Eagle* (Whitesburg, Ky.), 23 Oct. 1991, p. 7.

On John Mellencamp, see Richard Harrington in the *Washington Post*, 9 Dec. 1985, p. C12.

On Sen. Conrad Burns (R-Mont.), see the *Washington Post*, 5 Mar. 1989, p. A4.

On the Grand and Glorious Order of the Hillbilly Degree, I am indebted to Jim Harris's self-published history of the same, privately printed as a stapled booklet in Milford, Ohio, in March 1982. In his office as Imperial Raban of the Hillbilly Degree, Jim Harris also graciously granted me permission to reproduce the hillbilly character in Figure 1. That logo has been superseded by one that emphasizes the Shriners' work for crippled children. On the Cincinnati controversy, see "Hillbilly Convention Drawing Criticism," *Cincinnati Enquirer*, 12 Oct. 1982, pp. C1–C2. (I am indebted to Phil Obermiller for supplying this source.) See also Christopher Quinn, "Hillbillies on Parade," *Winston-Salem Journal*, 26 Nov. 1989, p. S7. Julie Mullis's unpublished interview with Ed Schweiger, Raban of Hillbilly Clan No. 13 in Charlotte, N.C., and her personal essay about her own father, who is also a member of Clan No. 13, confirmed my impressions of the hillbilly identity's *positive* charge. This positive energy has been little appreciated by regional academics. The Cincinnati Appalachian activists who put a stop to the mayor's sanctioning of the Shriner hillbillies were also successful, in 1993, in influencing the language of a new citywide human rights code that banned discrimination "based on race, sex, sexual orientation, color, religion, disability or Appalachian origin."

The Estill Drew paragraphs are based on letters from Estill Drew, interviews with Estill and Dale Drew, and showings of Estill's movies on the campus of Appalachian State University on 30 Sept. and 1 Oct. 1986.

I have for a number of years collected memories of Womanless Wedding folk plays from members of Elderhostel classes at Appalachian State University. I have talked to people who witnessed events very similar to my Texas memories in Florida, Georgia, Alabama, Kentucky, Ohio, Michigan, and North Carolina. Almost all accounts feature the hillbilly garb and the hillbilly props—outlandish rural poverty enacted by and for small-town people. Francis Brown Baker of Greenville, Ky., remembered that her classmates in Greenville High School in 1943 observed a Hillbilly Day, when they all dressed in "overalls with tatters and

shirts with tatters. At that time, which was just after the major part of the Depression, these tattered clothes represented utter poverty. At that time we
would not be caught dead in a pair of blue jeans. The only children who wore
blue jeans to our school were children who were totally poverty-stricken."

Jane Woodside's thesis on Womanless Weddings does not emphasize hillbilly
clowning as an integral part of the events, though some of the scripts Woodside
found do feature an exaggerated hillbilly dialect. She found pregnant brides
more often in African American versions. Many of Woodside's examples were
performed as fundraisers by church groups and were considerably less vulgar
than the version I remember from west Texas. Woodside's summation is worth
quoting: "Across the South, for at least the past seventy years, grown men have
been hooking themselves into bras, then struggling into dresses and evening
gowns. They have added wigs and make-up, hats or other accessories and driven to the local community auditorium, where they joined other men from
town—some of whom were dressed as women, some costumed as men. In the
presence of their family, friends and neighbors, the men have then gone
through the motions of a marriage ceremony." See Jane Xenia Harris Woodside, "The Womanless Wedding: An American Folk Drama," M.A. thesis, University of North Carolina at Chapel Hill, 1986. I am indebted to Jane Woodside
for generously loaning me a copy of this important research. Woodside also
brought to my attention the work of Michael Taft; "The Mock Wedding in Western Canada: A Sense of Continuity," paper read at the meeting of the California Folklore Society, Los Angeles, 1991.

I am also indebted to Nancy Collins and Randy Crutchfield for memories
and photographs of Womanless Weddings.

I owe the phrase "anywhere the ground is uneven" to Jim Wayne Miller, who
developed it and related ideas from those of French critic Roland Barthes. See
Jim Wayne Miller, "Anytime the Ground Is Uneven: The Outlook for Regional
Studies and What to Look Out For," in *Geography and Literature: A Meeting of the
Disciplines*, edited by William E. Mallory and Paul Simpson-Housley (Syracuse,
N.Y.: Syracuse University Press, 1987), pp. 1–20.

### Ambiguity and the Meanings of Mountains

George F. Will, "The Lure of the Lurid," *Washington Post*, 10 Dec. 1989, p. C7.
For help in parsing the meaning of *ambiguity*, I thank my colleague Dan Hurley.

I am indebted to Robert C. Allen, *Horrible Prettiness: Burlesque and American
Culture* (Chapel Hill: University of North Carolina Press, 1991), for helping to
settle my thinking about ambiguity and the curious "ordination" that stage acts

achieve. See J. W. Williamson, "Hillbilly Gals and American Burlesque," *Southern Quarterly* (Summer 1994).

Marjorie Hope Nicolson, *Mountain Gloom and Mountain Glory* (New York: Norton, 1963). Also useful are Longinus, *On the Sublime*, translated by James A. Arieti and John M. Crossett (New York: E. Mellen Press, 1984), and Samuel Monk, *The Sublime: A Study of Critical Theories in 18th-Century England* (Ann Arbor: University of Michigan Press, 1960). Dante's attitudes toward mountains are put forward by John Ruskin, as quoted by Nicolson (*Mountain Gloom*, p. 48). The seventeenth-century diarist John Evelyn is quoted by Monk as saying that the Alps contained "the rubbish of the earth" (*The Sublime*, p. 206).

Thomas Burnet is discussed in Nicolson, *Mountain Gloom*, pp. 213–24.

### Everybody's Got One

W. H. (Bill) Ward's line, "Everybody's got a hillbilly," has been used repeatedly in the *Appalachian Journal* to headline excerpted news items showing the hillbilly stereotype at work around the globe. But I admit here that Bill stoutly maintains he was misquoted, that he really said, "Everybody's got a redneck." Same difference.

Betty MacDonald, *The Egg and I* (New York: Lippincott Co., 1945). MacDonald is discussed more fully in Chapter 2 under the subhead "Ma and Pa Kettle."

Arnold Toynbee made a big deal out of comparing American hillbillies to the hairy Ainus of Japan and to other "barbarians" in his twelve-volume *A Study of History* (Oxford: Oxford University Press, 1934–61). A catalog of Toynbee's sins, along with a devastating assessment of his Appalachian "evidence," can be found in James S. Brown, "An Appalachian Footnote to Toynbee's *A Study of History*," *Appalachian Journal* 6, no. 1 (Fall 1978): 29–32.

The examples of hillbilly status used in this section were excerpted in *Appalachian Journal* 10, no. 3 (Spring 1983): 226 (Ramapo Mountains); 16, no. 1 (Fall 1988): 25 (Maine's "nativist nihilists"); 12, no. 4 (Summer 1985): 292 (China's Guizhou Province); 18, no. 1 (Fall 1990): 34 (Japan's Ainu); 15, no. 4 (Summer 1988): 338–39 (New Hampshire "swamp Yankees"); and 16, no. 1 (Fall 1988): 27 ("Yankee versions of slack-jawed hillbilly feebs").

I am indebted to Anna Creadick for reminding me of Carolyn Chute's *The Beans of Egypt, Maine*. A movie version of *The Beans* was released late in 1994 by American Playhouse Theatrical Films/I.R.S. Media, starring Martha Plimpton, Kelly Lynch, and Rutger Hauer.

*Chapter 2*

I am indebted to Anna Creadick, Dan Hurley, Bill McNeil, Henry Shapiro, Chip Arnold, and Pam Williamson for valuable editorial suggestions and comments on this chapter.

William Willeford, *The Fool and His Scepter: A Study in Clowns and Jesters and Their Audience* (Evanston, Ill.: Northwestern University Press, 1969), pp. xv, xvi.

Enid Welsford, *The Fool: His Social and Literary History* (London: Faber and Faber, 1935; rpt., Garden City, N.Y.: Anchor Books, 1961). See also Sandra Billington, *A Social History of the Fool* (New York: St. Martin's Press, 1984), and Lowell Swortzell, *Here Come the Clowns: A Cavalcade of Comedy from Antiquity to the Present* (New York: Viking Press, 1978).

Willeford is especially provocative on the doctrine of the fool and his mirror. Willeford is the source for most of the illustrations in this section. See also J. W. Williamson, "Thackeray's Mirror," *Tennessee Studies in Literature* 22 (1977): 133–53.

I am indebted to Jim Wayne Miller for comments about Till Eulenspiegel.

On the contemporary interpretation of the fool, see especially Geoff Hoyle's stage act, "The Fool Show," which is reviewed and discussed by David Richards, *Washington Post*, 3 Feb. 1989, pp. B1, B7, and by Elizabeth Kastor, *Washington Post*, 21 Feb. 1989, pp. C1, C4.

### Hillbilly Clowning

"Still Dumb," by Charlie Gearheart, © 1990 Dry Line Music, BMI; used with permission. I am indebted to Jim Webb for introducing me to the music of the Goose Creek Symphony.

David Reynolds pointed out to me that the Man, W.Va., high school basketball team is called The Hillbillies. There may be others.

The original Yosef idea was hatched by annual editors James "Soup" Storie, Elizabeth South, and Lloyd Isaacs, all of whom were "mountain locals," assisted by Bill Mitchell of the Observer Printing Company of Charlotte. Storie and South later married. See John Idol, "The Origin of 'Yosef,'" *The Appalachian*, 30 Sept. 1955, p. 2.

"Corn Huskers to Crown Mr. and Mrs. Yosef; Hay Pitchers to Announce Typical Pair," *The Appalachian*, 21 Nov. 1947, p. 1.

"Newland Boys Blast Editor and Yosef," *The Appalachian*, 14 Jan. 1966, p. 2; "Effram's Ma Writes," *The Appalachian*, 18 Feb. 1968, p. 2.

"'A' Club Enshrines Mountaineers' Spirit: 'Yosef' Cast in Bronze," *The Appalachian*, 15 May 1958, p. 1; "Western's Wrath: Not Our Fault," and editorial cartoon, "Cats Who Are Rats," *The Appalachian*, 21 Jan. 1966, p. 2.

Yosef's editorial column, "Musings of a Mountaineer," first featured a picture of him in the 22 Nov. 1946 edition of *The Appalachian* (p. 3). I have also gleaned information from the following articles in *The Appalachian*: "Yosef Yodelin'," 19 Sept. 1947, p. 2; "Elocutionary Education—Mountain Style" (in which Yosef is called a "perennial freshman"), 12 March 1948, p. 2; "Yosef," 15 Oct. 1948, p. 1; untitled cartoon, 8 Sept. 1950, p. 3; "Ray Flinchum Portrays Fabulous Mountaineer Character Yosef," 12 Oct. 1951, p. 3; "Proclamation," 1 Feb. 1955, p. 1; "Yosef, the Apps' Mascot," 17 Sept. 1959, p. 4; and the "Homecoming '86" special issue, p. 4B. I am also indebted to Gerald Adams and the Yosef Club office staff for valuable information; to ASU registrar Brooks McLeod; to Eric Olson and Dean Williams of the William Leonard Eury Appalachian Collection at ASU; to John Dinkins and Steve Ferguson of Audio-Visual Services, ASU.

In the late 1970s, individual students ceased to act out the part of Yosef, who was embodied instead by a toned-down soft-sculpture mask worn on an otherwise anonymous student's head.

Bill Blanton, interview with author, 15 June 1992, Boone, N.C.

On both hillbilly clowning and the traps in same, see also the discussion of David Crockett in Chapter 3.

## Hillbilly Archaeology

On Sut Lovingood, I am indebted to Mary Dunlap; to Ormonde Plater, "The Lovingood Patriarchy," *Appalachian Journal* 1, no. 2 (Spring 1973): 82–93; to Jim Wayne Miller; and to the *Lovingood Papers*, published by the University of Tennessee Press for the Sut Society, 1963–67.

Census data is from the *Encyclopedia Americana* (Danbury, Conn.: Grolier, Inc., 1988), "United States Population Growth."

On illustrations of Sut, see M. Thomas Inge, "Sut and His Illustrators," in *Lovingood Papers, 1965*, edited by Ben Harris McClary (Knoxville: University of Tennessee Press for the Sut Society, 1967).

Hans Bungert, introduction to "Sut Lovengood: On the Puritan Yankee," in *Lovingood Papers, 1963*.

J. J. Hooper, *Some Adventures of Captain Simon Suggs*, introduction by Manly Wade Wellman (Chapel Hill: University of North Carolina Press, 1969). Inge ("Sut and His Illustrators") led me to Suggs.

Archie Green is very good on iconographical history, and I have benefited from his "Graphics" series in *JEMF Quarterly*, especially "Portraits of Appalachian Musicians: Graphics no. 49," vol. 15, no. 54 (Summer 1979): 99–106. Green has urged me to compare the iconographical history of the hillbilly-as-fool more directly to other American and much earlier British representations of "wild men," because the hillbilly is clearly a descendant not just of clowns and fools but also of *beaux savages*. Green writes: "In short, hillbilly pictorialists long ago *combined* elements of the fool, the wild Celtic father figure, and the coonskin-capped, Indianized frontiersman." I do take up these other dimensions of the hillbilly in subsequent chapters.

William Faulkner, in *Writers at Work: The "Paris Review" Interviews*, is quoted in *Lovingood Papers, 1963*, edited by Ben Harris McClary (Knoxville: University of Tennessee Press for the Sut Society, 1963), p. [7].

Edmund Wilson was married four times. The first three wives were Mary Blair, Margaret Canby, and novelist Mary McCarthy. Wilson's comments about Sut are found in Inge, "Sut and His Illustrators," and in Walter Blair, "Harris' Best," in *Lovingood Papers, 1965*. Milton Rickles's introduction to "Sut Lovingood Come to Life," in *Lovingood Papers, 1963*, discusses George Washington Harris as a "propagandist for Southern secession"; and Hans Bungert's introduction to "How Sut Lovegood Dosed His Dog," in *Lovingood Papers, 1963*, discusses Harris's southern crudities as they were exploited in the North.

I am grateful to Eric Olson for bringing T. C. Crawford's *An American Vendetta* (New York: Belford, Clarke, and Co., 1888) to my attention.

On the earliest appearance of the word *hillbilly*, I follow Archie Green's history in "Hillbilly Music: Source and Symbol," *Journal of American Folklore* 78 (July–Sept. 1965): 204–28; I am also indebted to Archie Green in the next section below.

Cratis D. Williams wrote much about the comparison between "white trash" and "hillbilly" in *The Southern Mountaineer in Fact and Fiction*. For a guide to his references, see the entry under "poor whites" in the index to the first seven volumes of *Appalachian Journal*, vol 7, no. 4 (1980).

The plot synopsis of *Billie—the Hill Billy* is quoted from J. W. Williamson, *Southern Mountaineers in Silent Films: Plot Synopses of Movies about Moonshining, Feuding, and Other Mountain Topics, 1904–1929* (Jefferson, N.C.: McFarland and Co., 1994).

It's possible, though in my judgment unlikely, that the cartoonized hillbilly type, without that name attached to him, may have appeared in nickelodeon comedies about mountain moonshiners or mountain feudists or rubes generally. Nickelodeon comedies detailed in *Southern Mountaineers in Silent Films* include *Higginses vs Judsons* (Lubin, 1911), *Ferdie's Family Feud* (Imp, 1912), *That Houn' Dawg* (Pathé, 1912), *Why Kentucky Went Dry* (Frontier, 1914), *Good Cider* (Lubin, 1914), *Who's Who in Hogg's Hollow* (Selig, 1914), *The Cub* (World Film, 1915), *Jerry and the Moonshiners* (Cub/Mutual, 1916), *Moonshine* (Paramount,

1918), *When Bearcat Went Dry* (Macauley Photoplays/World, 1919), and numerous others. Few of these movies survive intact, though there are a few feet of the comedy *Pansy* in the Library of Congress. *Pansy* was a satire of phony city masculinity as exhibited by a politician. To garner votes, the politician plans to fight off a bear attack staged with a tame bear. "Mountain people" learn of the plot and substitute a wild bear, which puts the blowhard politician to flight. In none of the surviving frames of *Pansy* is there any character approaching our hillbilly clown. In fact, none of the synopses of any of these early comedies suggest that the Yosef/Paul Webb type hillbilly had yet been visually conceived. In what does survive intact from the nickelodeon period—mainly Biograph's series of mountain melodramas that began in 1904—mountain people tended to look quite ordinary and unremarkable.

In the surviving Biograph films—*The Moonshiner* (1904), *A Kentucky Feud* (1905), *The Feud and the Turkey* (dir. D. W. Griffith, 1908), *The Mountaineer's Honor* (dir. Griffith, 1909), and *The Fugitive* (dir. Griffith, 1910), the first two of which happen to be the earliest of all movies about mountain people—the mountain characters, many of them desperate and rough, were costumed in regular working-class and middle-class clothes of the period. In *A Kentucky Feud*, "Sally" Hatfield sports a high-piled French chapeau through the whole 675 feet. If anything, mountain characters in these melodramas looked vaguely Western. Archie Green spoke the truth: "The line between mountain and cowboy movies was no stronger or higher than a barb wire fence." If the cartoonized hillbilly type had been *available* for Griffith to exploit, he would have exploited it, especially given what we know of his affection for easy stereotypes and cheap shots. In 1923 Buster Keaton made his second feature film, a comedy called *Our Hospitality* (Keaton Productions/Metro), which followed the same basic storyline first tried in *Ferdie's Family Feud* (1912): a bumbling city dude inherits a Kentucky feud, only he doesn't realize it until it's too late. Keaton too did not use cartoonized hillbillies to menace his main character. Rather, his feuding Canfields visually resembled aristocratic southerners. Again, either the cartoonized hillbilly did not yet exist, or Keaton was too original a filmmaker to use him. Keaton had also been in *Moonshine* (1918), another mountain comedy, with star Fatty Arbuckle, but none of the film's publicity stills in *Moving Picture World* show anything like our cartoon hillbilly.

On the stage production of *The Cub*, see *New York Times*, 2 Nov. 1910, p. 11. When Maurice Tourneur was preparing to make the first film version of the play in 1915, he took the interesting step of traveling by train to Bluefield, West Virginia, and then north to Mingo County to interview Devil Anse Hatfield himself for "authenticity." A photograph was made of Tourneur and his assistant talking with Devil Anse across a fence, the gate of which has not been opened. We can speculate that the fence is as far as Tourneur got. But the image of Devil Anse is suggestive and invites the interesting speculation that the cartoonized hillbilly was originally a specific parody of this real personage.

Snuffy Smith first materialized as a subsidiary character in the highly popular syndicated cartoon strip *Barney Google*. See M. Thomas Inge, "The Appalachian Backgrounds of Billy De Beck's Snuffy Smith," *Appalachian Journal* 4, no. 2 (Winter 1977), 120–32. I realize that the character Snuffy Smith is not exactly Yosef; he's short and dumpy. But the world of *Snuffy Smith* does contain Yosef-like ectomorphs. The same is true of *Li'l Abner*, wherein the title character himself and many of the other principals are *sui generis*.

Willeford's quote about fools not belonging to the human image is from his *The Fool and His Scepter*, p. 71.

On movie cartoons, I am indebted to Will Friedwald and Jerry Beck, *The Warner Brothers Cartoons* (Metuchen, N.J.: Scarecrow Press, 1981), and Leonard Maltin, *Of Mice and Magic: A History of American Animated Cartoons* (New York: McGraw-Hill, 1980).

## The Hillbilly Fool as Troubadour

Mrs. Andy Webb's quote is from an interview published in "He Shouted Loud, 'Hosanna, Deliverance Will Come,'" an insert in *Foxfire* 7, no. 4 (Winter 1973).

"Plime-blank" means "exactly." It's one of Kentucky writer James Still's favorite mountain terms.

On hillbilly music, I am indebted to Archie Green, "Hillbilly Music: Source and Symbol," *Journal of American Folklore* 78 (July–Sept. 1965): 204–28; to *The Country Music Story*, photos by Burt Goldblatt, text by Robert Shelton (Indianapolis: Bobbs-Merrill, 1966); to several items in Linnell Gentry, *A History and Encyclopedia of Country, Western, and Gospel Music*, 2d ed. (Nashville: Clairmont Corp., 1969); to Bill C. Malone, *Southern Music, American Music* (Lexington: University Press of Kentucky 1979) and *Country Music, U.S.A.*, rev. ed. (Austin: University of Texas Press, 1985); to Neil V. Rosenberg, *Bluegrass: A History* (Urbana: University of Illinois Press, 1985); and to Robert Cantwell, *Bluegrass Breakdown: The Making of the Old Southern Sound* (Urbana: University of Illinois Press, 1984).

By 1919 there were 2,230,000 phonographs in this country. *Historical Statistics of the United States, Colonial Times to 1957* (Washington, D.C.: Government Printing Office, 1965).

"National earache," "the epidemic of corn," "nasal twang": see Doron K.

Antrim, "Whoop-and-Holler Opera," *Collier's*, 26 Jan. 1946, pp. 18, 85; "Bull Market in Corn," *Time*, 4 Oct. 1943; both reprinted in Linnell Gentry's *History and Encyclopedia of Country . . . Music*.

The David Reisman statement is quoted by Archie Green in "Hillbilly Music."

Bob Snyder talked about "blurting" as "an urgency of candor" in mountain poetry in "Colonial Mimesis and the Appalachian Renascence," *Appalachian Journal* 5, no. 3 (Spring 1978): 348.

The story about Ralph Peer and the recording of Fiddlin' John Carson and the naming of Al Hopkins's band is found in Green, "Hillbilly Music." But see also Gene Wiggins, *Fiddlin' Georgia Crazy: Fiddlin' John Carson, His Real World, and the World of His Songs* (Urbana: University of Illinois Press, 1987); *The Country Music Story*, p. 32; and Kyle Crichton, "Thar's Gold in Them Hillbillies," *Collier's*, 30 April 1938, pp. 24–5, reprinted in Gentry, *History and Encyclopedia of Country . . . Music*.

Neil Rosenberg discusses the comic edge of "the hillbilly performance" in *Bluegrass: A History*: "The comedy segments were boldly executed in terms of physical action (slapstick) and social content (stereotype)" (p. 22); hillbilly music was "a way of seeing the world and sowing wild oats" (p. 27). Robert Cantwell is also instructive on the "wild and carefree" sound of the Skillet Lickers and others in *Bluegrass Breakdown*, pp. 52–53.

On the Weaver Brothers and Elviry, Bob Burns, and Judy Canova (and also Lum and Abner), see Wade Austin, "The Real Beverly Hillbillies," *Southern Quarterly* 19, nos. 3–4 (Spring–Summer 1981): 83–94. I am also indebted to William K. McNeil's special issue devoted to the Weaver Brothers and Elviry, in *Old Time Country* 5, no. 4 (Winter 1988). But see also Mary A. Bufwack and Robert K. Oermann, *Finding Her Voice: The Saga of Women in Country Music* (New York: Crown Publishers, 1993), especially chap. 2, "Southern Sentiments: Country Females in Nineteenth-Century Show Business."

On Ferlin Husky, I have used Melvin Shestack, *The Country Music Encyclopedia* (New York: T. Y. Crowell Co., 1974), and Irwin Stambler and Grelun Landon, *Encyclopedia of Folk, Country, and Western Music* (New York: St. Martin's Press, 1969).

On comic hillbilly Walter "Kid" Smith, see Norm Cohen's piece in the *JEMF Quarterly* 9, no. 3 (Autumn 1973): 128–32.

Albert Goldman, *Elvis* (New York: McGraw-Hill, 1981).

I am much indebted to my colleague William Lightfoot for the notion that bluegrass music induces a state of Dionysian release and for other information and insights.

Anent *Bonnie and Clyde*'s bluegrass soundtrack, Archie Green points out that no one in Bonnie and Clyde's own era ever heard "Foggy Mountain Breakdown"-style bluegrass, because it wasn't invented yet. Writes Green in a letter to me: "With a sense of musical history, the film director could have used a western swing classic of the period such as 'Osage Stomp' and achieved the same effect."

I am indebted to my students for reminding me of other musical hillbilly clowns, including Ray Stevens. Other more recent musical acts that play on hillbilly clowning include the hypercurrent Dan Baird, the Chapel Hill bar band Southern Culture on the Skids, and the now defunct Kentucky Headhunters. My student Suzanne Moffitt describes Southern Culture on the Skids: "The lead singer wears union station overalls, long johns, work boots, and a typical hillbilly hat. . . . They sing songs with names like 'I Left My Teeth on the Window Sill,' 'The Kudzu Limbo, or How Low Can You Grow,' and 'Eight Piece Box.' . . . For 'Eight Piece Box' they eat fried chicken and share with the audience. They also give audience members sticks and hubcaps so they can play along, and they invite audience members to limbo on stage. Their music seems to be a mixture of country, bluegrass, rock, and The Beach Boys." See also Nicole Arthur, "Southern Culture: Grand Ole Hokey," *Washington Post*, 5 April 1993, p. D9.

I am also indebted to Andrea Frye for mentioning Dan Baird's solo debut album, *Love Songs for the Hearing Impaired*, which got rave reviews in the mainstream press. Frye writes: "Interestingly, the album has been so lauded largely because of its cheerful disregard for political correctness. (Sample lyric: 'You got knocked up / I got locked up / Guess you could say we both got screwed.') . . . We use country music as a vicarious release. People in country songs are still rather hedonistic: they drink too much, smoke too much, cheat on their husbands and wives without fear of AIDS, and make uncomplimentary observations about members of the opposite sex." See also William Booth, "White Noise: Good Ol' Boy Dan Baird's World of Bad Bars, Bad Girls and Bad Love," *Washington Post*, 4 April 1993, pp. G1, G10. The Kentucky Headhunters blossomed and faded very quickly. At first they were called "unmarketable," and even after they were featured on the 1991 broadcast of the Grammy Awards, Tony Kornheiser commented: "Get a load of that crew. What were they smelling, the algae on the surface of a limited gene pool?" That comment and others about the Kentucky Headhunters are excerpted in *Appalachian Journal* 17, no. 4 (Summer 1990): 338; 18, no. 1 (Fall 1990): 37; 19, no. 1 (Fall 1991): 23, 27–28.

## Ma and Pa Kettle

I have used Michael G. Fitzgerald, *Universal Pictures: A Panoramic History in Words, Pictures, and Filmographies* (Westport, Conn.: Arlington House Publishers, 1977), to document the Ma and Pa Kettle opera: *Ma and Pa Kettle* (1949), *Ma and Pa Kettle Go to Town* (1950), *Ma and Pa Kettle Back on the Farm* (1951), *Ma and Pa Kettle at the Fair* (1952), *Ma and Pa Kettle on Vacation* (1953), *Ma and Pa Kettle at Home* (1954), and finally *Ma and Pa Kettle at Waikiki* (1955). There were two more Kettle movies, with first Arthur Hunnicut and then Parker Fennelly playing Pa: *The Kettles in the Ozarks* (1956) and *The Kettles on Old MacDonald's Farm* (1957).

Betty MacDonald, *The Egg and I* (New York: J. B. Lippincott, 1945).

I am indebted to my student Deborah Bell for correcting parts of my summary of the movie *The Egg and I* and for suggesting a completely different meaning of that film, centered on the Colbert character and her ambiguous pregnancy. Bell writes: "Colbert never announces she's pregnant. She runs away, back East to her family, fearing that Bob (Fred MacMurray) has been seduced by the female owner of a modern (and *model*) farm. He's been seduced all right, but by the farm and not its 'barnyard glamor girl.' When Betty finally returns with the baby, she finds that Bob has bought the fancy farm for her." The title *The Egg and I*, then, obviously signals a serious wrestling match with traditional motherhood.

The "astonishing commercial success" of the Kettle movies is covered in *Halliwell's Film Guide*, 5th ed. (New York: Charles Scribner's Sons, 1986).

On the popularity of *The Beverly Hillbillies*, see Erik Larson, "Watching Americans Watch TV," *Atlantic Monthly*, March 1992, p. 69. Larson reports that seven of the fifty highest-rated TV programs of all time were 1964 episodes of *The Beverly Hillbillies*. Thanks to Dan Hurley for bringing this article to my attention.

*The Beverly Hillbillies* movie, starring Jim Varney and Cloris Leachman and directed by Penelope Spheeris, premiered nationwide on 15 Oct. 1993. See "Meterology: Spheeris Clouds Drop No Water," in "Signs of the Times," *Appalachian Journal* 21, no. 3 (Spring 1994): 252.

Horace Newcomb, "Appalachia on Television: Region as Symbol in American Popular Culture," *Appalachian Journal* 7, nos. 1–2 (Fall–Winter 1979–80): 155–64.

## Andy Griffith as Clown

"Bumpkin to Big-Timer," *Newsweek*, 18 Jan. 1954, p. 60.

"Country Cousins: Your Search for Mayberry Ends Right Here," *Simple Plea-*

*sures* (Mt. Airy, N.C.), May 1988, p. 6; Dotson Rader, "Why I Listened to My Father," *Parade*, 4 Feb. 1990, pp. 4–5; Martha Sherrill, "Mount Airy, Adoring Andy," *Washington Post*, 1 Oct. 1990, pp. B1, B8; Paul Collins, "Town Gears Up for 'Mayberry Days,'" *Winston-Salem Journal*, 26 Sept. 1991, pp. 13, 17; Gilbert Millstein, "Greeting Griffith," *New York Times*, 16 Oct. 1955, Sec. 2, pp. 1, 3.

The play *No Time For Sergeants* opened on Broadway in September 1955, but it was staged on live TV, starring Griffith and produced by the Theatre Guild, on 15 Mar. 1955, six months before its Broadway opening. The live TV production is available on VHS videotape from Wood Knapp Video.

I am indebted to Randy Crutchfield for reminding me of Bill Murray in *Stripes*.

The movie version of *No Time For Sergeants*, released by Warner Brothers, was produced and directed by Mervyn LeRoy and featured Nick Adams, Myron McCormick, Murray Hamilton, Don Knotts, and Dub Taylor.

Other reviews of Griffith's performance in both the play and the movie version of *No Time For Sergeants*: "The Hillbilly's a Hit," *Newsweek*, 31 Oct. 1955, p. 55 ("a backwoods bonehead"); John McCarten, "Familiar, but Funny," *New Yorker*, 7 June 1958, pp. 64–65 ("a look of friendly idiocy"); Bosley Crowther, *New York Times*, 30 May 1958, p. 13; "Andy's Dandy," *Newsweek*, 9 June 1958, p. 79; "New Films from Books," *Library Journal*, 15 June 1958, p. 1913; "Another Time for Sergeants," *Life*, 9 June 1958, pp. 77–78.

For other sources on Griffith, see the Griffith section in Chapter 6 below.

I have some support for my belief in a certain ambiguous scapegoat's fury lodged deep inside Griffith-as-clown. Screenwriter and playwright Frank Levering has written a play based on Griffith's highly conflicted relationship to the community of Mount Airy (Andrea Frye, unpublished interview with Levering).

### The Hillbilly as Priapus

"Late burlesque leer": In this interpretation, I have been much influenced by Robert C. Allen, *Horrible Prettiness: Burlesque and American Culture* (Chapel Hill: University of North Carolina Press, 1991).

I should note here the earlier movie version of *Li'l Abner* (Astor Pictures, 1940, dir. Albert S. Rogell), an execrable film that Al Capp himself would never acknowledge. Interestingly, it featured Buster Keaton in a bit part. See Michael H. Price and George E. Turner, "Abner Goes Hollywood; Gets Lost in Shuffle," in *Li'l Abner: Dailies Volume Six, 1940* (Princeton, Wis.: Kitchen Sink Press, 1989).

I am indebted to Josh Wood for reminding me of *I Spit on Your Grave*.

David K. Frasier, *Russ Meyer—the Life and Films* (Jefferson, N.C.: McFarland and Co. Inc., 1990).

Jimmy McDonough and Bill Landis, "Hillbilly Heaven," *Film Comment*, Dec. 1985, pp. 55–59.

## Raising Arizona

*Raising Arizona*, written, produced, and directed by Ethan and Joel Coen, starred Nicolas Cage and Holly Hunter. The Stephen Schiff quotes are from *Vanity Fair*, April 1987, pp. 37–38.

My quotations from the movie were transcribed from screenings and may differ slightly from the published screenplay, which certainly differs in many respects from the movie as it was released. See Joel Coen and Ethan Coen, *Raising Arizona: The Screenplay* (New York: St. Martin's Press, 1988).

Students Tom Byland, Angel Rippy, Elaine Vann, and others contributed much to my understanding of *Raising Arizona*.

See Jack Barth, "Praising 'Arizona,'" *Film Comment*, April 1987, pp. 18–20, 22–24; about those snot-nosed brats, the Coen brothers, see "The Coen Mother: Raising Auteurs," in *Entertainment Weekly*, 28 Feb. 1992, p. 59.

## Chapter 3

I am indebted to Chip Arnold, Anna Creadick, Dan Hurley, and Pam Williamson for valuable editorial suggestions.

The Robert Southey usage of *woaded* is found in the *Oxford English Dictionary*. All other quotes about the Picts come from T. D. Kendrick, *British Antiquity* (London: Methuen, 1950).

Penelope B. R. Doob has a chapter on the wildman tradition in England in *Nebuchadnezzar's Children: Conventions of Madness in Middle English Literature* (New Haven: Yale University Press, 1974).

Rodger Cunningham, *Apples on the Flood: The Southern Mountain Experience* (Knoxville: University of Tennessee Press, 1987).

Archie Green made several suggestions about the connections between ancient Celtic savages and frontier Americans including hillbillies, and I am grateful to him for letting me quote from a personal communication. He suggested the text and plates in T. D. Kendrick's *British Antiquity*, which contains some of John White's work. But for more documentary illustrations of Carolina Algonquins, see Paul Hulton, *America 1585: The Complete Drawings of John White* (Chapel Hill: University of North Carolina Press and British Museum Publications, 1984). White's imaginary drawings of ancient Picts are in this same volume. For additional representations of American frontiersmen, see Blake Nevius, *Cooper's Landscapes: An Essay on the Picturesque Vision* (Berkeley:

University of California Press, 1976); and see the 1807 likeness of explorer Meriwether Lewis all woaded up in animal skins, in Marshall B. Davidson, *The Drawing of America: Eyewitness to History* (New York: Harry N. Abrams, Inc., 1983), Plate 105.

## The Thrill of Buckskin

See George Will, "There Is a Bit of Cooper's 'Hawkeye' in All of Us," *Mount Airy News*, 8 Oct. 1992, p. 4. Will described the central character thus: "Hawkeye, America's first great popular hero of fiction, is the man between—between forest and settlement, between tepee and drawing room, leading a life that is one long declaration of independence."

## Fooling with Coonskin:
## The One and Only Original American Hillbilly

Parts of the first two sections of this chapter first appeared under the title "Say It Ain't So, Davy!: David Crockett vs. the Real Backwoodsman in Us All," a review essay on the paperback edition of James A. Shackford's *David Crockett: The Man and the Legend* (Chapel Hill: University of North Carolina Press, 1956; pbk. rpt., 1986). See *Appalachian Journal* 15, no. 1 (Fall 1987): 44–51.

For the "gentleman from the cane" story (Mr. Mitchell in the Tennessee state legislature), and for the quotes about Crockett in the election campaign against Dr. Butler, see Shackford, *David Crockett*, pp. 52–53, 59, 63–64.

Crockett's campaign style is captured in the following, which he said that he said to Butler: "When I set out electioneering. . . . I [will] . . . have me a large buckskin hunting-shirt made, with a couple of pockets holding about a peck each; and . . . in one I [will] carry a great big twist of tobacco, and in the other my bottle of liquor; for I knowed when I met a man and offered him a dram, he would throw out his quid of tobacco to take one, and after he had taken his horn, I would out with my twist and give him another chaw. And in this way he would not be worse off than when I found him; and I would be sure to leave him in a first-rate good humour" (*The Autobiography of David Crockett*, introduction by Hamlin Garland [New York: Charles Scribner's Sons, 1923], pp. 109–10). In his democratic practice of every-man-a-potential-drinking-buddy, Crockett's cavorting with alcohol is another link to the hillbilly fool identity.

This is Crockett's own description of his first outing as a legislative candidate at a barbecue in Vernon, Tennessee, in 1821: "As good luck would have it, these big candidates spoke nearly all day, and when they quit, the people were worn out with fatigue, which afforded me a good apology for not discussing the government. But I listened mighty close to them, and was learning pretty fast about political matters. When they were all done, I got up and told some laughable story, and quit. I found I was safe in those parts, and so I went home, and didn't go back again till after the election was over. But to cut this matter short, I was elected, doubling my competitor, and nine votes over" (quoted in Shackford, *David Crockett*, p. 44).

On Crockett's break with Jackson, see Shackford, pp. 122–27. Shackford quotes Crockett's *Autobiography*: "During my first two sessions in Congress, Mr. Adams was president, and I worked along with what was called the Jackson party pretty well. I was re-elected to Congress in 1829, by an overwhelming majority; and soon after the commencement of this second term, I saw, or thought I did, that it was expected of me that I was to bow to the name of Andrew Jackson . . . even at the expense of my conscience and judgment. Such a thing was new to me, and a total stranger to my principles" (p. 122).

See Franklin Meine Jr., ed., *The Crockett Almanacks: Nashville Series, 1835–1838* (Chicago: Caxton Club, 1955); Michael A. Lofaro, ed., *The Tall Tales of Davy Crockett: The Second Nashville Series of Crockett Almanacs, 1839–1841* (Knoxville: University of Tennessee Press, 1987); Richard Boyd Hauck, "The Man in the Buckskin Hunting Shirt: Fact and Fiction in the Crockett Story," in *Davy Crockett: The Man, the Legend, the Legacy, 1786–1986*, edited by Michael A. Lofaro, pp. 3–20 (Knoxville: University of Tennessee Press, 1985); John Seelye, "A Well-Wrought Crockett: Or, How the Fakelorists Passed through the Credibility Gap and Discovered Kentucky," in ibid., pp. 21–45.

For good sense about the real David Crockett, one can hardly beat Paul Andrew Hutton, "Davy Crockett: Still King of the Wild Frontier," *Texas Monthly*, Nov. 1986, pp. 122–28, 130, 244–48. When Hutton was last heard from, he was writing the script for a new movie about Crockett, based on his own unfinished biography, *Sunrise in His Pocket*. Director Jerry Zucker was rumored to want Robin Williams for the role.

### King of the Wild Frontier

Frank Thompson, *Alamo Movies*, with a foreword by Fess Parker (East Berlin, Pa.: Old Mill Books, 1991).

*The Immortal Alamo* (Star Film Company/Gaston Méliès, 1911), filmed on location in San Antonio, Tex.; *Davy Crockett, in Hearts United* (New York Motion Picture Co., 1909). Some other early Crockett movies are: *Davy Crockett* (Selig, 1910), Lochinvar-Crockett and no Alamo; *Martyrs of the Alamo* (The Fine Arts Co., 1915, released through Triangle), "supervised by" D. W. Griffith but dir. by William Christy Cabanne; *Davy Crockett* (Pallas Pictures/Paramount, 1916),

Lochinvar-Crockett and no Alamo; *Davy Crockett at the Fall of the Alamo* (Sunset Productions, 1926), starring Cullen Landis; *Heroes of the Alamo* (Sunset Productions, 1937), with Lane Chandler as Crockett; *Davy Crockett, Indian Scout* (United Artists, 1950), starring George Montgomery in a Wild West shoot-'em-up with no Alamo; and *The Man from the Alamo* (Universal-International, 1953), with Trevor Bardette as Crockett.

I am indebted to William Eric Jamborsky and of course to Frank Thompson for the cataloging of Crockett movies.

*Davy Crockett, King of the Wild Frontier* was released theatrically in June 1955. It had been stitched together out of three separate episodes on *Disneyland*, beginning with the one broadcast in December 1954, and some of the original TV footage was lost in the transition to theater. The movie version is available from Buena Vista Home Video.

Margaret J. King has pointed out that the three-part Disney TV series aired very soon after "the coming of age of television—the widespread ownership of sets and television watching as a major leisure-time activity," and so there were millions of viewers drinking in the images. Perhaps a majority of those millions were children between the ages of two and seventeen, the "baby-boomers" of post–World War II. See King, "The Recycled Hero: Walt Disney's Davy Crockett," in Lofaro, ed., *Davy Crockett*, pp. 137–58.

Thomas Main, one of my students, pointed out that Crockett (and his "anti-expansionism" speech quoted in the text) arrived on the scene at a time when American expansionism was beginning to be seen widely as a problem, an embarrassment.

The Disney team obviously wanted to associate their backwoods hero with another powerful mythic mountain man, Sergeant Alvin York; Fess Parker, as Davy, adopts the same gesture of wetting his sights before "doin' some serious shootin'" that Gary Cooper used in *Sergeant York*.

### The Race Heroes: Boone, Jackson, Houston

Daniel Boone movies: *Daniel Boone: Or, Pioneer Days in America* (Edison, 1907); *The Chief's Daughter* (Selig, 1911); *Daniel Boone's Bravery* (Kalem, 1911); *The Life of Daniel Boone* (Republic, 1912); *Native State*, an episode in *The Son of Democracy* serial (Chapin/Famous Players–Lasky, 1918); *Daniel Boone* (Pathé, 1923); *In the Days of Daniel Boone*, serial (Universal, 1923); *Daniel Boone, through the Wilderness* (Sunset Productions, 1926); *Daniel Boone* (RKO, 1936); *Return of Daniel Boone* (Columbia, 1941); *Daniel Boone, Trailblazer* (Republic Pictures, 1956); *Daniel Boone, Jr.*, cartoon (Terrytoons, 1960).

Sam Houston movies: *The Conqueror* (Fox Standard Picture, 1917), starring

William Farnum; *Man of Conquest* (Republic, 1939), starring Richard Dix; *Houston: The Legend of Texas* (Taft Entertainment/CBS-TV, 1986), starring Sam Elliott.

Andrew Jackson movies: *The Gorgeous Hussy* (MGM, 1936); *The Buccaneer* (Paramount, 1937; dir. C. B. DeMille), with Hugh Sothern playing Jackson to Fredric March's Jean Lafitte; *The Buccaneer* (Paramount, 1958; remake of the previous item, also dir. C. B. DeMille), with Heston as Jackson to Yul Brynner's Lafitte; *The President's Lady* (Twentieth Century–Fox, 1953).

David Crockett in the 1950s: *Davy Crockett, Indian Scout* (United Artists, 1950), with George Montgomery; *The Man from the Alamo* (Universal-International, 1953); *Davy Crockett, King of the Wild Frontier* (Disney, 1956) and *Davy Crockett and the River Pirates* (Disney, 1957), both starring Fess Parker; *The Last Command* (Republic Pictures, 1955), a Jim Bowie movie with the great Arthur Hunnicut as Davy; and *The Alamo* (Batjac Productions/United Artists, 1960), with Duke Wayne Hisself as Davy.

### Buckskin Doubt in the Age of Eisenhower

*The Kentuckian* (United Artists, 1955); available on CBS/Fox Video. *The Kentuckian* was based on Felix Holt's novel *The Gabriel Horn* (New York: E. P. Dutton, 1951). The novel contained no feuding Fromeses.

My student David Reynolds pointed out a similarity between the theories of Robert Bly (discussed more fully below in Chapter 7) and Burt Lancaster's character in *The Kentuckian*:

> Robert Bly's theory about the modern breed of "soft males" made passive by the corporate economic system is similar to Lancaster's theme in this movie. Big Eli, like Bly's mainstream American men, also had his "natural fierceness" sapped out of him by the business world and the pursuit of dollars. Big Eli is able to break free of this bondage by reclaiming his talismanic hunter's horn and lighting out for the wilderness of Texas. Bly's antidote for office nerds is the same: Pack your favorite talisman, travel to an isolated rural retreat, blow your horn, bang your drum, get nekkid, and reconnect with the natural man within yourself. Sample dialogue in the board meeting on Friday afternoon: "How about golf this weekend?" "Naw, I'm going to Big Sur, and I'm going to live it bold!" Of course Bly's disciples must return to the office on Monday morning, where they will once again be ground down to pinkboy slaves of the conspiracy. Now if they *really* wanted to get in touch with their primitive masculinity, they could take a canoe trip. . . .

### Crockett-dile Dundee, the Last Great Davy

*Crocodile Dundee* (Rimfire Films/Paramount, 1986). Cathleen McGuigan wrote in *Newsweek* at the time of the movie's release that the title character is "a throwback—a pre–Alan Alda hero who comes from a place where men are men and women are all called Sheila." The quote from Don Morris is in the same article: "Hogan's New Hero," *Newsweek*, 13 Oct. 1986, p. 91.

### *Chapter 4*

I am indebted to Chip Arnold, Anna Creadick, Dan Hurley, John Inscoe, and Pam Williamson for valuable editorial suggestions.

Eric Hobsbawm, *Primitive Rebels: Studies in Archaic Forms of Social Movement in the Nineteenth and Twentieth Centuries* (New York: Frederick A. Unger, 1963). See also Hobsbawm, *Bandits* (1969; rev. ed., New York: Pantheon, 1981).

The text of the Jesse James ballad is taken from *The Frank C. Brown Collection of North Carolina Folklore* (Durham: Duke University Press, 1952), 2:557–62.

The photographs appear in William A. Settle, *Jesse James Was His Name: Or, Fact and Fiction Concerning the Careers of the Notorious James Brothers of Missouri* (Columbia: University of Missouri Press, 1966). Perhaps I am stretching the point to see anything untoward in Jesse's protruding thumb, but his nickname was "Dingus," an expletive he uttered when he pinched (on a saddle horn) an unspecified part of his anatomy and a word that seemed to delight his male club (see Settle, p. 32).

Michael Fellman, *Inside War: The Guerrilla Conflict in Missouri during the American Civil War* (New York: Oxford University Press, 1989).

### Rube-in-Hoods

The attacks on Hobsbawm are exhaustively detailed by Gilbert M. Joseph, "On the Trail of Latin American Bandits: A Reexamination of Peasant Resistance," *Latin American Research Review* 25, no. 3 (1990): 7–53. (I am grateful to David Whisnant and Jeff Boyer for bringing this essay to my attention.)

Kent L. Steckmesser, "Robin Hood and the American Outlaw: A Note on History and Folklore," *Journal of American Folklore* 79 (1966): 348–55.

Billy Jaynes Chandler is quoted and summarized in Gilbert Joseph, "Latin American Bandits," pp. 14–15.

The Carleton Beals quote is in ibid., p. 10.

For the literature on "pukes," see Fellman, *Inside War*, pp. 13–15, 160–61. The long quote about the popular press is on p. 11.

For a recent discussion of ordination in the context of American burlesque, see Robert C. Allen, *Horrible Prettiness: Burlesque and American Culture* (Chapel Hill: University of North Carolina Press, 1991), especially the section "Burlesque as a Cultural Phenomenon," beginning on p. 30.

For the robbery of the Ocobock Brothers Bank, see Settle, *Jesse James Was His Name*, pp. 43–44.

Homer Croy, *Jesse James Was My Neighbor* (New York: Duell, Sloan, and Pearce, 1949). The long quote from Croy comes from his introduction to Carl W. Breihan, *The Complete and Authentic Life of Jesse James* (New York: F. Fell, 1954). Croy's quoted statistic about 450 dime novels, below, is also in Breihan.

The pro-capital quote from the governor of Missouri is in Richard White, "Outlaw Gangs of the Middle Border: American Social Bandits," *Western Historical Quarterly* 12, no. 4 (Oct. 1981): 396. The Frank James quote about "greed and manhood" is from the same source. White bases his theory about Jesse James as a reactionary image of masculinity on Gerald F. Roberts, "The Strenuous Life: The Cult of Manliness in the Era of Theodore Roosevelt," Ph.D. diss., Michigan State University, 1970, pp. 134–62.

The elderly Frank James—by 1902 a reformed intellectual, as he had always wished to be—sought a court order to prevent a traveling production of the play *The James Boys in Missouri* from being staged in Kansas City. His concern for the minds of adolescent boys is very interesting: "I am told the Gilliss Theater was packed to the doors last night, and that most of those there were boys and men. What will be the effect on these young men to see the acts of a train robber and outlaw glorified?" (quoted in Settle, *Jesse James Was His Name*, p. 176).

Jesse James is not invariably romanticized for juveniles in American pop culture. My student Deirdre Cecil told me about an episode of *The Brady Bunch* in which Bobby, the youngest son of the Brady family, develops an inappropriate fixation on the Jesse James myth: "Every adult around him tried to explain that Jesse James was not a hero but a villain, and his parents and teachers were all extremely worried about him." Finally, a frightening dream about the *real* outlaw jolts young Bobby out of his infatuation.

Robert Bly, *Iron John: A Book about Men* (Reading, Mass.: Addison-Wesley Publishing Co., 1990). Bly's work is discussed further in Chapter 7, "The Mama's Boys," below.

The *New York Daily Graphic* front page is reproduced in Settle, *Jesse James Was His Name*, following p. 148.

## Social Bandit Meets the Silver Screen

References to a film version of the play *The James Boys in Missouri* are in *Moving Picture World*, 18 Apr. and 9 May 1908. The description of the plot of the play comes from Settle, *Jesse James Was His Name*, pp. 175–76.

For *Jesse James under the Black Flag*, see *Moving Picture World*, 2 Oct. 1920 (p. 677), 20 Nov. 1920 (p. 367), 18 Dec. 1920 (p. 904), and 25 Dec. 1920 (ad). Settle mistakenly labels this the "first motion picture about Jesse James."

*Jesse James* (Paramount, 1927), starring Fred Thomson. See *Moving Picture World*, 16 Apr. 1927 (pp. 627, 647), 27 Aug. 1927 (pp. 588, 597), 1 Oct. 1927 (p. 275), 8 Oct. 1927 (p. 344), 22 Oct. 1927 (p. 514). For Jesse James Jr.'s lawsuit against Thomson and Paramount, see *Variety*, 17 Apr. 1929 (p. 6), 1 May 1929 (p. 5), 22 May 1929 (p. 4). The public outrage over the erecting of a monument to Jesse in the Kearney, Mo., cemetery is effectively surveyed in *Literary Digest*, 29 Oct. 1927, pp. 44, 48, 50.

*Jesse James* (Twentieth Century–Fox, 1939). Quotes from the script are taken from Nunnally Johnson's "final script," dated 1 June 1938, in the Henry King and Larry C. Bradley Collections, University of Wyoming Archives, American Heritage Center. I am grateful to the archives for supplying the script and many clippings about the production in Pineville, Mo. I am also indebted to Mrs. Roy H. Collins of Christiansburg, Va., step-niece of Henry King, who told me about the King papers at the University of Wyoming and who gave me very generous access to her own King files.

David Reynolds pointed out that a year later, in 1940, director John Ford again cast Henry Fonda and Jane Darwell in the roles of sainted rurality in *The Grapes of Wrath*, and he presented them in the same grip of cruel capitalism: "A salt-of-the-earth family is being run off their farm by moneyed interests." However, when the money men arrive on the farm in *Grapes*, Hank Fonda isn't there to send them packing and protect his ma.

John H. Lenihan, *Showdown: Confronting Modern America in the Western Film* (Urbana: University of Illinois Press, 1980), p. 92, and see the still on p. 142.

## Saving Jesse's Face

I am most indebted to students Randy Crutchfield and David Reynolds, who deepened my reading of *The Long Riders*. I have added paragraphs to my discussion that are based on their insights.

Other Jesse James movies: *Days of Jesse James* (Republic, 1939); *The Return of Frank James* (Twentieth Century–Fox, 1940), starring Henry Fonda; *Jesse James at Bay* (Republic, 1941), starring Roy Rogers as both a good Jesse and an evil look-alike twin; *I Shot Jesse James* (Screen Guild, 1949), the story of Bob Ford, starring Preston Foster and John Ireland, directed by Samuel Fuller; *Jesse James's Women* (United Artists, 1954); *The True Story of Jesse James* (Twentieth Century–Fox, 1957), starring Robert Wagner and apparently based on the 1939 Nunnally Johnson script for the same company; *The Great Northfield Minnesota Raid* (Roberts and Associates Productions/Universal, 1972), starring Cliff Robertson as Cole Younger and Robert Duvall as a decidedly unhinged Jesse. This last movie may be the strangest Jesse James film ever, as producer/star Robertson skews the story away from Jesse in favor of the more normal Cole Younger. My friend Chip Arnold insisted that this movie deserved its own extensive discussion in this chapter. And what can I say, except *de gustibus ain't what dey used to be.*

As this book was going to press, there was news that bad-boy brat-packer Rob Lowe had signed on to play Jesse James in a new movie to be called *Frank and Jesse* and shot at least partly on location in the Arkansas Ozarks.

### Chapter 5

I am indebted to Chip Arnold, Anna Creadick, Dan Hurley, and Pam Williamson for valuable editorial suggestions and comments.

#### The Fountainhead: *Thunder Road*

*Thunder Road* (DRM Productions, 1958), story by Robert Mitchum, produced by Robert Mitchum, and starring Robert Mitchum, directed by Arthur Ripley. Most quotes are from the final shooting script dated 15 Aug. 1957. I am indebted to Bill Ross, who was an extra in *Thunder Road*, for a copy of this script.

Biograph's *The Moonshiner* and the hundreds of other silent moonshining movies are discussed and detailed in my book, *Southern Mountaineers in Silent Films: Plot Synopses of Movies about Moonshining, Feuding, and Other Mountain Topics, 1904–1929* (Jefferson, N.C.: McFarland and Co., 1994).

DRM Productions was Mitchum's own company. Other actors in the movie were Gene Barry as the lawman, Trevor Bardette as Kogan (Bardette had played Davy Crockett in *The Man from the Alamo* in 1953), Keely Smith as Francie, and James Mitchum as Doolin's younger brother. Robert Porterfield, founder of the Barter Theater in Abingdon, Va., had a bit part as the preacher in the church scene. Charlie Elledge, long a fixture in Boone's outdoor drama *Horn in the West*, had a small speaking part as one of the Rillow Valley moonshiners (and later appeared in other moonshining movies such as *Hot Summer in Barefoot County*). Exteriors were filmed on location in and around Asheville, N.C. But so powerful was this myth of the lone wolf that people from any number of mountain locales claim the film was made in or near their hometowns. I've heard people from Harlan County, Ky., say the film was definitely made there. And I've heard people in Knoxville claim it for east Tennessee (perhaps because the "road to Memphis" also figures prominently in the script).

Alex Gabbard claims to have partly uncovered the original true events on which Robert Mitchum based the *Thunder Road* script, though there are conspicuous holes in Gabbard's account. See *Return to Thunder Road: The Story behind the Legend* (Lenoir City, Tenn.: Gabbard Publications, 1992). And see the review of Gabbard's book in *Appalachian Journal* 21, no. 2 (Winter 1994): 198–202.

Wesley Saylors pointed out a certain similarity between Luke Doolin's relationship to his mother and the "mama's-boys" relationships discussed at length in Chapter 7.

The story of doomed resistance was similarly romanticized in *Thelma and Louise* (Percy Main Productions/MGM-Pathé, 1991). In both movies, the experience of death at the end is made irrelevant by the thrill of the gesture of ultimate defiance.

*Thunder Road*'s successful illusion of reality has prompted some claims that the character and exploits of Luke Doolin were based on real-life hillbilly bootlegger Junior Johnson, who was arrested at his father's still in Wilkes County, N.C., in 1955, three years before *Thunder Road*. Johnson himself has seemed to encourage the speculation that he was the inspiration for Doolin: see the interview with Mike Mulhern, *Winston-Salem Journal*, 14 Jan. 1990, p. A11. But in a telephone interview on 1 Oct. 1991, Johnson said Luke Doolin was more likely a composite of several country boys. One of those others may have been NASCAR star Tim Flock. Flock told Sylvia Wilkinson a story that bears a striking resemblance to the opening sequences in *Thunder Road*: Gene Barry's revenuer car has a set of bumper locks that grab hold of Luke Doolin's back bumper and would have held him, except that Luke pulls a lever and the bumper detaches, and he speeds away to freedom. In Tim Flock's account, "they [revenue agents] come up with these cowcatchers on their bumpers. They were like big old-timey ice tongs and they'd run up behind you and pinch onto the bumper and hold you. . . . So we come up with putting the bumper on the back of our cars with coat hanger wire. They'd run up and grab on, then we'd give it the gas and it would break loose and roll up under the front of their car and get all tangled up." See Sylvia Wilkinson, *Dirt Tracks to Glory: The Early Days of Stock Car Racing as Told by the Participants* (Chapel Hill, N.C.: Algonquin Books, 1983), pp. 33–34.

Mitchum was already forty-one years old when he played Luke Doolin.

*Thunder Road* was a low-budget film and looked it, with glaring lapses of continuity. For example, in the opening sequence, Robert Mitchum attempts a bootleg turn but goes into a skid and rolls his black car. Immediately after the roll, the same car is seen sitting upright in a cloud of dust without a dent in it. Mitchum then speeds away and escapes the cops. The camera stays with Mitchum in the black car as the credits roll. But by the end of the credits, though there's never been a cutaway, he's driving up to the homeplace in a *white* car.

Bill Davidson, "The Many Moods of Robert Mitchum," *Saturday Evening Post*, 25 Aug. 1962. For the marijuana bust, see the *New York Times*, 2 Sept. 1948 (p. 1), 3 Sept. 1948 (p. 16), 4 Sept. 1948 (p. 8), 8 Sept. 1948 (p. 22), 9 Sept. 1948 (p. 28), 30 Sept. 1948 (p. 24), 13 Nov. 1948 (p. 18), 1 Nov. 1949 (p. 34), 10 Feb. 1949 (p. 37), 1 Feb. 1951 (p. 21), 10 May 1955 (p. 24), 12 June 1955 (sec. 2, p. 5).

Steve Smith speculated on why *Thunder Road* makes Luke Doolin drive all the way to Memphis instead of to the more obvious middle-Tennessee destination of Nashville: "The music used in the night club scene was supposed to show that Luke had gone out of the hills and into the sophisticated world. Even though Nashville was a sophisticated Southern financial and political center, it already had the image of being a hillbilly town, due to the Grand Ole Opry. But Nashville probably had more of those type of supper clubs depicted in the movie than did Memphis. Printers Alley, just a block from the Tennessee State Capitol, had a number of fancy supper clubs for business lobbyists to wine and dine legislators. But since nationally Nashville was stereotyped as a hillbilly town, Mitchum apparently decided to bypass it in favor of a jazzier Memphis."

### The Sons of Doolin

For Roseanne Arnold's interview with Kevin Sessums, see *Vanity Fair*, Feb. 1994, p. 116.

*Moonrunners* (United Artists, 1974), written and directed by Gy Waldron, filmed on location in Coweta County, Ga. For the background on Jerry Rushing, I am indebted to Mike Knepper, "Moonrunner!" *Motor Trend*, July 1984, pp. 61–62. On the career of "redneck auteur" Earl Owensby, see Nancy M. Collins's interview with him in *Appalachian Journal* 21, no. 3 (Spring 1994): 280–301, and see the Owensby filmography beginning on p. 301 for other films featuring Jerry Rushing.

*Moonshine County Express* (Universal, 1976), directed by Gus Trikonis. Besides Saxon, Conrad, and Howard, the movie featured Jeff Corey and Dub Taylor. It was filmed at Nevada City and Grass Valley, Calif.

*Thunder and Lightning* (Twentieth Century–Fox, 1977). Besides Carradine and Jackson, it featured Roger C. Carmel as Mr. Big and Sterling Holloway as an old moonshiner.

Other good-old-boy movies not mentioned above in the text: *Moonshine Mountain* (Herschell Gordon Lewis Motion Picture Enterprises, 1964); *White Lightnin' Road* (J. R. T. Films/Ormond Organization, 1965); *Moonshiner's Woman* (Worldwide Films, 1968); *The Road Hustlers* (Saturn Productions, 1968); *Girls from Thunder Strip* (Borealis Enterprises, 1970); *Preacherman* (Preacherman Corp., 1971), discussed in Chapter 2; *Hot Summer in Barefoot County* (Preacherman Corp., 1974); *Bootleggers* (Howco International, 1974); *Dixie Dynamite* (Dimension Pictures, 1976); *Hooch* (American National Enterprises, 1977). For a comprehensive listing, see the *Southern Mountaineers Filmography* on the Appalachian State University gopher (appstate.edu).

One of the most bizarre riffs on the moonshine theme was *The Moonshine War* (Filmways/MGM, 1970), starring Alan Alda (of all people) as a Kentucky moonshiner trying to protect his stash of outstanding pre-Prohibition whiskey from both government men and a ludicrous bunch of bad guys.

In the interest of completeness, I should mention the handful of *anti*moonshining films, beginning with *The Devil's 8* (American International, 1969), an obvious ripoff of *The Dirty Dozen* (1967) in which a gang of misfit cons are recruited to break up a notorious moonshining ring. Also among the *anti*s were the several versions of the Buford Pusser story: *Walking Tall* (Bing Crosby Productions, 1973), *Walking Tall, Part 2* (American International, 1975), *Walking Tall—the Final Chapter* (American International, 1977), and *A Real American Hero* (Bing Crosby Productions, CBS-TV, 1978).

### Bad Georgia Road

*Bad Georgia Road* (Producers Group Inc., 1977), produced and directed by John C. Broderick (who also shared credit for the script), cinematography by Tak Fujimoto. Besides Lockwood, it starred Carol Lynley as Molly Golden and Royal Dano as Pennyrich.

### The Biopix

I am indebted to Charles Alan Watkins and the Junior Johnson materials in the Appalachian Cultural Museum at Appalachian State University.

The quote from Tim Flock is in Wilkinson, *Dirt Tracks to Glory*, along with all the quotes from Soapy Castles and Wendell Scott.

*Greased Lightning* (Warner Brothers, 1977), directed by Michael Schultz. Besides Pryor, Grier, and Bridges, it featured Cleavon Little, Vincent Gardenia (as the bumptious sheriff), Richie Havens (as a mechanic), and Georgia state legislator Julian Bond in a small speaking part.

Richard Schickel, "Vroomy Movie," *Time*, 15 Aug. 1977, p. 61.

*The Last American Hero* (Twentieth Century–Fox, 1973), directed by Lamont Johnson. Besides Bridges, Lund, and Lauter, it featured professional hillbillies Gary Busey and Ned Beatty, along with Geraldine Fitzgerald (very good as Junior's mother) and Valerie Perrine (sunk again in another bimbo part as a racetrack groupie). The exteriors representing Wilkes County were shot around Kings Mountain, N.C. Watauga County beekeeper Bob Cole plays a noncartoonized sheriff in early scenes.

In a telephone interview in October 1991, Junior said that although the movie did not accurately represent his "whole life," it was in his estimation dead accurate about the grinding economics of stock-car racing.

Pauline Kael's review is in the *New Yorker*, 1 Oct. 1973, pp. 114–18.


## Chapter 6

I am indebted to Chip Arnold, Anna Creadick, and Pam Williamson for valuable editorial suggestions and comments.

Theodore Roosevelt, *The Winning of the West* (New York: Review of Reviews Co., 1904–5).

*Deliverance* (Warner Brothers, 1972), directed by John Boorman. For more on this film, see below.

One *Deliverance* ripoff was *Hunter's Blood* (Cineventure, 1986). The similarities were explored in Josh Wood's unpublished paper, "Preposterous Violence in Hillbilly Horror: Titillating and Teaching the Adolescent Male."

*The Evil Dead* and *The Evil Dead II* (Renaissance Pictures, 1983, 1986), directed by Sam Raimi (assisted by Ethan and Joel Coen on the first movie).

*Pumpkinhead* (Lion Films/United Artists, 1988), directed by Stan Winston, who did the creature effects in *Aliens*. The similarity between monsters is thus explained if not exactly forgiven.

### Ferociousness without the Monstrousness:
### Or, All Balls, No Strikes

*The Mountain Men* (Columbia, 1980), directed by Richard Lang; starring Charlton Heston and Brian Keith. Roger Ebert's opinion was offered on his TV show with Gene Siskel.

*The Man from Snowy River* (Cambridge Films, 1982), directed by George Miller.

*Overboard* (MGM/United Artists, 1988), starring Goldie Hawn and Kurt Russell.

*The Winter People* (Nelson Entertainment, 1989), adapted from John Ehle's novel, directed by Ted Kotcheff; starring Kelly McGillis and Kurt Russell. The plot I have emphasized here is but one of two plots in the movie. Some might consider the other plot the main one. That one involves a dilemma faced by the mountain woman (Kelly McGillis): whether to give up her baby to save the rest of her family (i.e., the men of her family). It was this other plot that led Chip Arnold to dub the film "Sophie Yokum's Choice."

*Next of Kin* (Lorimar, 1989), directed by John Irvin; starring Patrick Swayze. Rita Kempley's crack was in the *Washington Post*, 21 Oct. 1989, p. C2. See also J. W. Williamson, interview with Jean Ritchie on the making of *Next of Kin*, in *Now and Then* (East Tennessee State University, Center for Appalachian Studies) 8, no. 3 (Fall 1991): 23–24, 26; and Anndrena Belcher's essay about the same thing in the same issue of *Now and Then*: "Relatively Strange: On the Set of *Next of Kin*," pp. 22, 25–26.

Bruce Curtis, "The Wimp Factor," *American Heritage*, Nov. 1989, pp. 40–50. Also contributing to my understanding of contemporary American masculine anxiety are the following: Steve Olson, "Year of the Blue-Collar Guy," *Newsweek*, 6 Nov. 1989, p. 16; Henry Allen, "The Mystique of Guns: From Daniel Boone to Dirty Harry, America's Fascination with Firearms," *Washington Post*, 19 Apr. 1989, pp. D1, D2; James B. Twitchell, "Our Preposterous Violence," *Washington Post*, 10 Dec. 1989, pp. C1, C2 (see also Twitchell's book, *Preposterous Violence* [New York: Oxford University Press, 1989]); Duncan Spencer and Reed Phillips, "Hunting the He-Man Vote," *Washington Post*, 12 Feb. 1989, p. C5; Marjorie Williams, "The Battle and the Sexes," *Washington Post*, 18 Feb. 1991, pp. C1, C10–C11; Don Colburn, "The Way of the Warrior: Are Men Born to Fight?," *Washington Post*, Health supplement, 29 Jan. 1991, pp. 11–12; Tom Spain, "Lights, Camera, Violence!," *Washington Post*, 19 July 1990, p. B7; Hal Crowther, "Red Sails in the Sunset," *Independent*, 29 Aug. 1990, p. 5; Courtland Milloy, "The Painful Games That Boys Play," *Washington Post*, 30 Apr. 1991, p. B3; Rita Kempley, "The HIMBO: The Brawn Derby—Uncovering the Men of Hollywood," *Washington Post*, 17 June 1988, pp. D1, D2; Rupert Wilkinson, *American Tough: The Tough-Guy Tradition and American Character*, Contributions in American Studies no. 69 (Westport, Conn.: Greenwood Press, 1984); J. A. Mangan and James Walvin, eds., *Manliness and Morality: Middle-Class Masculinity in Britain and America, 1800–1940* (New York: St. Martin's Press, 1987); Donald Spoto, *Camerado: Hollywood and the American Man* (New York:

New American Library, 1978). I am grateful to Robert J. Higgs and Steve Fisher, respectively, for bringing the last two items to my attention.

### Ed and Lewis and Bobby and Drew: The Monster in the Mirror

The quote by Mrs. Andy Webb comes from "He Shouted Loud, 'Hosanna, DELIVERANCE Will Come,'" oral history interviews by Barbara Taylor, Mary Thomas, and Laurie Brunson, *Foxfire* 7, no. 4 (Winter 1973): special insert.

*The Silence of the Lambs* (Strong Heart–Demme/Orion, 1991), directed by Jonathan Demme; starring Jodie Foster, with Anthony Hopkins as Hannibal the Cannibal.

*Cape Fear* (Amblin Entertainment/Universal, 1991), directed by Martin Scorsese; starring Robert De Niro as the psychotic hillbilly. De Niro apparently learned his accent partly by listening to audiotapes obtained from my colleague Howard Dorgan, who is an authority on mountain religion.

*Deliverance* (Warner Brothers, 1972), directed by John Boorman, screenplay by James Dickey and John Boorman; starring Burt Reynolds, Ned Beatty, Jon Voight, and Ronny Cox. Based on the novel by James Dickey. Some quotations here and in the following section are taken from the "second draft" script dated 12 Jan. 1971.

Rodger Cunningham, *Apples on the Flood: The Southern Mountain Experience* (Knoxville: University of Tennessee Press, 1987), pp. 122–31.

"The multitude of male-on-male glances . . . open the narrative to all sorts of speculation": My memory is that the literary criticism of Dickey's novel often mentioned the homosexual undercurrent.

*The Emerald Forest* (Embassy Pictures, 1985), directed by John Boorman; starring Powers Boothe, Meg Foster, and Charley Boorman. On *The Emerald Forest*, see Harlan Kennedy, "The Brits Have Gone Nuts," *Film Comment*, Aug. 1985, pp. 51–55; and John Boorman, "The Greening of the Emerald Forest," excerpted from *The Emerald Forest Diary* (New York: Farrar, Straus and Giroux, 1985) in *American Film*, Sept. 1985, pp. 34–35, 38–39.

David Reynolds updated the figures on the "Deliverance syndrome": between 1972 and 1975, seventeen people drowned in the Chattooga. A vigorous safety program implemented in 1976 was credited with saving lives.

### *Deliverance* on Location

All the quotes by people on location come from "He Shouted Loud," oral history interviews by Barbara Taylor, Mary Thomas, and Laurie Brunson.

Although I agree with David Reynolds that the *Foxfire* interviewees mainly *said* they enjoyed their brush with Hollywood, they often betrayed a great deal of aversion. For example, Louise Coldren, who catered much of the food for the cast and crew, related this story: "One morning about five o'clock I was serving breakfast in the dining room [of a local Rabun County hotel]. Until that time hippies were not as prevalent in Rabun County as they are today. I saw a man come in with his hair tied in a cord. He was clean, he was ragged, and he carried a briefcase. I think to myself, 'I'm glad he is coming in this early, maybe he'll eat his breakfast and leave before many people come in here.'"

The impact of *Deliverance* on popular culture cannot be exaggerated. "Squeal like a pig" long ago entered the demotic vocabulary. A particularly obnoxious episode of *Designing Women* was devoted to replaying for cheap laughs the implications of country people's menacing of city dwellers. David Reynolds remembered a *Deliverance*-inspired skit on *Saturday Night Live*: "I don't recall the specifics of the skit, but I think Ed, Lewis, Bobby, and Drew were all homosexual leather-boys wearing biker caps. I think the premise was that they were camped on the river for the express purpose of engaging in anal sex or that they were *hoping* to be raped by hillbillies." Suzanne Moffitt remembered a different skit on *Saturday Night Live*: "Two hillbillies are ravenously tearing away at their food, when one suggests that after dinner, they go have some fun with the pigs. Before they do, however, both get sick, vomit, eat more, and then go out the door to the barnyard, the sty of pleasure."

See the special section, "Twenty Years after 'Deliverance,'" *Atlanta Journal and Constitution*, 18 Mar. 1990. I am grateful to John Inscoe for providing me with a copy of this special section.

### Andy Griffith as Masculine Monster

*A Face in the Crowd* (Warner Brothers, 1958), produced and directed by Elia Kazan, written by Budd Schulberg; featuring Walter Matthau and Anthony Franciosa in addition to the stars mentioned in the text. The movie also featured Rod Brasfield, the country-music clown of Ferlin Husky's *Country Music Holiday*, as Lonesome's sidekick.

Rita Kempley, "The HIMBO. The Brawn Derby: Uncovering the Men of Hollywood," *Washington Post*, 17 June 1988, pp. D1–D2.

Elia Kazan, *Elia Kazan: A Life* (New York: Knopf, 1988), esp. pp. 566–69.

"The depths of Arkansas": Bosley Crowther, "The Great Man Myth: A Television Person Exploded in a Film," *New York Times*, 2 June 1957, sec. 2, p. 1.

Elia Kazan, "Paean of Praise for a Face above the Crowd," *New York Times*, 26 May 1957, sec. 2, p. 5.

Gilbert Millstein, "Strange Chronicle of Andy Griffith," *New York Times*,

2 June 1957, p. 17. See also Lawrence Elliott, "Andy Griffith: Yokel Boy Makes Good," *Coronet*, Oct. 1957, pp. 105–10; Bosley Crowther, "The Rise and Fall of a TV 'Personality,'" *New York Times*, 29 May 1957, p. 33; John McCarten, "More TV Villainy," *New Yorker*, 8 June 1957, pp. 86, 88; "Loud-Lunged Satire," *Newsweek*, 3 June 1957, p. 101; "Guitar-Thumping Demagogue," *Life*, 27 May 1957, p. 68; Mary Ellin and Marvin Barrett, "On Our List," *Good Housekeeping*, Aug. 1957, p. 70; and Arthur Knight, "Monster on the Make," *Saturday Review*, 25 May 1957, p. 23.

Deborah Bell wrote about *A Face in the Crowd* as a "mirror of early television": "When Lonesome started making fun of the commercials and the sponsor's product, I was reminded of Arthur Godfrey, who used to do the same thing and who also got into trouble for it, just like Lonesome. Interesting, isn't it, that Rhodes mentions getting Arthur Godfrey to sub for him on his show? Of course, some of those commercials were something to ridicule, especially the old-style cartoon ones they used then."

In 1986 and again in 1987, news leaked out that Whoopi Goldberg had "set her sights on playing the lead [Lonesome Rhodes] in a remake of *A Face in the Crowd*," with Don Johnson in the Patricia Neal part, all fetching and vulnerable to seduction. See the *Washington Post*, 30 Jan. 1986, p. B7, and the *Wilmington [N.C.] Morning Star*, 10 Mar. 1987, p. 2D.


*Chapter 7*

I am indebted to Chip Arnold, Anna Creadick, Dan Hurley, and Pam Williamson for valuable editorial suggestions and comments, as well as to others named below.

Helen Gurley Brown, quoted in *Time*, 1 Nov. 1982, excerpted in *Appalachian Journal* 10, no. 3 (Spring 1983): 221.

Frederick J. Hoffman, *The Twenties: American Writing in the Postwar Decade*, rev. ed. (New York: Collier Books, 1962), pp. 21–22.

All the mama's boys undergo boy-to-man initiations through violence. The message in every one of these films is that the American adolescent male must be capable of killing (though *Stark Love* has a conflicting position on that capacity). Both *Tol'able David* and *Sergeant York* were propaganda films. Both were made in close proximity to world wars, and both saw America as an unblooded and innocent rural boy until knighthood called, and then America became the knight perfected by justified violence, remaining miraculously innocent through fields of blood. *Tol'able David* and *Sergeant York* saw self-fathering as no problem. They were bucolic, romantic, and wildly popular at the box office in their day. The other two movies summarized in this group failed, perhaps because they were openly ambivalent about the implications of the "mountain" in men's natures. *Stark Love* treated the pioneer in our past with irony; in that movie, no adult male is anything but a self-centered brute, and the one good but weak boy can't beat his giant in the end. In fact, he has to flee the mountains entirely even to survive. But *At Close Range* gave fullest voice to the ambiguity of fathering ourselves into manhood.

Robert Bly, *Iron John: A Book About Men* (Reading, Mass.: Addison-Wesley Publishing Co., 1990). See also Skip Hollandsworth, "The Call of the Wildman," *Texas Monthly*, Jan. 1990, pp. 107–11, 148–50; Phil McCombs, "Men's Movement Stalks the Wild Side: Lessons in Primitivism for the Modern Male," *Washington Post*, 3 Feb. 1991, pp. F1, F6. Bly has been much attacked; see, for one example, Fred Pelka, "Robert Bly and Iron John: Bly Romanticizes History, Trivializes Sexist Oppression, and Lays the Blame for Men's 'Grief' on Women," *On the Issues*, Summer 1991, pp. 17–19, 39. (I am indebted to Steve Fisher for bringing this last item to my attention.)

I thank David Reynolds for trying to help me clarify the connection between Bly's "father hunger" and what Reynolds himself has dubbed "the syndrome" of the mama's boy. I have paraphrased Reynolds's class journal a time or two in the text in addition to quoting from it below.

On the usefulness of Bly's analysis for interpreting *Tol'able David*, Reynolds wrote: "Perhaps Bly's theories can help explain the surprising success of *Tol'able David* in 1922. The years following World War I saw a rise in the emphasis on Big Business, the economic system which sapped the physical aggressiveness and strength from men, replacing it with urban sophistication. If indeed American men were already "father hungry" at this point (and not having read Bly, they might not have known it yet), *Tol'able David* offered an idealized version of an unassuming male who proved to be more dangerous than he appeared. The film was a validation for those in the audience who wanted to believe that one need not be rough-and-ready to be a true man."

### Tol'able David

Exhibitors' comments come from *Moving Picture World* 54, no. 5 (4 Feb. 1922): 457; 55, no. 7 (15 Apr. 1922): 756; 56, no. 1 (6 May 1922): 83; 57, no. 6 (5 Aug. 1922): 444; 56, no. 7 (12 Aug. 1922): 523; 58, no. 2 (9 Sept. 1922): 132; 58, no. 9 (28 Oct. 1922): 795; 59, no. 5 (2 Dec. 1922): 451; 59, no. 6 (9 Dec. 1922): 567; and 59, no. 9 (30 Dec. 1922): [868]. The excerpts quoted in the text and cited here represent but a fraction of the favorable mentions *Tol'able David* received in *Moving Picture World* (hereafter cited as *MPW*) throughout 1922.

Exhibitor comment in 1925: "This is a little old but it is a real picture and a wonderful story" (Worthington, Ind.), *MPW* 72, no. 7 (14 Feb. 1925): 684.

"The oblivion of obsolescence": In 1921 there was no American Film Institute, and no cinema appreciation society or university archive trying to document and save Hollywood products. There were so many of those products, and the demand for novelty was so unrelenting, that prints were regularly destroyed after their short runs for the silver content in the film stock. For a complete chronological presentation of silent film stories dealing with southern mountaineers—company-published synopses—see J. W. Williamson, *Southern Mountaineers in Silent Films: Plot Synopses of Movies about Moonshining, Feuding, and Other Mountains Topics, 1904–1929* (Jefferson, N.C.: McFarland and Co., 1994).

"Best Picture of 1922" *Photoplay* award: see *MPW* 60, no. 3 (20 Jan. 1922): 263.

"Questionnaire Shows Richard Barthelmess Is Strong Favorite with America's Women," *MPW* 62, no. 6 (9 June 1923): 507; "Richard Barthelmess Pictures to Be Handled by Associated–First National," *MPW* 50, no. 3 (21 May 1921): 278; "'Tol'able David' First Barthelmess Film for First National Release," *MPW* 50, no. 6 (11 June 1921): 629; "The Rise of Richard Barthelmess," *MPW* 41, no. 4 (26 July 1919): 491.

On the celebration of Barthelmess as "Our Dick," see "Richard Barthelmess Is Made 'One of the Family' of First National at Dinner to Franchise Holders," *MPW* 53, no. 5 (3 Dec. 1921): 553. At the dinner at the Hotel Astor in New York City, First National sneak-previewed *Tol'able David* for its franchise holders. Barthelmess was guest of honor, his black hair slicked into a jet Valentino helmet, and he had to submit to being symbolically "adopted." First National solemnly presented him with official-looking adoption papers and got him to sign on as "son"—"another manifestation . . . that First National is one big family," said the press release. The actor, very much the beholden and dutiful boy, did not look at the camera when the publicity still was made. He sat in stiff profile, head bowed like the fawn he was, signing his "adoption" papers.

The moonshining and feuding bona fides of southern mountaineers in American movies before *Tol'able David* are fully exposed in Williamson, *Southern Mountaineers in Silent Films*. By the end of World War I, any new hillbilly movie prompted groans aplenty, much as Westerns did in the 1960s. The industry began to mock its own plot formulas and character types in slapstick comedies like *Maybe Moonshine* (Kalem, 1916), *Jerry and the Moonshiners* (Cub/

Mutual, 1916), *Moonshine* (Paramount, 1918, starring Fatty Arbuckle with Buster Keaton), *His Noisy Still* (Sunshine Comedy, 1920), *Moonshine* (Educational Film Corp., 1921), *Bone Dry* (Hal Roach/Pathé, 1922), *Torchy's Feud* (Educational Film Corp., 1922), etc. In 1920, the market strategists at *Moving Picture World* advised theater owners to book the Fox Company's new Tom Mix movie *The Feud* with great caution: "This title will not sell readily. It is trite and suggestive of a theme badly overworked" (*MPW* 42, no. 8 [20 Dec. 1919]: 1008). New movies that tried to make serious emotional hay with mountain types were hooted at derisively. By 1922 few companies attempted serious use of mountain types, although Universal made *Wolf Law,* and independent Wistaria Productions made *Anne of Little Smoky.* Of the first film (which starred the dashing Frank Mayo), an exhibitor wrote *Moving Picture World*: "Nothing against Mr. Mayo, but the theme is out of date" (*MPW* 62, no. 8 [23 June 1923]: 663). And *Anne of Little Smoky* was considered "of average interest" because it was "built on an oft-used theme . . . the habits of the natives of the mountainous region" (*MPW* 54, no. 4 [28 Jan. 1922]: 427). By the late 1920s, *Variety* remarked in its trademark no-fleas-on-us style that movies with rural settings "have lost a large measure of popular appeal, forcing producers to recognize the public demand for modern themes. . . . centered around big town activity" (6 June 1928, p. 48).

The early movie mountaineers did not so much die as transmigrate. The dying "Easterns" went West and survived for a long time by trading on the same thrills and chills, the same symbolic characters and symbolic struggles, done this time on horseback and in rawhide behind the very same rocks that had served earlier for moonshiners and feudists. From about 1910 onward, the majority of southern mountain actioners were shot in California and adjoining states. Because the Western retooled so well the myth of male brute force and consolidation—violent rural aggression and domination as mythic self-definitions of American character—the Western became the only rural projection of itself supported persistently by a large portion of the urban American audience after World War I and into the 1950s. Anna Creadick has asked, "But if Westerns are merely transmigrations of Southern mountain adventures about land acquisition, why are hillbillies a source of fear and loathing while cowboys are a source of fantasy and admiration? Because cowboys *shave*?" In response, Nancy Collins has suggested that cowboys were always safe abstractions of a mythic past, and "they obligingly rode off into the sunset." In other words, they were a version of the past that *stayed* in the past. There were no such sunset-laws for hillbillies. "The hillbilly is more ornery," writes Collins, a personage from an ambiguous frontier past who stubbornly hangs on into the present. Julie Mullis puts it this way: "The wild, wild West was a desirable fantasy world to the audience, whereas Hillbillyland is a past that their families had only recently escaped. . . . Hillbillies are those who refused to change," and in that sense they can be viewed as paradoxical renegades from history (from "progress") who continue to stink up the present.

"Old-fashioned rural melodrama" and *Way Down North*: see *MPW* 48, no. 1 (1 Jan. 1921): 96.

On Mary Pickford in *The Eagle's Mate*, see reviews in *MPW* 21, no. 1 (4 July 1914): 81; and 21, no. 3 (18 July 1914): 412. The film was successfully re-released in 1918: see *MPW* 37, no. 10 (7 Sept. 1918): [1359]; and 38, no. 2 (12 Oct. 1918): 279. Mary Miles Minter's *The Call of the Cumberlands* survives in the Library of Congress collection; on *Melissa of the Hills*, see *MPW* 33, no. 5 (4 Aug. 1917): 810; on *Her Country's Call*, see *MPW* 34, no. 2 (13 Oct. 1917): 251. Mabel Normand's turn in *Mickey* was one of the most hyped performances of the World War I era; see especially *MPW* 35, no. 1 (5 Jan. 1918): 101; 35, no. 2 (12 Jan. 1918): 249; 35, no. 5 (2 Feb. 1918): 658; 35, no. 6 (9 Feb. 1918): 836; 35, no. 8 (23 Feb. 1918): 1110; 35, no. 11 (16 Mar. 1918): 1529; 35, no. 13 (30 Mar. 1918): 1839; these are only a few examples. Normand's role as the title character in *Sis Hopkins* was only slightly less ballyhooed; see, for example, *MPW* 38, no. 8 (23 Nov. 1918): 848; 38, no. 12 (21 Dec. 1918): 1372; 38, no. 13 (28 Dec. 1918): 1499; 39, no. 5 (1 Feb. 1919): 659; 39, no. 6 (8 Feb. 1919): 711, 798; 39, no. 7 (15 Feb. 1919): 841.

On rural adolescent male David Kinemon as ideal American, I am indebted to Gerald C. Wood, "The Pastoral Tradition in American Film before World War II," *The Markham Review* 12 (Spring 1983): 52–60. Wood led me to Clifford B. Anderson, "The Metamorphosis of American Agrarian Idealism in the 1920's and 1930's," *Agricultural History* 30 (Oct. 1961): 182–88.

On the mama's-boy as incipient knight, think of Sir Gawain, who had the Virgin painted on the inside of his shield so he could look to her in the heat of battle.

Wesley Saylors has noticed "the disquieting delay of justice" in *Tol'able David*, another failure of manhood that David must redeem: "Perhaps this is a message to those who would allay the feelings of decisive justice—revenge—the neutering of male instinct."

Ben Grimm, "Find Woman: Arouse Her Curiosity; That's One First Step in Practical, Everyday Motion Picture Showmanship or in Any Other," *MPW* 40, no. 7 (17 July 1919): 1023.

*The Hill Billy* (1924), "not a woman's picture": see *MPW* 68, no. 6 (7 June 1924): 556.

On the location shoot, see entry for *Tol'able David* in *West Virginia Heritage*

*Encyclopedia* (Richwood, W.Va.: Jim Comstock, 1976), 21:4690–91; *West Virginia: A Guide to the Mountain State*, compiled by workers of the WPA Federal Writers' Project (New York: Oxford University Press, 1941), 506–7.

On Henry King, I am indebted to King's niece, Edythe King Collins of Christiansburg, Va., for interview material, clippings, and correspondence, to the Henry King Collection at the University of Wyoming, and to Gene Phillips, S.J., at the Department of English, Loyola University, Chicago. See Rev. Gene Phillips, S.J., "Hollywood Royalty: Conversations with Henry King," *American Classic Screen* 5 (Fall 1981): 14–22. See also *MPW* 29, no. 12 (16 Sept. 1916): 1839; 33, no. 11 (15 Sept. 1917): 1690; 32, no. 3 (21 Apr. 1917): 440.

My characterization of Arnold Toynbee's association of barbarism with the supposed descendants of the Celts in Appalachia is based on James S. Brown, "An Appalachian Footnote to Toynbee's *A Study of History*," *Appalachian Journal* 6, no. 1 (Fall 1978): 29–32.

*Tol'able David* is available on VHS tape from Reel Images/Video Yesteryear, Box 137-M, Monroe, Conn. 06468.

William E. "Bill" Lightfoot is my colleague in the Department of English at Appalachian State University, a folklorist and an expert in mountain music.

*Bill Apperson's Boy* survives in the Library of Congress collection. On Jack Pickford's version of *The Little Shepherd of Kingdom Come*, see *MPW* 41, no. 12 (20 Sept. 1919): 1832; 42, no. 8 (20 Dec. 1919), unpaginated ads; 43, no. 9 (28 Feb. 1920): 1522–23. On Pickford in *The Hill Billy*, see *MPW* 66, no. 1 (5 Jan. 1924): 54; 66, no. 5 (2 Feb. 1924): 377; 67, no. 3 (15 Mar. 1924): 171; 67, no. 4 (22 Mar. 1924): 317; 67, no. 5 (29 Mar. 1924): 335, 359; 67, no. 7 (12 Apr. 1924): 525.

On Barthelmess in *Kentucky Courage*, see *Variety*, 16 May 1928, p. 13, and the full-page ad in the same issue.

On *Driven*, see *New York Times*, 12 Feb. 1923, sec. 13, p. 4; and *MPW* 59, no. 6 (9 Dec. 1922): 572–73; 60, no. 8 (24 Feb. 1923): 767 and unpaginated ad; 61, no. 1 (3 Mar. 1923): 81, 83, 85; 61, no. 2 (10 Mar. 1923): 164; 61, no. 4 (24 Mar. 1923): 457. For the Saranac Lake exhibitor, see *MPW* 64, no. 4 (22 Sept. 1923): 349.

On *Sun-Up*, see *MPW* 74, no. 1 (2 May 1925): 79; 74, no. 7 (13 June 1925): 793; 75, no. 9 (29 Aug. 1925): 918; 76, no. 1 (5 Sept. 1925): 82. I am also indebted to Jean H. Speer, who has researched the career of Lula Vollmer and who graciously consented to read this section and comment on it.

*Tol'able David* was remade by Columbia Pictures in 1930 as a "talkie," with Richard Cromwell as the title character and Noah Beery as Luke Hatburn, but this remake failed to capture an audience and did nothing whatsoever for

Cromwell's career. So disastrously did this film play at the box office, *Variety* quoted Columbia's Harry Cohn in 1931 as saying he was "cured of remakes." Cohn said he preferred from now on "to let other studios take the gamble on talker versions of silents," no matter how big a hit they had been previously (see *Variety*, 4 Feb. 1931, p. 6). For additional coverage, see *Variety*, 14 May 1930, p. 4; 19 Nov. 1930, p. 21; and the full-page ads in 5 Nov. 1930 (p. 31), 12 Nov. 1930 (p. 29), and 19 No. 1930 (p. 29).

### Stark Love

I am indebted to the following people, who read an early draft of this section and made many helpful suggestions: Chip Arnold, Steve Fisher, Gordon B. McKinney, Henry D. Shapiro, Jean H. Speer, Charles A. Watkins, David E. Whisnant, and John Alexander Williams.

This discussion relies heavily on writer/director Karl Brown's own account of the making of *Stark Love*, first published in *Appalachian Journal* under the title "Hollywood in the Hills: The Making of *Stark Love*," with an introduction by Kevin Brownlow (18, no. 2 [Winter 1991]: 174–220). I am indebted to Kevin Brownlow for making available Brown's unpublished manuscript "The Paramount Story," from which the *Appalachian Journal* text was extracted. Brownlow's pioneering work on *Stark Love* was my starting point: see his first piece on the movie in *Film* 53 (Winter 1968–69): 15–18 (published by the British Federation of Film Societies). See also Brownlow, "Stark Love," in *The American Film Heritage: Impressions from the American Film Institute Archives* (Washington, D.C.: Acropolis Books, 1972), pp. 110–14; and Brownlow, *The War, the West, and the Wilderness* (New York: Knopf, 1979), pp. 499–507. I also thank Frank Thompson for sharing a letter from Karl Brown, dated 27 June 1983, in which Brown discussed the location for *Stark Love* and the shoot.

For the comments in *Variety*, see the issue of 2 Mar. 1927.

For the Paramount ad in *Moving Picture World*, see 86, no. 7 (18 June 1927): 501.

For Karl Brown's career before *Stark Love*, see his book *Adventures with D. W. Griffith* (New York: Farrar, Strauss and Giroux, 1973).

For historians' comments on *The Covered Wagon*, see Brownlow, *The War, the West, and the Wilderness*, p. 380.

The first installment of Lucy Furman's *The Quare Women* ran in the *Atlantic* in May 1922, and extreme isolation was a featured element in the very first chapter.

For Brown's 1927 interview on the isolation of mountain people, see "Primitive Mountaineers Filmed in Native Nooks," *New York Times*, 20 Feb. 1927, sec. 7, p. 6. See also "Mountaineers in Picture," *New York Times*, 29 Aug. 1926, sec. 7, p. 5; and "Where Man Is Vile: 'Stark Love' a Realistic Reproduction of Life of Mountaineers," *New York Times*, 6 Mar. 1927, sec. 7, p. 7. Brownlow quotes Brown's comment about "only 5,000 mountaineers left" in "Stark Love," cited above. See also the reviews in *MPW* 85, no. 3 (19 Mar. 1927): 214, and in *New York Times*, 28 Feb. 1927, sec. 22, p. 3.

Irene Hudson [pseud.], "The Schoolma'am of Sandy Ridge," *Atlantic*, Jan. 1921, pp. 11–22. The desert island quote is on p. 13.

See David C. Hsiung, "How Isolated Was Appalachia? Upper East Tennessee, 1780–1835," *Appalachian Journal* 16, no. 4 (Summer 1989): 336–49. See also Gene Wilhelm Jr., "Appalachian Isolation: Fact Or Fiction?," in *An Appalachian Symposium: Essays Written in Honor of Cratis D. Williams*, edited by J. W. Williamson (Boone, N.C.: Appalachian State University Press, 1977), pp. 77–91.

No one has found any surviving evidence of Brown's visit to Berea College. On the subject of on-location moviemaking in Appalachia during the silent era, I have collected some evidence and cataloged some films: see Williamson, "On-Location in Appalachia: Silent Movies, 1910–1927," paper presented at the University of Kentucky's Seventh Annual Conference on Appalachia, "The State of the Arts in Appalachia," 5–7 November 1992. Jenny Lee Henderson of Wilmington, N.C., has gone much further than I in documenting movies made on location in North Carolina, but so far as I know she has not yet published any of her research.

On Horace Kephart, I am indebted to George Ellison's introduction to *Our Southern Highlanders* (Knoxville: University of Tennessee Press, 1976).

Once I knew that Robbinsville, N.C., had been Karl Brown's base for the filming of *Stark Love*, I made several trips there and corresponded with several longtime Graham County residents and spoke on the phone with others. I am indebted to the kindness, no less than to the wealth of memory, of the following people: Amanda Roberts Blankenship, Bill Breedlove, Wanda Brooks, Jerry and Sherry Collins, Ollie Crisp Collins, Blaine Denton, Marian Ingram, Nancy L. Love, Oleta Nelms, Mabel C. Orr, Harry Owens, Bob Roberts, Elmer Rogers, Genevieve Hooper Rogers, Ollie Mae Holland Stone, Henry Stuart, and Earl Wall. I thank Teresa Hollifield, Sue Phillips, and Gary Pressley of the Graham County Library for videotaping interviews with Bob Roberts and Earl Wall. I am also indebted to the Friends of the Graham County Library for arranging two showings of *Stark Love*, for inviting me to introduce them, and for arranging for me to meet many of the people named above. I especially want to thank the indefatigable Ruth Harrold and Bob and Betty Smith, Dave and Dot Grosvenor, and John and Shirley Stage for facilitating two of my visits to Graham County, for arranging for local showings of *Stark Love*, and for their kind hospitality.

Ollie Mae Stone passed away in late November 1990, a few months after she told me the story of being approached to play the girl in *Stark Love*.

On the whereabouts of Helen Mundy: Carson Brewer, a columnist for the *Knoxville News-Sentinel*, published two columns (30 July 1979 and 6 Aug. 1979) about her mysterious disappearance from history. In the second piece, Brewer claimed to have located her under her married name of Mrs. Donald Barringer in Galesburg, Michigan. But my follow-up investigation found that claim to be totally erroneous. Helen Mundy's whereabouts and her history after *Stark Love* remain a mystery. But memories of her in Graham County are still pungent. I have a letter from Graham County native Paul Rogers that describes her as something of a local scandal during the making of *Stark Love*: "Some of us guys were loafing around Cole Ghormley's Cafe when the actress [Helen Mundy] came up through the alley to get her mail. While passing us, her safety pin came loose on her skirt. I am afraid she didn't have much more on. Hoke Phillips can vouch for this." See also Myrtle West's profile of Helen Mundy, "Of All the Luck!" *Photoplay*, Jan. 1927, pp. 84, 113–14.

After reading Karl Brown's account of the making of *Stark Love*, David Reynolds wrote: "Brown comes off as especially insensitive and self-important. Well aware that his project is exploitative, he proceeds as planned, concealing his true intent from those he plans on exploiting. He is interested in what he perceives to be their plight, but he does not empathize with or attempt to understand them, confident that there was not 'anything good about their lives from our point of view.' This though does not taint Brown's achievement. *Stark Love* is a masterful film, and his work with an all-rookie cast is impressive. I found it to be a superior film in comparison to *Tol'able David*, especially in terms of pacing."

### Tol'able Alvin: *Sergeant York*

I am indebted throughout this section to David D. Lee, *Sergeant York: An American Hero* (Lexington: University Press of Kentucky, 1985).

George Pattullo, "The Second Elder Gives Battle," *Saturday Evening Post*, 26 April 1919, pp. 3–4, 71, 73–74.

"Kinogram Shows Home of Sergeant York," *Moving Picture World* 40, no. 10 (7 June 1919): 1534.

The Thedford's Black Draught newspaper ad was found by Dean Williams in the *Brevard News* [N.C.], 9 Apr. 1920, p. 12.

On biographers Cowan and Skeyhill, I am indebted to David Lee, *Sergeant York*, chap. 6, "The Legend Makers."

On Sergeant York as embodiment of Americanism without necessarily being an embodiment of regionalism, David Reynolds has written: "His heroism is a symbol of American virtue, not Appalachian virtue, even though those qualities which earned him hero status—his moral convictions and his sharpshooting ability—are a direct result of his Appalachian upbringing. However, these attributes have also been used to portray Appalachians in a negative light, as primitive fundamentalists with a propensity for violence. The mountains end up with the lasting negative stereotypes, while the mountain-born heroes are claimed by the Nation. While *Sergeant York* made Americans feel good about themselves, it did not also make them feel good about Appalachians."

One scene in particular establishes a connection between York and Daniel Boone. As Alvin and his brother George set off hunting one day, the camera tracks past a tree with the following inscription carved in its trunk: "D. Boon kilt a bar." I had always assumed the scene was pure Hollywood symbol-mongering, but it turns out that indeed an ancient beech tree *was* still standing in 1916 in east Tennessee (if not exactly in Alvin York's neighborhood), inscribed as follows: "D. Boone Cilled a Bar On Tree In Year 1760." I am indebted to George Ellison for this piece of arcana; see his article, "Entering an Extended Stand of Beech Trees Is Like Penetrating a Special Zone," *Smoky Mountain Neighbors* insert in the *Asheville Citizen-Times*, 27–28 Sept. 1989, p. 7. Later I read that the "Boon" inscription in the beech tree was probably a hoax. So who knows?

Though York had script approval, he left in at least one howler about shooting turkeys. Randy Crutchfield noticed it: "After York enters Army training, there's a scene in which he tells his new buddy Pusher and the others in the barracks about the best way to shoot turkeys. He lines up a row of shell casings to represent a flock of turkeys flying overhead. 'Now, which one do you shoot first?' Pusher guesses the first one. Wrong. York says you pick off the last one first and work your way backward up the line. York's suggestion that turkeys fly in formation, as do certain types of migratory birds, is glaringly incorrect. Turkeys only fly to roost. A small flock of 20 or fewer turkeys might take 30 minutes to fly up to roost. They move individually without regard for one another. Spooked by a man or dog, some turkeys will fly into a tree if one is handy, while most will run. Turkeys rely more on their feet than their wings." Why York didn't correct the errors of the scriptwriters is unknown.

On the issue of social class in the York saga, Deborah Bell, who grew up in middle Tennessee, remembers family folklore: "My maternal grandmother liked to say she thought Alvin York was 'a big, dumb country boy who got lucky when he ran into and captured all those Germans.' Her viewpoint was part contempt for the rural: she was born, reared, and lived all her life in the city of Nashville. But it also reflected class-consciousness. She was also the daughter and granddaughter of successful Nashville contractors and the wife of a successful Nashville banker."

I am indebted to Deborah Bell for pointing out to me that the melody of "Beulah Land" is also the melody of the former state song of Tennessee:

The fairest of the fair we see,
The bravest of the brave have we,
The freest of the noble free
In battle-scarred old Tennessee.


## Chapter 8

I am indebted to Anna Creadick and Pam Williamson for helping organize and shape this chapter and to David Reynolds for editorial suggestions. Parts were originally published as "Hillbilly Gals and American Burlesque," *Southern Quarterly* (Summer 1994): 84–96; for their sound advice during the writing of that earlier essay, I am grateful to Chip Arnold, Steve Fisher, Dan Hurley, and Jim Williams.

### The *Thunder Road* of Feminism

I am grateful to Randy Crutchfield, who found the *Women and Guns Magazine* subscription info in *Harper's*.

Anna Creadick pointed out to me a basic similarity between *Thelma and Louise* and *Fried Green Tomatoes*, especially in the use of female duos to reinforce female bids for freedom. In *Fried Green Tomatoes*, there are two such duos. In the central plot, the cross-dressing hillbilly gal Idgie (played by Mary Stuart Masterson) helps her married friend (played by Mary Louise Parker) escape the cruel domination of a psychotic husband. And in the framing plot, mousy housewife Kathy Bates comes into her female power under the influence of nonagenarian Jessica Tandy.

About the ending of *Thelma and Louise* and the credits sequence that immediately followed it, David Reynolds has written: "The suicidal dive off the edge of the canyon is perfect. But I would have liked to have seen the freeze-frame of the Thunderbird suspended in mid-flight as the final image of the film. No sell-out. We should have either held on that image or faded to black as the credits roll. Instead, the emotional power is lost immediately as we see stills of Thelma and Louise in happier, more carefree times. Smiling yes, happy maybe, but not yet 'crossed over' and not yet fully powerful. I'd like to believe that the decision to end with this fluff was not the director's but the studio's. Perhaps my ending would be perceived as too radical, too unrelenting by a studio that wants to ease the tension before sending its customers back out into the sunlight."

Reynolds continues: "What explains Thelma's newfound strength? Is it because she has finally been laid properly, finally achieved equality in the bedroom? Gender equality in bed translates to equality out in the world. What's wrong with that? We're all in this together."

## Uppity Women: Seen but Not Heard

We know these earliest movies primarily from company-written plot synopses; most of the actual film footage does not survive. See J. W. Williamson, *Southern Mountaineers in Silent Films: Plot Synopses of Movies about Moonshining, Feuding, and Other Mountain Topics, 1904–1929* (Jefferson, N.C.: McFarland and Co., Inc., 1994).

*Heart o' the Hills* survives in the collection of the Library of Congress.

Other examples of uppity women in silent movies: The title character in *Jane of the Soil* (Essanay, 1915) is "a mountain girl, wild and rough," who thinks she killed a man who was sexually assaulting her. But by the end she is let off the hook (the man isn't really dead after all) and placed firmly again under the physical protection of her sweetheart. Also, see *A Mountain Tragedy* (Reliance, 1912), *Her Moonshine Lover* (Nestor, 1914), *The Shrine of Happiness* (Balboa, 1915), *Moonshine Blood* (Big U/Universal, 1916), *A Magdalene of the Hills* (Rolfe Photoplays/Metro, 1917), *Patsy* (Fox, 1917), *Morgan's Raiders* (Bluebird, 1918), *Riders of the Night* (Metro, 1918), *Wild Primrose* (Vitagraph, 1918), *A Woman of Redemption* (World Pictures, 1918), *The Rebellious Bride* (Fox, 1919), *Sis Hopkins* (Goldwyn Pictures, 1919), *Anne of Little Smoky* (Wistaria Productions, 1921), and *A Daughter of the Hills* (Fox, 1921).

## Cross-Dressers: Who's Wearing the Pants?

*Annie Get Your Gun*, with music and lyrics by Irving Berlin, opened in New York on May 16, 1946, with Ethel Merman playing Annie. The stage musical was turned into an MGM movie in 1950, with Betty Hutton in the title role. The story was revived on stage by the San Francisco Light Opera Company in 1957, starring Mary Martin, and on November 27, 1957, the Mary Martin version was performed live on NBC-TV (that broadcast is available on VHS tape from Hen's Tooth Video). In all three versions, Annie Oakley's hillbilly credentials are established with the song "Doin' What Comes Natur'lly," which is quite explicit in its challenge to conventional propriety. A more serious version of the Annie

Oakley story was the 1935 movie *Annie Oakley* (RKO Radio), starring Barbara Stanwyck and Preston Foster. Though it was no comedy, this movie, too, placed gender roles and gender politics very much at the heart of the story.

*Calamity Jane* (Warner Brothers, 1953; dir. by David Butler) is available on Warner Home Video. Jean Arthur played Calamity Jane opposite Gary Cooper in *The Plainsman* (Paramount, 1936, dir. Cecil B. DeMille). The character was featured again in a routine Western programmer for Universal-International called *Calamity Jane and Sam Bass*, with Yvonne de Carlo and Howard Duff. Calamity Jane appeared again in 1984 in the made-for-TV movie *Calamity Jane*, starring Jane Alexander and Frederic Forrest. According to Steven Scheuer's *Movies on TV*, 11th ed. (New York: Bantam Books, 1985): "Ms. Alexander's 'Calamity' is not the tomboy next door . . . but a grimy, gritty, independent woman who prided herself on being able to compete with men on an equal basis."

My friend Bob Snyder objects on principal to assigning any sort of "threat" to a movie starring Doris Day, and he has a very good point.

In *Calamity Jane*, gender-bending spreads like a contagion. Wild Bill, the man's man, loses his bet that Calamity can't bring Adelaid Adams back from Chicago to Deadwood, so he appears before all the other men dressed as an Indian squaw carrying a papoose. Another sequence shows a female impersonator (though he claims he's never done this before) selling himself in song as a seductive woman ("I've got a hive full of honey for the right kind of honey bee"). Until his wig is accidentally removed, he gets away with the imposture, making fools of the men in the saloon. He takes his drag parade among the tables, allowing the sex-starved and evidently myopic men to pinch his cheek, fondle him, rub up against him, and roll their eyes.

### Mannish Misfits

*Spitfire* was adapted from Lula Vollmer's Broadway play *Trigger* and co-starred Robert Young and Ralph Bellamy.

Most regrettable in *The Ballad of the Sad Cafe* is director Simon Callow's relentless crackerization of southerners as ignorant villagers who seem to be practicing for roles as extras in a remake of *Night of the Living Dead*.

### Heidi and the Poverty Mamas:
### Fooling with Economics

For early Heidi plots in silent movies, see *The Heart of the Hills* (Victor/ Universal, 1914), *Diana of Eagle Mountain* (Bison, 1915), *Mickey* (Mack Sennett, 1918), and *In Old Kentucky* (First National, 1920).

*Tammy and the Bachelor* (Universal-International, 1957), directed by Joseph Pevney; starring Fay Wray and Mildred Natwick.

On *Coal Miner's Daughter*, see Edwin T. Arnold's perceptive interview with scriptwriter Tom Rickman, "Hollywood in the Hills," *Appalachian Journal* 10, no. 4 (Summer 1983): 335–49, reprinted in J. W. Williamson and Edwin T. Arnold, eds., *Interviewing Appalachia: The Appalachian Journal Interviews, 1978–1992* (Knoxville: University of Tennessee Press, 1994). The *People* magazine quote is from the 19 May 1980 issue, pp. 79–80.

For plot details from *Big Business*, I have relied on Rita Kempley's review in the *Washington Post*, 10 June 1988, pp. D1, D4.

Tommy Fletcher, the Inez, Kentucky, coal miner visited by Lyndon Johnson in 1964, has sadly resurfaced in the public press, apparently as shocking evidence of the failed programs of political liberalism. John Egerton wrote about Fletcher in *Shades of Gray: Dispatches from the Modern South* (Baton Rouge: Louisiana State University Press, 1991), and more recently Doug J. Swanson did a feature story on Fletcher and his background of notoriety for the *Dallas Morning News*; his article was excerpted in *Appalachian Journal* 20, no. 2 (Winter 1993) under the title "Johnson's Poverty Poster Boy on the Brink, in the Clink."

"The in-depth hillbilly feature story": Examples are legion. The *Appalachian Journal* has been excerpting and mocking them for years in its "Signs of the Times" section. Sometimes they cause a great furor in the mountains, as did CBS's *48 Hours* broadcast on Muddy Gut Hollow in Floyd County, Kentucky, in December 1989. For this and other examples, see especially the index to vols. 8–18 of the *Appalachian Journal*, published as vol. 18, no. 4 (Summer 1991), under the entries for "Appalachia, Negative Stereotypes" and "Television."

### Hillbilly Gals and Burly Cue

The Dolly Parton quote is in Rita Kempley, "Dolly Parton, Going for Glitter," *Washington Post*, 17 Nov. 1989, p. D2, excerpted in *Appalachian Journal* 17:4 (Summer 1990), 361–3.

Robert C. Allen, *Horrible Prettiness: Burlesque in American Culture* (Chapel Hill: University of North Carolina Press, 1991); see esp. "The Intelligibility of Burlesque," pp. 25–30, and "Burlesque as a Cultural Phenomenon," pp. 30–36. The Seph Weene quotes are on p. 286. In introducing the paradox of "the low-other," Allen uses the vocabulary of Peter Stallybrass and Allon White, from their *Politics and Poetics of Transgression*.

On the issue of whether stage freedom amounts to real freedom, Allen cites Terry Eagleton on carnivalesque disruptions of the dominant social order: insofar as such disruptions are sanctioned, allowed to happen, they are actually instruments of social control and not expressions of freedom. Therefore any pop entertainment takes place by definition in what Allen calls "a politically ineffective space." I see his point, but I don't think his pronouncement settles the matter.

On nineteenth-century origins of women performers—with many hillbilly gal prototypes—see Mary A. Bufwack and Robert K. Oermann, *Finding Her Voice: The Saga of Women in Country Music* (New York: Crown Publishers, 1993), esp. chap. 2, "Southern Sentiments: Country Females in Nineteenth-Century Show Business."

David Lida, *Interview* magazine, Dec. 1989, pp. 70, 72–73, 124.

"She boiled men like lobsters": I am indebted to Allen for this conceit, which is not idle decoration (see *Horrible Prettiness*, pp. 214–17).

John Ed Bradley, *Washington Post Magazine*, 10 Dec. 1989, pp. 26–27. This and other press clippings on Blaze Starr were excerpted in *Appalachian Journal* 17, no. 4 (Summer 1990): 364–66; 16, no. 1 (Fall 1988): 26; and 16, no. 4 (Summer 1989): 313.

Dolly Parton's "about my look" quote comes from her interview with William Stadiem in *Interview* magazine, July 1989. This and other press clippings about Parton used in this section were excerpted in *Appalachian Journal* 8, no. 4 (Summer 1981): 246; 11, no. 3 (Spring 1984): 178; 12, no. 1 (Fall 1984): 7; 12, no. 4 (Summer 1985): 304; 13, no. 2 (Winter 1986): 150; 13, no. 3 (Spring 1986): 255, 334; 14, no. 1 (Fall 1986): 16, 17; 14, no. 4 (Summer 1987): 402; 15, no. 2 (Winter 1988): 102; 15, no. 3 (Spring 1988): 217–18; 17, no. 1 (Fall 1989): 19–20; 17, no. 4 (Summer 1990): 361–63; 18, no. 1 (Fall 1990): 36, 38; 18, no. 2 (Winter 1991): 252; 19, no. 1 (Fall 1991): 21, 22–23, 29–31.

On Parton's remark that she is "very outgoing and ballsy" like Mae West, my colleague Dan Hurley has commented: "*Ballsy* may be a tribute to strength and independence, but it is also a participation in male-dominance semantically. Does public courage always have to be testicular in origin? If so, has Dolly bought her breasts but earned her balls? Making a woman an honorary ball-carrier doesn't seem like much progress."

# Index

Page numbers in boldface refer to illustrations.

Duff, Howard, 304
*Dukes of Hazzard, The*, 133, 135
Dunaway, Faye, 52
Duncan, Tony, 31, 32
Dunlap, Mary, 268
Durante, Jimmy, 59
Duvall, Robert, 284

*Eagle's Mate, The*, 180, 296
Earle, Steve, 8
Ebert, Roger, 152, 288
Ebsen, Buddy, 83–84
*Ed Sullivan Show*, 57
Egerton, John, 305
*Egg and I, The*: book, 20, 274; movie, 53–55, 56, 274
Ehle, John, 289
Elkins, West Virginia, 249
Elledge, Charlie, 284
Elliott, Sam, 280
Ellison, George, 199, 299, 301
Embry, Dink, 49
*Emerald Forest, The*, 161–62, 290
Erasmus, 24, 26; *Praise of Folly*, **27**
*Esquire* magazine, 40, 143, 146
Eulenspiegel, Till, 25, 267
*Evil Dead, The*, 150, 288
*Evil Dead II, The*, 150, 288

*Face in the Crowd, A*, 167–72, **171**, 291–92
Fairbanks, Douglas, 39
Farnum, William, 280
*Father Knows Best*, 5
Faulkner, William, 34, 69, 269
Fellman, Michael, 101, 104, 281
Femininity: and music-hall clowns, 49–50; in *Raising Arizona*, 68; and rural resistance, 116, **117**; in *Thun-*

*der Road*, 127–28; in good-old-boy movies, 132–33, 134–35, 135–41; in *Silence of the Lambs*, 153, 156; mothers and adolescent male initiations, 174; in *Stark Love*, 206; and guns, 225; "hillbillyland" and freedom for women, 225–32; and violence, 232–34; symbolic cross-dressing, 235–42; mannish misfits, 242–47; "poverty mamas," 247–53; burlesque freedom, 253–61
Fennelly, Parker, 274
Fentress County, Tennessee, 209, 211, 214, 216–17, 224
*Ferdie's Family Feud*, 269, 270
*Feud, The* (1920), 295
*Feud and the Turkey, The*, 270
*Feuding Fools*, 43
Feuds and feuding, 44, 189, 234, 235, 294–95; *The Cub* as satire of, 39; feud melodramas, 178–79; motif in *Tol'able David*, 186–88. *See also* Hatfield-McCoy feud
*Feud There Was, A*, 43
*Fighting Kentuckian, The*, 89–90
First National Pictures, 178, 294
Fisher, Steve, 290, 293, 298, 302
Fitzgerald, Geraldine, 288
Flaherty, Robert, 191–92
Flatt, Lester, 8
Flatt and Scruggs, 52–53
Fleming, Fanny Belle. *See* Starr, Blaze
Fletcher, Tommy, 251, 305
Flock, Tim, 141, 285, 287
Floyd County, Kentucky, 305
Fonda, Henry, **111**, **113**, 283
Fonda, Jane, 245, 252
Fools. *See* Clowns, clowning
Forbes, Ralph, 88

Hoffman, Frederick J., 174–75, 176, 292

Hogan, Paul, 94–97, **95**, **96**

Holbein, Hans, 26; *Praise of Folly*, **27**

Holloway, Sterling, 287

Holm, Celeste, 55

*Hooch*, 287

Hooper, J. J., 34, 268

Hooper, Sim, 204

Hope, Bob, 59

Hopkins, Al, 47–48, 49, 272

Hopkins, Anthony, 290

Hopkins, Joe, 48

*Horn in the West*, 284

*Hot Summer in Barefoot County*, 64, 284, 287

Houston, Sam, 86, 88, 279–80

*Houston: The Legend of Texas*, 280

Howard, Justin H., 33, **34**

Howard, Susan, 134

Hoyle, Geoff, 267

Hsiung, David C., 197, 299

Hubbert, Cork, 246

Hudson, Irene, 196–97, 299

Humphrey, Hubert, 251

Hunnicut, Arthur, 55, 133–34, 274, 280

Hunter, Holly, 67, 245, 276

*Hunter's Blood*, 288

Hurley, Dan, 265, 266, 274, 276, 281, 284, 292, 302, 306

Husky, Ferlin (Simon Crum), 50–51, 272, 291, **51**

Hutton, Betty, 303

Hutton, Paul Andrew, 278

*I Love Lucy*, 5

*I'm From Missouri*, 50

*Immortal Alamo, The*, 82, 278

Incest: part of hillbilly stereotype, 6, 263

*Incredible Journey of Dr. Meg Laurel, The*, 252

Indians. *See* Native Americans

Inge, M. Thomas, 268, 271

*In Old Kentucky*, 304

Inscoe, John, 281, 291

*In the Army Now*, 59

*In the Days of Daniel Boone*, 88, 279

*Intolerance*, 191

*Invasion of the Space Preachers*, 241

Ireland, John, 284

Isaac, Bobby, 141

*I Shot Jesse James*, 283–84

Isolation, myth of, 196–98, 200, 298–99

*I Spit on Your Grave*, 62, 275


Jackson, Andrew, 9, 80, 81, 89, 278; as movie character, 83, 84, 85, 86, 88–89, 280

Jackson, Kate, 135

Jamborsky, William Eric, 279

James, Forrest, 203–4, 205, **205**

James, Frank, 99, **100**, 101, 104, 105–6, 111, 112, 115, 118, 120, 282, 283

James, Jesse: in real life, 99–106, 227, 281–82, **100**, 101; in movies, 107–21, 123, 283–84

James, Jesse, Jr. (Jesse Edwards James), 108, 109–10, 283

James, Jessie Edwards, 110

*James Boys in Missouri, The*: movie, 107–8; play, 108, 282, 283

*Jane of the Soil*, 303

*Jeepers Creepers*, 49

*Jerry and the Moonshiners*, 269, 294–95

Martin, Quinn, 188

*Martyrs of the Alamo*, 82, 278

Masculinity, 2, 6, 35; and aggression, 31; idealized as street-smart, 57; southern manliness, 58; and the military, 59; in *Raising Arizona*, 66, 68–69; American Masculine Ideal, 78; as idealized by Davy Crockett, 82; testosteronized fighter, 83; as frontier virility, 86; as "Rooseveltian care for underdog," 88; and Andy Jackson, 88–89; and dread of loss of virility, 90–94; American frontier virility migrated to Australia, 94–97; and Jesse James myth, 106; in *Thunder Road*, 123, 126, 127–28, 130; in good-old-boy movies, 132–33; Primitive ideal in *Bad Georgia Road*, 136–41; proper masculinity, politics, and the movies, 151–55; and women, 167; in *A Face in the Crowd*, 168; "self-fathering" and "father hunger," 173–77; America as cornered adolescent male, 209; patriotic dimensions of manhood, 213; First Male as arbitrager, 236; sources on contemporary masculine anxiety, 289–90

Massys, Quentin, 23

Masterson, Mary Stuart, 302

*Matewan*, 7

Matthau, Walter, 91, 291

*Maybe Moonshine*, 294

Mayo, Frank, 295

*Medium Cool*, 252

*Melissa of the Hills*, 180, 296

Mellencamp, John, 9, 264

Men. *See* Masculinity

Merman, Ethel, 303

Metro-Goldwyn-Mayer, 216

Meyer, Russ, 62, 275

*Miami Vice*, 76

*Mickey*, 180, 296, 304

Middler, Bette, 250

Miller, Clell, 115, 116, 117

Miller, Ed, 118

Miller, Jim Wayne, 265, 267, 268

Miller, Slim, 49

Millstein, Gilbert, 169, 275, 291–92

Milsap, Ronnie, 8

Mimms, Zerelda (Zee), 112–13, 115, 116, 117

Mingo County, West Virginia, 255, 256

Minter, Mary Miles, 180, 233, 296

Miracle, Silas, 203

Missionaries, 196–97

Mitchell, James C., 80–81

Mitchum, James, **125**, 130, 133, 284

Mitchum, Robert, **125**, 127, 128–29, 130, **131**, 256, 284–86

Mix, Tom, 295

Moffitt, Suzanne, 273, 291

Monmouth, Geoffrey of, 75

Montgomery, George, 279, 280

*Moonrunners*, 133–34, **134**, 286

Moonshine, 62, 63, 189, 232, 233–34, 235, 245, 284–85, 286–87, 294–95; moonshine-running movies, 123–47, 178–79

*Moonshine*: 1918, 269, 270, 295; 1921, 295

*Moonshine Blood*, 303

*Moonshine County Express*, 134–35, 286

*Moonshine Mountain*, 287

*Moonshiner, The* (1904), 124, 179, 232, 270, 284

Womanless Weddings, 15–17, **16**, 264–65

*Woman of Redemption, A*, 303

Women. *See* Femininity

Wood, Gerald C., 296

Wood, John, 5

Wood, Josh, 275, 288

Woodfill, Sgt. Samuel, 209

Woodside, Jane, 265

Wopat, Tom, 133

World War I, 174–75, 181, 182, 188, 189, 207–10, 213, 292–93

World War II, 189, 213, 217, 218

Wray, Fay, 305

Wuhl, Robert, 256

Wycherly, Margaret, 216, 218–19, **221**, **222**

Yoakam, Dwight, 8, 263–64

York, Alvin, 177, 207–24, **212**, **217**, 300–301

York, Gracie (Mrs. Alvin), **212**, 216, 219, 220, 224

York, Mother Mary, 211–12, **212**, 216, 219, 220–22, 224

Yosef (hillbilly clown mascot), 28–32, **30**, **32**, 33, 38, 39, 43, 45, 49, 267–68, 270, 271

Young, Robert, 304

Younger, Cole, 115, 116, 117–18, 135, 284

Younger, Jim, 115, 118

*You're in the Army Now*, 59

Zanuck, Darryl F., 110

Zimmer, Hans, 227

Zucker, Jerry, 278

Zukor, Adolph, 109, 192